The Translation of Art

Essays on Chinese Painting and Poetry

RENDITIONS Special Art Issue

Centre for Translation Projects
The Chinese University of Hong Kong

Clothbound edition distributed by
University of Washington Press
Seattle and London

RENDITIONS No. 6

Special Art Issue

GUEST EDITOR

James C. Y. Watt

This issue is published with the aid of the
Wing Lung Bank Fund for Promotion of Chinese Culture

Renditions is published twice a year, in Spring and Autumn. Address all editorial and advertising correspondence to: *Renditions*, Centre for Translation Projects, The Chinese University of Hong Kong, Shatin, New Territories, Hong Kong. SINGLE COPY and ANY AVAILABLE BACK ISSUE: HK$12.00 (£1.80 or US$3.00), obtainable by writing to the Centre for Translation Projects or the Publications Office of the Chinese University of Hong Kong, Shatin, New Territories, Hong Kong, and authorized distributors. SUBSCRIPTION: 1 year HK$24.00 (£3.60 or US$6.00); 2 years HK$42.00 (£6.30 or US$10.50); 3 years HK$60.00 (£9.00 or US$15.00), surface-mail postage included. The contents of this magazine are copyrighted; no part of it may be reproduced without written permission from the Publisher. Copyright © 1976 The Chinese University of Hong Kong, Library of Congress Catalog Card Number 74-641755
The clothbound edition of this book is distributed by the University of Washington Press, Seattle and London. Library of Congress Catalog Card Number (for the clothbound edition): 76-28572. ISBN (for the clothbound edition): 0-295-95535-X 0577

Printed in Hong Kong by Dai Nippon Printing Company (Hong Kong) Ltd.

CONTENTS

RENDITIONS is published by the Centre For Translation Projects
The Chinese University of Hong Kong

Editor's Note

The idea of a Special Art Issue for *Renditions* was first proposed by George Kao, who has created the journal and now serves as its Editor-at-Large. The task of executing the idea has fallen upon this writer; but without the enthusiastic support of others on the editorial staff and the generous response from contributors near and far, this volume would not have come into existence. The result of this joint effort is the present collection of essays and pictures covering most periods of Chinese art and interpreting its every aspect, particularly in relation to poetry.

We are fortunate in securing original and important contributions to the study of Chinese art by some of the most distinguished scholars and translators in the field. Some topics have much to do with translation, such as Hin-cheung Lovell's comments on titles given to Chinese paintings in the West. Hsio-yen Shih's article on Ku K'ai-chih includes new translations of Chang Hua's "Admonitions of the Imperial Preceptress", Ts'ao Chih's famous and several-times translated "Lo-shen *Fu*", and Ku K'ai-chih's own untranslatable prose-poem on "Thunder and Lightning". Wang Fang-yu's translation and commentaries on Chu Ta's riddle-like poems will help some readers to gain an insight into one aspect of painterly art in China in recent centuries. The relationship between painting and poetry is discussed by Jonathan Chaves and Laurence Tam, who provide their own translations of poems of the Sung and Ch'ing periods respectively.

In a way, to write about the art of one country in the language of another is an act of translation. Certainly Richard Edwards' exposition on landscape painting is a perfect example of translating Chinese thought and artistic ideals into a Western mode of expression as well as into a Western language, thus making the unfamiliar more immediately understandable to our Western readers.

The contributions by Ellen Laing, Chu-tsing Li and Thomas Lawton reflect one of the most important trends in recent scholarship in the study of Chinese art, that is the direct use of Chinese sources rather than translated or related material. Writing of this nature must also include original translations, and these articles will be of interest to both the specialist and the general reader.

Hsiang Ta's well-known essay on Western influences on Chinese art, written in the 'Thirties, is presented in this volume in a translation with annotations by Wang Teh-chao, himself a scholar in this field. As to art historical writing in China and Hong Kong today, Kao Mayching's translation of Chih Kung's article in *Wen Wu* 1972 is complete, while Jao Tsung-i's paper presented to the Paintings Symposium held at the Art Gallery of this University last year has been only given an abridged rendering, mainly because of the translator's inability to put into English the esoteric language, especially the poetic language, of the literati of the late Ming.

Readers who are concerned about contemporary Chinese art, and its immediate past and future, may wish to read the last article first. It is both a personal and scholarly statement by Nelson Wu in his dual role as creative writer and art historian.

Grateful acknowledgement is due to Penelope Jordan, Rebecca Mok and John Gannon, who read and suggested improvement to some of the translations; to the Director of the Palace Museum in Taipei, to the Director of the Freer Gallery, to the Trustees of the British Museum, and to Mr. Jean-Pierre Dubosc, who have all given permission to reproduce paintings in this issue. Individual acknowledgement of ownership follows the caption to each painting.

JAMES C. Y. WATT
Curator, Art Gallery
The Chinese University of Hong Kong

Poetry Illustration and The Works of Ku K'ai-chih

By Hsio-yen Shih

THE CONNECTION between calligraphy, painting and poetry as allied arts for Chinese scholars from the 11th century A.D. on is well-known. Before the Northern Sung dynasty the question of whether painting was a suitable activity for scholars at all remained a subject of debate, the ultimate defence for its worthy status being given by Chang Yen-yüan 張彥遠 in the *Li-tai ming-hua chi* 歷代名畫記 (ca. A.D. 847).[1]

Our knowledge of pre-10th century painting has been largely restricted to funerary works or tomb decoration, and religious subjects. Despite the great masses of information offered in treatises written from the 5th century on, concerning both the lives of painters and the names of their works, we are barely able to form an image of what their styles may have been, though we can often discover something of their pictorial concerns. The vicissitudes of centuries, in which precious collections formed by Chinese connoisseurs have been repeatedly dispersed and destroyed, have robbed us of authentic examples. Only one figure has emerged with any degree of clarity in the early history of painting through the survival of perhaps original works or at least early copies. Happily, Ku K'ai-chih 顧愷之 (ca. 345-406) was considered one of the greatest painters of all time, as well as a scholar of distinguished literary gifts.

Ku's life was given extensive coverage by Chang Yen-yüan, and most discussions of him by Western scholars have depended upon this source and his biography in the *Chin shu* 晉書 (Dynastic History).[2] Many translations are, therefore, available of the two basic descriptions of his career and character. A recent Chinese publication has, moreover, added some minor anecdotes selected from other texts.[3] A chronological

---

[1] Book 1, "Hsü hua chih yüan-liu" 敍畫之源流 (On the Origins of Painting)—"Now, painting is a thing which perfects the civilized teachings, and helps the social relationships. It penetrates completely the divine permutations of Nature, and fathoms recondite and subtle things. Its merit is equal to that of the Six Classics, and it moves side by side with the Four Seasons. It proceeds from Nature itself, and not from either (human) invention or transmission....
夫畫者，成教化，助人倫，窮神變，測幽微，與六籍同功，四時並運。發於天然，非由述作。
"Painting is a great treasure of the Empire, containing the strands and leading ropes which can regulate disorder.... What has this in common with the mental activity required for (mere amusements like) chess or checkers? Without doubt, painting is one of the things which may be enjoyed within the teachings of Confucianism."

圖畫者，有國之鴻寶，理亂之紀綱。……豈同博奕用心？是名教樂事。

[2] See Arthur Waley, *An Introduction to Chinese Painting* (London, 1923), pp. 45 ff; and Osvald Sirén, *Chinese Painting: Leading Masters and Principles* (London, 1956), Part I, pp. 26 ff. For a translation of Chang Yen-yüan, *Li-tai ming-hua chi*, Book 5's entry on Ku, see William R.B. Acker, *Some T'ang and Pre-T'ang Texts on Chinese Painting* (Leiden, 1974), Vol. II, pp. 43 ff. Also consult Ch'en Shih-hsiang 陳世驤, *Chinese Dynastic Histories Translations* (Berkeley, 1953), no. 2.

[3] Ma Ts'ai 馬采, *Ku K'ai-chih yen-chiu* 顧愷之研究 (Shanghai, 1958); also P'an T'ien-shou 潘天壽, *Ku K'ai-chih* (Shanghai, 1958); Yü Chien-hua 俞劍華 et al, *Ku K'ai-chih yen-chiu tzu-liao* 資料 (Peking, 1962).

summary of the major events reported may be compiled from these various histories.

Ku's father was a *pieh-chia* 別駕 (Chevalier-in-waiting) to Yin Hao 殷浩 (d. 356) when the latter was Governor of Yang-chou 揚州 ca. 346. After Yin was deposed in 354, Ku Yüeh-chih 悅之 became a *shang-shu tsa-ch'eng* 尚書左丞 (Assistant Secretary in the Imperial Secretariat). According to the *Ching-shih ssu chi* 京師寺記,[4] as quoted by Chang Yen-yüan, K'ai-chih was poor in early life, and he may have been engaged in classical and Buddhist studies at this time, living a modest life despite his father's official position. Huan Wen 桓溫 (312-373) became *ta ssu-ma* 大司馬 (Grand Marshall) in 363, and at about this time K'ai-chih entered his service as a *ts'an-chün* 參軍 (Aide-de-Campe). After this we learn that Ku became Aide-de-Campe to Yin Chung-k'an 殷仲堪 (d. 399), when the latter was Governor of Ching-chou 荊州 (Hupei). This must have been between 392 and 399, the span of Yin's service there. Ku returned to Yang-chou in 404, and was appointed *shan-ch'i ch'ang-shih* 散騎常侍 (Cavalier Attendant in Ordinary, an honorific post) the next year.

SOME REVELATION of Ku's literary imagination may be discovered in various anecdotes. One is reported in both the *Shih-shuo hsin-yü* 世說新語, compiled by Liu I-ch'ing 劉義慶 (403-444), and the *Chu-kung chiu-shih* 渚宮舊事 by Yü Chih-ku 余知古 (T'ang).[5]

> As Marshall of the West, Huan constructed many beautiful sites in the city of Chiang-ling 江陵. He gathered guests and companions upon a river ferry and said: "Whoever is able to describe this town appropriately will receive a prize." Ku K'ai-chih was present as Huan's Aide-de-Campe, and, looking, said: "Regarding this terraced town from afar, red towers appear to be rosy clouds." Huan then rewarded him with two female slaves.

> 溫征西治江陵城甚麗，會賓僚出江津云：「若能目此城者賞。」顧愷之
> 為參軍在坐，目曰：「遙望層城，丹樓如霞。」溫郎賞以二婢。

It is, perhaps, not too far-fetched to see a distinctly visual translation in Ku's poetic couplet. Two other episodes also demonstrate the painter's awareness of pictorial symbolism.

> Once he wishes to paint the portrait of Yin Chung-k'an who had long suffered from an eye disease and, persistently excused himself (from being portrayed). He said: "Your Excellency may rely on my hiding the eyes, for if the pupils are dotted in clearly, and then flying white is brushed on, the result will be like light clouds concealing the moon."

> 嘗欲寫殷仲堪眞，仲堪素有目疾，固辭。長康曰：「明府當緣隱眼也，
> 若明點瞳子，飛白拂上，使如輕雲蔽月。」

[4]The *Shui shu* 隋書 "I-wen chih" 藝文志 (Bibliographical Section) 2 lists two works by this title; one by Liu Ch'iu 劉璆 and one by T'an-ching 曇景. For speculations about these lost works, cf. Paul Pelliot, "Les déplacements de fresques en Chine sous les T'ang et les Song," *Revue des Arts Asiatiques*, Vol. 8 (1934), p. 206 note 4.

[5]Cf. Yü Chien-hua, *op. cit.*, p. 123.

He also painted a portrait of P'ei K'ai 裴楷 (act. ca. 265-290) upon which he added three hairs to the chin, saying: "K'ai looked handsome and brilliant and was full of wisdom. These (hairs) are precisely (the signs of) his wisdom." Spectators examining it decided that its brilliance of spirit was exceptionally forceful.[6]

又畫裴楷眞，頰上加三毛，云：「楷俊朗有識具。此正是其識具。」觀者詳之，定覺神明殊勝。

Finally, the direct liaison between Ku's pictorial and literary imaginations is most clearly demonstrated in the following passages.

He also painted Hsieh Yu-yü 謝幼興 (i.e. K'un 鯤, 280-322) in a cave. People asked him why and Ku replied: "In (the environment of) hills and vales, he considered himself surpassing. This person is most appropriately placed within a cave."[7]

又畫謝幼興於一巖裏。人問所以。顧云：「一丘一壑，自謂過之。此子宜置巖壑中。」

He admired Hsi K'ang 嵇康's (223-262) four-word poems and painted illustrations of them. He once said: "*My hand sweeps over the five strings* 手揮五絃 is easy to paint, but *My eye bids farewell to homing geese* 目送歸鴻 is difficult."[8] It would seem that, in Ku's creative impulse, a concrete image was more adaptable to pictorial expression than an emotive mood suggested by a physical event.

[6]For the first account, Chang Yen-yüan's version accords with the *Chin shu*'s Book 92, which has one additional phrase in Ku's speech of persuasion—"... the moon, and would this not be beautiful?' Then Chung-k'an consented." 「……月，豈不美乎！」仲堪乃從之。
A *Shih-shuo hsin-yü* Section 21 version is very similar, but has Yin declining—"My form is ugly. Would it not only be vexing?" 「我形惡，卿不煩耳。」

The second episode also appears in both earlier texts, with the *Shih-shuo* ... version ending—"Those who looked at the painting examined and decided that the additional three hairs have given it brilliance of spirit, making it look much better than without the hairs." 看畫者尋之，定覺益三毛如有神明，殊勝未安時。

[7]Chang Yen-yüan's text must have followed the *Chin shu* 49 biography of Hsieh K'un, which reads— "Ming Ti (reigned 323-326) met him in the Eastern Palace and was most warmly respectful to him, asking: '(I have heard) speakers who feel that you, sir, are equal to Yü Liang (d. 340). What would you yourself say?' He replied: 'Correct and relaxed in temple and hall, setting a standard for all officials, in this K'un cannot equal Liang. In (the environment of) hills and vales, I consider myself surpassing him.' "
賞使至都，明帝在東宮見之，甚相親重。問曰：「論者以君方庾亮，自謂何如？」答曰：「端委廟堂，使百僚準則，鯤不如亮。一丘一壑，自謂過之。」

Both versions may have depended upon the *Shih-shuo* ... Section 21 anecdote.

[8]The lines come from a poem also supposed to have been illustrated by the Chin Emperor Ming. The fourth of five verses on "Tseng hsiu-ts'ai ju-chün" 曾秀才入軍五首 (offered to the First Degree Graduate upon his Entering the Army) dedicated to Hsi K'ang's older brother Hsi 熹, in the *Wen hsüan* 文選, compiled by Hsiao T'ung 蕭統 (501-531), Book 24—

"I leave my attendant to rest in the Epidendrum Garden;   息徒蘭圃，
I leave my horse to graze on the Brilliant Mountain;   秣馬華山。
I trail my arrow string and stone weight over flat marsh;   流磻平皐，
I hang my fishing line in the long river.   垂綸長川。
My eye bids farewell to homing geese,   目送歸鴻，
My hand sweeps over the five strings.   手運五絃。
In a moment, I obtain A free heart in the Great Mystery;   俯仰自得，遊心泰玄。
I marvel at that Old Fisher, Who caught fish and forgot the net.   嘉彼釣叟，得魚忘筌。
The man of Ying has passed. With whom can I still have speech?"   郢人逝矣，誰與盡言。

WHEN WE TURN to historical records of Ku's attributed œuvre to determine the extent of his literary interests as expressed in painting, the evidence is meagre. In this context general mythological themes have been excepted as not directly related to specific literary works. Of seventeen scrolls listed in P'ei Hsiao-yüan 裴孝源's *Chen-kuan kung-ssu hua-lu* 貞觀公私畫錄 (preface of 639), not a single title suggests literary and/or especially poetic inspiration. Only one in thirty-six subjects recorded by Chang Yen-yüan refers directly to poetry.[9] Mi Fu 米芾's (1052-1107) *Hua shih* 畫史 is the earliest text to mention a handscroll of the *Nü-shih chen t'u* 女史箴圖 (Admonitions of the Imperial Preceptress) in the collection of one Liu Yu-fang 劉有方. Mi also refers to a T'ang copy of a *Lieh-nü chuan t'u* 列女傳圖 (Illustrious Women), the original attributed to Ku, mounted upon carved boards to form a fan, and with figures in the same scale as the handscroll (i.e. about three inches in height). The *Lo-shen fu t'u* 洛神賦圖 (Nymph of the River Lo) title did not appear until ca. the mid-14th century in T'ang Kou 湯垕's *Hua chien* 畫鑑 as attributed to Ku, though such a work had been given to the Chin Emperor Ming, Ssu-ma Shao 司馬紹, in both the *Chen-kuan . . .* and *Li-tai ming-hua chi*.

Of the three subjects allied to Ku's name in existing works, that of the *Admonitions . . .* has been most discussed. It is the earliest of his literary illustrations to have a lineage, being recorded by Mi Fu, in the *Hsüan-ho hua-p'u* 宣和畫譜 (preface of 1120) Book 1, and in Chou Mi 周密's (1232-?) *Yün-yen kuo-yen lu* 雲煙過眼錄. Two versions exist of it today; one in the British Museum, and the other in the Peking Ku Kung Museum. Controversy over whether the London scroll is an original or a copy still rages. On the credit side is cited the number of seals and inscriptions which testify that it was considered to be a genuine example of Ku's painting from an early period. Its provenance can be traced back to the 8th century. Beginning with the Hung-wen kuan 弘文館, a department of the Han-lin Academy 翰林院, it was subsequently in the collections of Yen Sung 嚴嵩 (1481-1518), Ku Cheng-i 顧正誼 in the 1570s, Hsiang Yüan-pien 項元汴 (1525-1590), Liang Ch'ing-piao 梁清標 (1620-1691), An Ch'i 安歧 (1683-after 1742), Yang Shih-ch'i 楊世齊 between 1693 and 1700, the Ch'ing imperial collection from at least the Ch'ien-lung reign (1736-1796) on,[10] and finally entered the British Museum in 1903. Mi Fu identified the painting as by Ku and its calligraphy as by Wang Hsien-chih 王獻之 (344-386). The script form of the phrases identifying various scenes is, however, not in 4th century style, and this was recognized long before any doubt of the painting's origin had been admitted. A second suggestion was put forth by Ch'en Chi-ju 陳繼儒 (1558-1639) in the *Ni-ku lu* 妮古錄 that the painting is of Sung origin, and its calligraphy by the Emperor Kao-tsung 高宗 (reigned 1127-1173). Hu Ching 胡敬's (1769-?) *Hsi-ch'ing cha-chi* 西清劄記 (preface of 1816), Book 3 notes it as a T'ang

[9] The title is given as "Ch'i-hsien Ch'en Ssu-wang shih" 七賢陳思王詩 (Poems to the Seven Sages) by Ts'ao Chih 曹植, 192-232. These Seven Sages were also known as the "Chien-an ch'i-tzu" 建安七子 (Seven Masters of the Chien-an Period), being Ying Yang 應瑒 (d. 217), Hsü Kan 徐幹 (170-217), Wang Ts'an 王粲 (177-217), K'ung Yung 孔融 (153-208), Ch'en Lin 陳琳 (d. 217), Yüan Yü 阮瑀 (d. 217) and Liu Chen 劉楨 (d. 217). The six who died in the same year had all been infected by the same plague. See Wei Wen Ti 魏文帝's letter to Wu Chih 吳質 (d. 230) in the *Wen hsüan* Book 42. *Op. cit.*, Books 20 and 24 contain several poems by Ts'ao Chih to the first three figures named above.

[10] *Shih-ku-t'ang shu-hua hui-k'ao* 式古堂書畫彙考, compiled by Pien Yung-yü 卞永譽, preface dated to 1682, Book 8.

copy, with a long calligraphic exercise by the Emperor Hui-tsung 徽宗 (reigned 1101-1126) appended to it. Japanese and Western scholars have wavered between these various opinions, but there is general agreement that the "signature" is a later addition. The most recent study has given it to the Five Dynasties or Sung period, i.e. 10th-11th century, on the basis of a particular leaf stylization to be seen in the landscape representation.[11] The subject is, however, not one upon which much more could be said. The difficulty in dating might not have arisen had the work not been of such superior quality.

The scroll is an illustration of a text by Chang Hua 張華 (232-300) supposedly written to ridicule the Chin Dynasty Empress Chia 賈 at a time when the rise of her clan threatened the stability of the throne.

Admonitions of the Imperial Preceptress

女史箴

"FROM THE chaotic cosmos were *yin* and *yang* separated;

From emanate force and amorphous form were they moulded and shaped.

With P'ao-hsi as ruler were the divine and the human distinguished.

Thus began male and female, the ruler and ruled.

The family's *tao* is regulated and the ruler's *tao* stabilized.

Feminine virtue honours yielding, holding within codes of moral behaviour;

Submissive and meek is the female's proper role within the household.

Having assumed matrimonial robes, she should reverently prepare the offerings;

Dignified and grave in deportment, be a model of propriety.

To influence King Chuang of Ch'u, the Lady Fan ate no meat for three years;

To reform Duke Huan of Ch'i, the Lady Wei ignored her own love of music;

Their firm wills and lofty ideals changed the minds of two rulers.[12]

When the black bear escaped its cage, the Lady Feng hastened forward.

How was she not in fear but, aware of mortal danger, she did not hesitate.

茫茫造化,
二儀既分。
散氣流形,
既陶既甄。
在帝庖羲,
肇經天人。
爰始夫婦,
以及君臣。
家道以正,
王猷有倫。
婦德尚柔,
含章貞吉。
婉嫕淑慎,
正位居室。
施衿結褵,
虔恭中饋。
肅慎爾儀,
式瞻清懿。
樊姬感莊,
不食鮮禽。
衛女矯桓,
耳忘和音。
志厲義高,
而二主易心。
玄熊攀檻,
馮媛趨進。
夫豈無畏,
知死不恡。

---

[11] Michael Sullivan, "A Further Note on the Date of the Admonitions Scroll", Burlington Magazine, XCVI (1954), pp. 307-309.

[12] King Chuang thereupon giving up his love of bloody sports and warfare, and Duke Huang relinquishing his taste for licentious popular music. Both stories are recorded in Liu Hsiang 劉向's (80-9 B.C.) *Lieh-nü chuan* 列女傳 (Biographies of Illustrious Women), Book 2 "Hsien-ming" 賢明 (The Enlightened).

The Lady Pan declined, despite her desire, to ac-
company the Emperor in his palanquin.
How could she not have been sad but, forfending the
unseemly, she acted with prudence.[13]
The *tao* never flourishes but to deteriorate,
All matter must have its moment of florescence then
decay;
For the sun rises to its zenith then sets,
And the moon comes to fullness then wanes.
Acquisition of virtue may be compared to the pace of
earth building up in layers;
Decline of values can occur with the suddenness of an
arrow shooting from the crossbow.
Men all know how to improve their visages, but not
to refine their characters,
An unrefined character will fall short of propriety.
One should sculpt and embellish one's own character,
and discipline oneself to become a sage.
If the words which one speaks are good, they will be
heeded for a thousand miles;
If one defies this rule of conduct, then even one's
bedmate will doubt one.
Now, even though one makes a seemingly insignificant
utterance, yet from it issues one's triumph or
failure;
No matter that one is in obscurity, spirits, without
image, can still examine one;
No matter that one is in a boundless waste, spirits,
without sound, can still hear one.
Do not pride yourself on your eminence, for Heaven
detests such conceit;
Nor boast of your prosperity, for magnificence will
dim.
Observe how the tiny stars were made free and
content, and learn it as a lesson;
Make your heart like the grasshopper's, then you will
multiply your kind.[14]
Favour must not be abused, and love must not be
exclusive.

班婕有辭，
割驩同輦。
夫豈不懷，
防微慮遠。
道罔隆而不殺，
物無盛而不衰。
日中則昃，
月滿則微。
崇猶塵積，
替若駭機。
人咸知飾其容，
而莫知飾其性。
性之不飾，
或愆禮正。
斧之藻之，
克念作聖。
出其言善，
千里應之。
苟違斯義，
則同衾以疑。
夫出言如微，
而榮辱由茲。
勿謂幽昧，
靈監無象。
勿謂玄漠，
神聽無響。
無矜爾榮，
天道惡盈。
無恃爾貴，
隆隆者墜。
鑒于小星，
戒彼攸遂。
比心螽斯，
則繁爾類。
驩不可以黷，
寵不可以專。

[13]Both stories are recorded in the *Ch'ien Han shu* 前漢書 Book 97B "Wai-ch'i chuan" 外戚傳 (Biographies of Consorts). The Lady Pan 班倢伃's words to the Emperor Ch'eng the Filial 孝成帝 (32-7 B.C.), in declining his invitation, are supposed to have been—

"When one sees the paintings of the ancients, wise and virtuous rulers were always accompanied by noted officials. Only at the decline of the Three Dynasties (Hsia, Shang and Chou) were they surrounded by concubines. Now, if I were to be in the same palanquin as your Imperial Majesty, would it not be comparable to the events of the Three Dynasties?"
「觀古圖畫，賢聖之君皆有名臣在側，三代末主乃有嬖女，今欲同輦，得無近似之乎？」

[14]The couplet implies humility and generosity as the two virtues to be cultivated by women.

ADMONITIONS OF THE IMPERIAL PRECEPTRESS: Handscroll attributed to Ku K'ai-chih, illustrating the poem by Chang Hua. All sections reproduced here are from the British Museum version, courtesy of the Board of Trustees, British Museum, London.

Plate 1   THE ADMONITIONS SCROLL: *"When the black bear escaped its cage, the Lady Feng hastened forward."*

Exclusive love breeds coyness and extreme passion is fickle.

專實生慢，
愛極則遷。

All that has waxed must also wane, and this principle is sure.

致盈必損，
理有固然。

Admire your own beauty if you will, but that brings misfortune.

美者自美，
翻以取尤。

Seeking to please with a seductive face, you will be despised by honourable men;

冶容求好，
君子所讎。

If the bond of love is severed, this is the cause.

結恩而絕，
職此之由。

Thus it is said:

故曰，翼翼矜矜，

Prosperity is fostered with caution; honour will attend those who reflect.

福所以興。
靖恭自思，
榮顯所期。

The Imperial Preceptress rules these admonitions and respectfully instructs the imperial concubines.[15]

女史司箴，
敢告庶姬。

The British Museum version begins with the Lady Feng episode to continue for a total of nine scenes.[16] A second copy in the Peking Ku Kung Museum is unquestionably of much later date, but includes the two earlier scenes of Lady Fan and Lady Wei.[17] However, these are highly suspect as evidence for the composition of sections lost from the London scroll. Though the rest of the Peking copy appears to be quite close to the London painting, albeit feebler (as, for example, the bear in the Lady Feng scene which has been transformed by an incompetent hand to an insignificant rodent-like creature), its first two scenes betray a markedly different character. Lady Fan and King Chuang of Ch'u stand facing one another quite calmly to indicate nothing of the matter in dispute, to be followed by a repetition of the

[15]The *Wen-hsüan* Book 56.

[16]The British Museum scroll is best reproduced in

Osvald Sirén, *op. cit.*, Part III, Pls. 11-15.

[17]The Peking Ku Kung scroll is partially reproduced in Ma Ts'ai, *op. cit.*, Pls. 5 ff. (seven scenes in all).

Plate 2   THE ADMONITIONS SCROLL: *"The sun rises to its zenith then sets, and the moon comes to fullness then wanes."* (British Museum version)

Lady Fan kneeling before an empty table. The Lady Wei tale is depicted with a single female figure seated before two musicians playing upon bells and chimes. Both illustrations lack the explicitness and drama of visual interpretation which are to be seen in most of the other scenes. This dullness and lack of insight into literary content are products of a less imaginative painter. Very likely, the copyist decided to fill the gaps in his model, perhaps the British Museum scroll, and added two compositions of his own invention. An additional betrayal of their late conception may be seen in the furnishings and musical instruments which are unlike any found in Six Dynasties work. Their brushwork, too, have lost any similarity to the original. The Peking scroll is, therefore, of little help in forming an idea of what has been considered to be the style of Ku K'ai-chih.

Facial and figural forms on the London scroll, on the other hand, are very close to such excavated examples of Six Dynasties pictorialization as the "Seven Sages of the Bamboo Grove" stamped on bricks of a tomb near Nanking, and the Taoist themes moulded and painted on bricks of a tomb at Teng hsien 鄧縣, Honan.[18] The fine, even movement of lines in drapery rendering etc. is equally in accord. Some of the British Museum version's male figures show a bulky roundness of body structure less in keeping with a 4th century work. This is particularly evident in the Lady Pan scene, where the palanquin form is drawn in the same manner as this motif at Teng hsien,[19] but with its bearers moving in complicated curvilinear rhythms for which there seems no adequate motivation. Such a stylization evidences a departure from the angularity we generally expect in Chin dynasty style. Two other details are also anomalous. In the landscape scene, neither the mountain nor the figure resemble known Six Dynasties work. The plasticity of accumulated boulder shapes alternated with flat surfaces of paths is much more three-dimensional, and conceived in terms

[18] Alexander C. Soper, "A New Chinese Tomb Discovery: the Earliest Representation of a Famous Literary Theme," *Artibus Asiae*, XXIV: 2 (1961), pp. 79-86; and Honan sheng wen-hua chü 河南省文化局, *Teng hsien ts'ai-seh hua-hsiang chuan-mu* 鄧縣彩色畫象磚墓 (Peking, 1958).

[19] *Teng hsien . . .*, no. 32.

Plate 3 THE ADMONITIONS SCROLL: *"People all know how to improve their visage, but not to refine their characters."* (British Museum version)

of mass rather than the successive overlapping planes of 4th to 6th century formalizations. Similarly, a crude pyramidal arrangement of the family group seems incongruous. It is less satisfactory in giving an idea of recession than the usual Six Dynasties device of diagonal placement on an imaginary ground-line. The problems presented by the London scroll are, therefore, not merely a question of whether it is an original or a copy, for the first possibility must be excluded. Even the placement of its exact date of execution is less important than whether it reflects Ku's conception more or less clearly.

For this reason, it is in its visual interpretation of literary content that the London painting may prove particularly revealing. In the Lady Feng episode, two court ladies in smaller scale are shown moving off towards the right while the Emperor sits impassively facing left towards the onrushing beast which leaps at the erect lady while being attacked by two lancers. Following is a single lady representing the Imperial Preceptress herself to introduce the Lady Pan episode. The expression of a truly idiosyncratic creative intelligence is most clearly displayed in the contrasts provided for this scene. The virtuous lady follows behind the Emperor whose head is seen, above the side of his litter, looking backward with a lugubrious face while another lady is seated beside him, and his bearers seem to be moving under their burden with immense effort. The next scene, illustrating a metaphysical statement in poetic terms rather than a story with narrative elements, is most interesting if awkward. The pictorial image uses a mountain as its central motif, to the right of which is the sun and its symbols, and to the left the moon and its symbols. A man rests on one knee at the left, almost half the height of this peak, aiming a bow and arrow at a tiger on the slope. This animal is also exaggerated in size. By contrast, pheasants, rabbits and other beasts are smaller in scale and, at least, plausible in relation to the land mass. Similarly, the trees and landscape details

Plate 4 THE ADMONITIONS SCROLL: *"Make your heart like the grasshopper's, and you will multiply your kind."* (British Museum version)

are somewhat diminished in size to relate to the whole. There seems to be no obvious reason for these discrepancies in proportions. At the same time, there may appear to have been a failure of imagination in the literalness with which every concrete image (sun and moon, "earth building up in layers" and "an arrow shooting from the crossbow") was seized upon and transferred. It has been said that this scene represents the text in terms of symbols alone,[20] but these symbols are the equivalents of poetic similes, and their very combination in a noticeably artificial construct echoes the allusive quality of their textual origin. The difficulties of conveying metaphorical significance are also demonstrated in the next scene which shows one figure applying facial make-up while another seated figure is having his hair dressed by a standing female figure. Here, the details of dressing-stand, mirror and cosmetic boxes all fit with what we know of Han and Six Dynasties accoutrements. The artist's sense of humour and human acumen are again visible in the illustration of the couplet on true and false speech, with a gentleman addressing his spouse while seated on the edge of a bed, and she sitting inside as far away from him as the restricted space of this piece of furniture would permit. The inadequacy of the family scene as a formal composition has already been noted, but it is also less effective than other sections in conveying the gist of its verbal communication. The second to last group chose to represent two elements: a lady approaching a gentleman is rejected by him with a warding-off gesture from his left hand, and another lady is seated quietly alone, presumably perfecting her "commitment to compassion". Finally, the Imperial Preceptress is seen writing on a scroll before two court ladies.

[20] Alexander C. Soper, "Life-Motion and the Sense of Space in Early Chinese Representational Art," *Art Bulletin*, XXX: 3 (Sept. 1948), p. 178.

THE SECOND best known attribution to Ku is the illustration to the *Lo shen fu* which now exists in three known versions.[21] This title appeared within Ku's œuvre in the Yuan dynasty. It was next listed in Mao Wei 茅維's (act. ca. 1596) *Nan-yang ming-hua piao* 南陽名畫表. Wang K'o-yü 汪珂玉's *Shan-hu-wang* 珊瑚網 (1543) Book 1 describes a heavily coloured version on much damaged silk, with Sung dynasty mounting. Hu Chin's *Hsi-ch'ing cha-chi* Book 2 briefly mentions a scroll of this title attributed to Ku, but without signature. The 1744 imperial catalogue *Shih-ch'ü pao-chi* 石渠寶笈 describes a version with a Ch'ien-lung imperial inscription dated to 1741, four seals of the Jurchen Chin dynasty's Ming-ch'ang 明昌 reign (1190-1196) and five colophons, in Book 36. While in the collection of K'o Chiu-ssu 柯九思 (1312-1365), it had been seen by Chao Meng-fu 趙孟頫 (1254-1322) whose seals appeared on the scroll and whose inscription of the prose-poem itself in the calli-graphic style of Wang Hsi-chih 王羲之 (303-361) was on a separate piece of paper attached to the painting. After Chao's inscription of 1299, colophons were added by Li K'an 李衎 (1245-1320) in 1307, Yü Chi 虞集 (1272-1348), Shen Tu 沈度 (act. ca. 1401 on) in 1417 and Wu K'uan 吳寬 (1435-1504) in 1470. Finally, in the late Ch'ing dynasty, a connoisseur and dealer Li Pao-hsün 李葆恂 recorded, in his *Hai-wang-ch'un shuo-chien shu-hua lu* 海王村所見書畫錄 Book 1, what seems to have been another version from the imperial collection, with a seal of Li Kung-lin 李公麟's (ca. 1040-1106) collection, various seals of Liang Ch'ing-piao, an inscription by Tung Ch'i-ch'ang 董其昌 (1555-1636) and seals of the Ch'ien-lung emperor. Li also noted that there were many copies of Sung and later date, from Li Kung-lin's efforts onward.

The Freer Gallery scroll is clearly fragmentary, with only four episodes, but fits Li Pao-hsün's description, and entered the U.S.A. from the Tuan-fang 端方 (1861-1911) collection. The Peking Museum's more complete version in eight scenes arranged as a continuous composition is not inscribed with the prose-poem itself, and may be the one seen by Hu Ching. Finally, the Tung-pei Museum's freer render-ing is also partial, but contains one scene not found on either of the two other paint-ings, and having as well the text inscribed in sections and Ch'ien-lung seals.

OF THE THREE, the Peking scroll reveals the most amazing fidelity to the prose-poem's text.[22] A comparison between the poetic and pictorial descriptions will indicate what its illustrative attitude was.

---

[21] One in the Peking Ku Kung Museum is repro-duced in Ma Ts'ai, *op. cit.*, Pls. 1 ff. (seventeen in all), and in two details from *A Selection of Figural Paintings from Various Dynasties* (Shanghai, 1959). The scroll in the Freer Gallery of Art, Washington, D.C., is reproduced in Osvald Sirén, *op. cit.*, Part III, Pls. 9 and 10. The version in the Tung-pei Museum, Shen-yang, is also reproduced in Ma Ts'ai, *op. cit.*, Pl. 2 ff. (five in all). A fourth copy is supposed to exist but its where-abouts has not been noted; cf. Wen Chao-t'ung 溫肇桐,

"Ku K'ai-chih ti 'Lo-shen fu' t'u chüan" 顧愷之的洛神賦圖卷 (*The Nymph of the River Lo* Handscroll by Ku K'ai-chih), *Mei-shu* 美術, III (1957), p. 47.

[22] *Wen-hsüan* Book 19. Ts'ao Chih 曹植's (192-232) poem has been partially and rather freely translated by Arthur Waley, *op. cit.*, pp. 60-62. Unless otherwise acknowledged, all translations in this article are by its author.

NYMPH OF THE RIVER LO: Handscroll attributed to Ku K'ai-chih, illustrating the poem by Ts'ao Chih. This and Plates 7, 9, 11 are reproduced from the Ku Kung Museum version, Peking.

Plate 5 NYMPH OF THE RIVER LO: *"She moves with the lightness of wild geese in flight; with the sinuous grace of soaring dragons at play."*

Nymph of the River Lo

洛神賦

IN THE YEAR 223, after being at court in the capitol, I returned by the River Lo. According to the ancients, the deity of this river is named Mi-fei. Remembering Sung Yü 宋玉's (290-222 B.C.) account of the tale of the divine maiden and the King of Ch'u, I composed this prose-poem, its words being—

黃初三年，余朝京師，
還濟洛川。
古人有言：
斯水之神名曰宓妃。
感宋玉對楚王神女之事，
遂作斯賦。其辭曰：

LEAVING THE capitol and returning to my fief in the
    east,
With back to towering I-ch'üeh Mountain I crossed
    the tortuous Huan-yüan Pass;
Penetrated the great T'ung Valley and traversed the
    Ching Peak.
As the sun descended westward, horses and chariot
    were weary,
So we unhitched them upon a flowery bank, grazing
    the steeds amidst perfumed fields.

余從京域，言歸東藩。
背伊闕，
越轘轅。
經通谷，
陵景山。
日既西傾，
車殆馬煩。
爾乃稅駕乎蘅皋，
秣駟乎芝田。

The first scene of the Peking scroll shows two grooms by three horses gambolling and feeding in a meadow.

Then I rested within a willow grove, casting glances
    at the River Lo.
Suddenly, my spirits were startled and my thoughts
    scattered.
Bowing down I could see nothing, but looking up I
    beheld wonder:
I perceived a beauty at the foot of a precipice.

容與乎陽林，
流眄乎洛川。
於是精神移駭，
忽焉思散。
俯則未察，
仰以殊觀。
覿一麗人於巖之畔。
乃援御者而告之曰，
爾有覿於彼者乎。

Plate 6 NYMPH OF THE RIVER LO:
This detail and Plates 8, 10, 12, 13, 14 are
reproduced from the Freer Gallery version,
courtesy of the Smithsonian Institution,
Freer Gallery of Art, Washington, D.C.

Then I seized an attendant and asked:
"Do you see that person over there?
Who is she with so fair a form?"

The attendant replied: "I have heard of the Nymph
    of the River Lo, whose name is Mi-fei.
Perhaps that is whom Your Honour sees.
But what of her form? For I truly wish to know."
I replied: "She moves with the lightness of wild geese
    in flight;
With the sinuous grace of soaring dragons at play.
Her radiance outshines the autumn chrysanthemums;
Her luxuriance is richer than the spring pines.
She floats as do wafting clouds to conceal the moon;
She flutters as do gusting winds to eddy snow.
From afar she gleams like the sun rising from dawn
    mists;
At closer range she is luminous like lotus rising from
    clear waves.

彼何人斯，
若此之艷也。
御者對曰，
臣聞河洛之神，
名曰宓妃。
然則君王所見，
無乃是乎。
其狀若何，臣願聞之。
余告之曰，其形也，
翩若驚鴻，婉若游龍。
榮曜秋菊，華茂春松。
髣髴兮若輕雲之蔽月，
飄颻兮若流風之迴雪。
遠而望之，
皎若太陽升朝霞。
迫而察之，
灼若芙蕖出綠波。

In the scroll, a group of men, Ts'ao and his attendants, are represented gazing to the left at the nymph who stands on the surface of the waves. The artist has chosen to convey Ts'ao's eulogy, with its profusion of similes, by simply representing the objects to which she is compared. Thus, two geese in flight and an ascending dragon appear in the sky to the right of her figure, a sun with its crow symbol rises from behind clouds to the left, while lotus flowers emerge from the waters below.

Her height and girth fit exactly in proportion;
Her shoulders are sculptured forms, and her waist
    pliant as a bundle of silk.

襛纖得衷，修短合度。
肩若削成，腰如約素。

Plate 8   NYMPH OF THE RIVER LO: *"P'eng-i beat his drums, and Nü-wa trilled her song."* (Freer Gallery version)

Her slender neck and tapered nape reveal a glowing surface,
Without application of scent or fragrant powders;
Her hair coils in cumulus clouds and her brows curve in silken threads;
Her cinnebar lips gleam without, with snowy teeth pure within;
Her bright eyes glance charmingly, and dimples decorate her cheeks.
Her deportment is superb and her attitude tranquil;
Her manner is gentle and elegant, and her speech bewitching;
Her unusual dress is that of another world and her form worthy of depiction.
Wrapped in brilliant gauzes, she is adorned with earrings of rich jade,
And hair ornament of gold and feathers; her body glistens with strings of pearls.
She treads upon "far-roaming" patterned slippers, trailing a skirt of misty silk;
She skims among fragrant growths of delicate orchids and wafts by the mountain slopes."

延頸秀項，皓質呈露。
芳澤無加，鉛華弗御。
雲髻峨峨，修眉聯娟。
丹唇外朗，皓齒內鮮。
明眸善睞，靨輔承權。
瓌姿艷逸，儀靜體閑。
柔情綽態，媚於語言。
奇服曠世，骨像應圖。
披羅衣之璀粲兮，
珥瑤碧之華琚。
戴金翠之首飾，
綴明珠以耀軀。
踐遠遊之文履，
曳霧綃之輕裾。
微幽蘭之芳藹兮，
步踟躕於山隅。

The nymph is seen placed in a setting of hills and flowers, and is elaborately garbed.

Then, suddenly, she straightened herself and took to random play,
On her left a brilliant banner, and on her right a cassia flag.

於是忽焉縱體，
以遨以嬉。
左倚采旄，右蔭桂旗。

Plate 9 NYMPH OF THE RIVER LO: A section from the Ku Kung Museum version, depicting the same scene as Plate 8.

She bent her wrist to a fairy bank to pluck a dark
    reed from the shallows.
Thrilled by her beauty, my heart moved restlessly,
Lacking a go between to join us in happiness, I
    entrusted my message to the rippling waters.
Wishing to express my sincerity, I removed a jade
    pendant as pledge of my vow.
How courteous the fair one was, how refined in
    propriety and poetry!
For she offered precious gems in acceptance, and
    pointed to the mysterious depths in promise.
But, realizing the vicissitudes of love, I feared the
    spirit would betray me.
For I remembered how Chiao-fu was once deceived,[23]
So was I cunningly forewarned and wary as a fox.
I composed my expression and quieted my mind;
I assumed an air of dignity and held myself aloof.
Whereupon, the Nymph of the River Lo was moved;
    she wavered and faltered;
Her divine light flickered, now darkening and again
    gleaming.
She tensed her light frame like a crane erect, about to
    fly but yet with wings furled;
She trod along the clove-spun path, spreading fragrance
    of the herbs.
She uttered a long cry of eternal love, a sound sorrow-
    ful and enduring.

攘皓腕於神滸兮，
采湍瀨之玄芝。
余情悅其淑美兮，
心振蕩而不怡。
無良媒以接懽兮，
托微波而通辭。
願誠素之先達兮，
解玉珮以要之。
嗟佳人之信修兮，
羌習禮而明詩。
抗瓊珶以和予兮，
指潛淵而爲期。
執眷眷之款實兮，
懼斯靈之我欺。
感交甫之棄言兮，
悵猶豫而狐疑。
收和顏而靜志兮，
申禮防以自持。
於是洛靈感焉，
徙倚傍徨。
神光離合，乍陰乍陽。
竦輕軀以鶴立，
若將飛而未翔。
踐椒塗之郁烈，
步蘅薄而流芳。
超長吟以永慕兮，
聲哀厲而彌長。

[23]Chiao-fu exchanged vows with two immortal maidens who immediately disappeared.

Plate 10 NYMPH OF THE RIVER LO: *"Wishing to express my sincerity, I removed a jade pendant as pledge of my vow."*(Freer Gallery version).

At this, the multitude of spirits came flocking to proclaim their amity.
Some splashed through the clear waves and others winged amidst the sacred isles;
Some gathered brilliant pearls and others kingfishers' plumes.
Together came the two queens of the Hsiang River, and she who roamed the bank of the River Han.
They sang the doleful song of the Ladle Constellation that knew no mate, and pealed the ballad of the Herdboy's loneliness.

爾乃衆靈雜遝，
命儔嘯侶。
或戲清流，或翔神渚，
或采明珠，或拾翠羽。
從南湘之二妃，
攜漢濱之遊女。
嘆匏瓜之無匹兮，
詠牽牛之獨處。

There is a break at this point in the Peking scroll, for the landscape elements do not match at the join of silk lengths. The Tung-pei version has the first group of Ts'ao and his attendants immediately followed by the nymph's figure moving left towards the noble backed by only three attendants (of eight in the first scene). At no other point and on no other copy is any group represented with a strong counter-movement to the right as seen here. Could this have been a replacement for a missing section? We would expect some illustration of the exchange of vows, Ts'ao's uneasiness and its consequences.

The nymph, her light mantle fluttering in the wind, trailing her long sleeves, stood still for a while.
Then, swift as a bird on the wing, with the elusiveness of an immortal,
She passed lightly over the waves, her silken stockings rousing fine dust.
Her movements were unpredictable, at once unsure and calm, seeming to advance and to retreat.

揚輕袿之猗靡兮，
翳脩袖以延佇。
體迅飛鳧，飄忽若神。
陵波微步，羅襪生塵。
動無常則，若危若安。
進止難期，若往若還。

Plate 11 NYMPH OF THE RIVER LO: *"She summoned the flying fish to guard her chariot, and the sound of jade chimes mark her departure."* (Ku Kung Museum version).

She turned her glittering eyes backward, which lit up
   her jade-like face;
She withheld her words, only exhaled the fragrance
   of rare orchids.
Her beauty was such as to make me forgetful of self.

轉眄流精，光潤玉顏。
含辭未吐，氣若幽蘭。
華容婀娜，令我忘飱。

The nymph is repeated four times, thrice accompanied by a spirit attendant of whom one is depicted in the peculiar attitude of moving on her knees. This unusual detail is also to be seen on the Tung-pei scroll.

Then the Storm God lulled the winds and the Water
   God stilled the waves;
P'eng-i beat his drums, and Nü-wa trilled her song.
The nymph summoned the flying fish to guard her
   chariot,
And the sound of jade chimes mark her departure.
Six dragons, majestic in even line, pulled the floating
   cloud chariot;
Whales and dolphins gambolled at its wheelside, while
   water fowl flew as escort.

於是屛翳收風，
川后靜波。
馮夷鳴鼓，女媧清歌。
騰文魚以警乘，
鳴玉鸞以偕逝。
六龍儼其齊首，
載雲車之容裔。
鯨鯢踊而夾轂，
水禽翔而爲衞。

Ts'ao is shown seated, partially surrounded by five attendants, watching the departure of the nymph. The Washington fragment begins at this point. All the deities of earth and sky cited in the poem are depicted to the left of the nymph. Following this section, the Peking scroll again appears to have suffered a loss. There is another clear break in its join of two pieces of silk between the official group and the nymph seated upon the Jade Phoenix. On the Freer example, the distance between the two protagonists is fairly long, while it is too short on the Ku Kung copy to create a suitable effect of increasing separation between the worlds of immortal and man. In both versions, the nymph's head is turned back to the right.

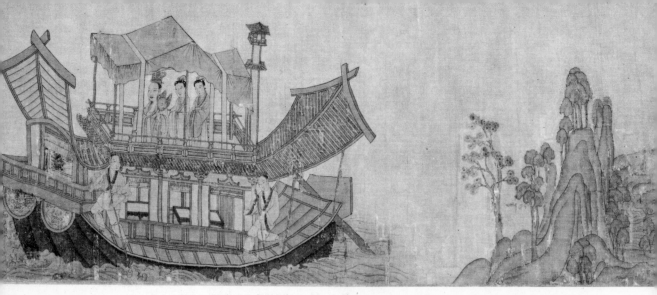

Plate 13 NYMPH OF THE RIVER LO: *"I floated on the long stream forgetting to return, my thoughts like tangled threads, my longing ever increasing."* (Freer Gallery version).

All three copies retain the section with her unearthly mode of travel, though the Peking scroll is the simplest in its depiction and the Washington version the most elaborate.

Having crossed the northern islet and passed the southern mound,
She turned her smooth neck and gazed back with clear eyes.
She moved her red lips and slowly spoke of the rules of friendship,
Of her regret that the ways of man and divinity are separate, and her sorrow at the waste of her prime of life.
She raised her damask sleeve to conceal the tears which coursed in streams onto her collar;
She grieved at the eternal severance of this love, and mourned the finality of her departure.
"Unable to return the slightest affection for your love, let me offer you this bright pearl of the South.
Though I stay concealed in the Great Darkness, my heart will long be entrusted to you, my lord."

於是越北沚，過南岡。
紆素領，迴清揚。
動朱唇以徐言，
陳交接之大綱。
恨人神之道殊兮，
怨盛年之莫當。
抗羅袂以掩涕兮，
淚流襟之浪浪。
悼良會之永絕兮，
哀一逝而異鄉。
無微情以效愛兮，
獻江南之明璫。
雖潛處於太陰，
長寄心於君王。

The Peking scroll shows the nymph clearly with her head turned back and mouth open as if in speech, though the last detail is less clear in the two other versions.

Suddenly, I no longer see where she was, for the divinity had disappeared, and her light had faded.
Then, descending from the high mountain, I walked away, but my heart remained.

忽不悟其所舍，
悵神宵而蔽光。
於是背下陵高，
足往神留。

My mind dwelt upon her image, and, looking about,
  I became depressed.
Hoping that the divinity would resume her form,
I embarked upstream on a swift boat to begin my
  search.
I floated on the long stream forgetting to return,
My thoughts like tangled threads, my longing ever
  increasing.
At night, disquieted I could not sleep, and, soaked by
  the dew, I remained awake till dawn.

遺情想像，顧望懷愁。
冀靈體之復形，
御輕舟而上遡。
浮長川而忘返，
思綿綿而增慕。
夜耿耿而不寐，
霑繁霜而至曙。

All copies show Ts'ao in a boat, attended by two ladies, and then seated on the shore with a pair of lighted candles by his side to suggest the sleepless night. The Freer copy has a detail of a landscape scroll hanging within the boat and visible from its bow through a window, which is thought to date it as a Southern Sung dynasty work.[24]

I ordered the grooms to hitch the chariot, and was
  about to resume the eastern road.
I seized the reins and raised the whip; yet, depressed
  and undecided, I could not leave.

命仆夫而就駕，
吾將歸乎東路。
攬騑轡以抗策，
悵盤桓而不能去。

Both the Peking and Tung-pei versions terminate with this scene of Ts'ao seated in a chariot and looking back to the river, while the Freer copy ends with his night watch. Interesting in both scrolls in China is the presence of a lady seated beside Ts'ao in the chariot, a contradiction of the expressed sentiment, and perhaps a satirical note which echoes that already described for the Lady Pan episode of the *Admonitions* . . . scroll.

[24]Taki Seiichi 瀧拙庵, "Ku K'ai-chih's Illustration of the Poem of Lo-shen," *Kokka* 國華, No. 582 (May 1939), pp. 139-144.

The Ku Kung example offers one striking difference from the Freer one in terms of formal rendering; that is, a less distressing incongruity of scale. Though trees are in all versions not much taller than human figures, in the Peking scroll, they offer a greater impression of mass through close grouping and fullness of foliage. The spatial continuum is more closely defined in it as well. An extended landscaped ground reaches to about the midpoint of the scroll's height and is defined through use of colour as well as line. In the other two copies, the landscape elements in the immediate foreground are distinctly represented with line and colour, but contours tend to dissolve into soft washes with recession. Figural types also differ from each other. The Peking copy's bulky figures with smooth flowing draperies to emphasize their mass recall T'ang dynasty types. However, its female divinities with slender bodies and garments in active movement remain closer to what we can reconstruct of Chin dynasty forms. The Washington copy shows uniformly slim figures, but not elongated bodies with small heads such as are familiar in Six Dynasties archaeological finds. Their lines, too, are stiffer and straighter than in the Peking work. Finally, the Tung-pei copy betrays temporally the latest figural style, with its emphasis upon hard lines and more complicated drapery folds which return to a non-descriptive pattern of schematization. All three show some fidelity to Six Dynasties costume, hair arrangements and tree stylizations. There can be little doubt that efforts were made to recapture original effects.

Certain points may be established about the appearance of the original from the evidence of these copies. First, the horizontal scroll form was in use, but organized as separate and closed scenes. Movement from one part to the next was prompted by the action of main figures in a single direction. Second, landscape setting was conceived in terms of "space cells". Emphasis upon an accumulation of landscape motifs in the immediate foreplane, with only occasional definitions of rocks and trees behind, indicates that it was felt unnecessary to enclose the space in which figures were set. Third, plant motifs were executed with a limited range of foliage patterns. An exact definition of leaf contours prevented a correct relationship between the parts of trees or shrubs. Finally, decorative lines were exploited in seemingly wind-blown drapery, and in the scrolled stylizations of waves and clouds.

Common to all three versions is a certain charming naivité in the illustration of narrative. Compartmentalization of the continuous scroll form was adapted to a temporal and spatial sequence. Their elements of representation are specific and concrete; thus, all metaphorical allusions were translated into visible images. The reading of such a painting is literary as well as pictorial in its demands upon an understanding of standard symbols.[25]

IF WE TURN to examine Ku K'ai-chih's own literary production, will we discover a special quality of visualization expressed through verbal means? Fortunately, the most complete of his extant writings is also in the *fu* (prose-poem) form; the *Lei-tien fu* 雷電賦 (Prose-Poem on Thunder and Lightning) being, therefore, comparable to the *Lo-shen fu* and its illustration. Ku's composition has been described by Ch'en Shih-hsiang as follows—

> "Its word-power is as enchanting as that of any other good work in this *fu* genre. But remarkable is the occasional demonstration of an artist's insight into the visual attraction of the raging natural elements in a sublime landscape."[26]

The late Professor Ch'en then offered a partial translation "to show its quality". His version is a masterful one, but for the sake of consistency in English literary style, it has been thought preferable to offer another translation of the entire poem.[27]

Prose-Poem on Thunder and Lightning   雷電賦

> In ordering of the cosmic chaos and purification of
>   the primal ether,
> *Yin* and *yang* coalesced to produce thunder and
>   lightning.

太極紛綸，
元氣澄練。
陰陽相薄，
爲雷爲電。

---

[25] The third attribution to Ku is a *Lieh-nü chuan t'u* 列女傳圖 (Illustrations to the Biographies of Illustrious Women) which may be reflected in a handscroll also in the Peking Ku Kung Museum, reproduced in Ma Ts'ai, *op. cit.*, six scenes; P'an T'ien-shou, *op. cit.*, Pls. 11-24; and Yü Chien-hua, *op. cit.*, Pls. 35-38. A woodblock printed edition of Liu Hsiang 劉向's text appeared in 1063, with a preface identifying its illustrations as copies after Ku's work. Chang Yen-yüan, *op. cit.*, Book 5 does specify a "Maiden of the Ah Valley" among Ku's œuvre, and her story is included in the *Lieh-nü chuan* Book 6 as a model of "penetrating argument". The blocks were recarved in 1825 by Yüan Fu 元福, whose sister Chi-lan 季蘭 was responsible for copying the illustrations. Extant copies of this edition show that very little of the original's style could have survived after passing through the hands of first Sung then Ch'ing artisans. The Ku Kung painting is fragmentary. A Sung inscription by Wang Chu 汪注 notes that the original had fifteen scenes containing twenty-four male figures, twenty-one female figures and four children. A version extant in the Sung dynasty had eight scenes composed of fifteen male figures, nine female figures and four children. Later, another copy was discovered in a private collection. This was executed on paper and had fourteen scenes, lacking only five figures of the original. These were again copied to remedy omissions in the previous copy. Only twenty-seven figures have been reproduced. Their hard lines, very much schematized in drapery folds, indicate that they are of late production, probably post-Sung. However, the compositions and general illustrative approach are closely related to the *Admonitions* . . . scroll, though adding very little to our further understanding of Ku's literary and pictorial interpretations. The figures are grouped simply, moving in dignified poses against a plain background. The subjects are identified more clearly in inscription than through expressive or animated action. Furthermore, all other elements reflect this scroll's later origin. Even the garments, vessels and furniture are of post-Sung, and possibly Ming types.

[26] Ch'en Shih-hsiang, *op. cit.*, pp. 9-11.

[27] The former Professor of Chinese at the University of California at Berkeley was certainly influenced in his English poetic style by the generation of Oxford aesthetes just after the First World War, for he was a student of Harold Acton's at Ch'ing-hua University 清華大學; cf. Harold Acton, *Memoirs of an Aesthete* (London, 1948).

They battled (the sacrilegious) Wu-i by the Yellow
   River, demonstrating his punishment by ex-
   ecution;
They shook the temple of the Chan clan, exposing a
   concealed crime.
Thus it was that Confucius himself would suddenly
   alter his respectful visage (at their phenomena).
For (thunder's) noise is without fixed outbreak and
   (lightning's) flash is without constant gleam,
But like the deafening crash of rolling wheels and the
   secrative flickers of dodging flames.
When the yin sinks and the yang rises,
Torpid insects emerge, their vitalized spirits first to
   respond
In multitudes gently vibrating, neither agitated nor
   passive.
When the (yin musical mode of) Lin-chung rules the
   season of humid heat and shimmering haze,
Stars and moon blur, and clothing feels aflame,
Then, to usher in a pure breeze gusting away dust and
   dirt,
Richly rumbling the sound breaks and jaggedly the
   clouds are rent apart.
Then it is that worn faces open to renewed vigour;
Though disturbing one's peace and troubling one's
   rest,
(Thunder and lightning) arouse the vital essence and
   stimulate the spirit.
When the wrath of Heaven is about to erupt, crimson
   lightning issues first,
Exposing cliffs from all sides, glaring or gleaming in
   double perfection.
Thunder and lightning are awesome enough to move
   the Earth's pivot,
Rebounding and disrupting so that mountains and
   oceans submit (to their greater might).
When noon and midnight are in balance, waters dry
   up and trees become bare,
Winter's second month is about to commence and
   concealed thunder bursts out,
Crashing and booming, flashing and blinding.
How could this be but 'sound and fury signifying
   nothing'?
For it banishes accord and injures life;
It reveals the ruler's loss of the just mean, and makes
   visible the secret of Heaven and Earth.

擊武乙於河,
而誅戮之罰明。
震展氏之廟,
而隱慝之誅見。
是以宣尼,
敬威忽變。
夫其聲無定響,
光不恒照。
砰訇輪轉,
倏閃藏曜。
若乃太陰下淪,
少陽初升。
蟄蟲將啟,
動靈先應。
殷殷徐振,
不激不憑。
林鍾統節,
溽暑烟熅。
星月不朗,
衣裳若焚。
爾乃清風前颾,
蕩濁流塵。
豐隆破響,
裂缺開雲。
當時倦容,
廓焉精新。
豈直驚安煉寐,
乃以暢精悟神。
天怒將凌,
赤電先發。
窺岩四照,
影流雙絕。
雷電赫以驚衡,
山海磕其奔裂。
若夫子午相乘,
水旱木零。
仲冬奮發,
伏雷先行。
磕磕隆隆,
閃閃夐夐。
豈隱隱之虛憑,
乃違和而傷生。
昭王度之失節,
見二儀之幽情。

Then again, sometimes, in the bright sun and cloud-
  less sky of an early morn,
That spiritual eye will raise its essence to flame
  fiercely;
The stalwart drum will burst the skies with its
  sonorous beats;
Then tombs and citadels roar (echoing) as if in
  expectation of down-fall;
Flat lands heave vertical as if about to disintegrate;
Mortal beings lose their lives before they knew it;
Dragons and demons are dislodged in tumultuous
  confusion;
Light startles (those) in river depths and noise vibrates
  beyond heaven's bounds.
It is like the scattering of the Great Dipper at the
  sacred birth (of the Yellow Emperor):
The shaking of K'un-yang when (Wang Meng) attack-
  ed the transgressor;
The falling of deer horns to caution (Hsia) Chieh;
The suicides (by T'ien Heng's followers) on the isle
  between two rivulets;
The tossing of fallen junipers up to Heaven's limits
  (when the Duke of Chou died);[28]
The grazing of soaring dragons at the clouds' borders.
Set the whole earth ablaze with your encircling glare;
Solemnize the Six Directions with your transforming
  power.
Moving within the sphere of spiritual virtue,
The ways of divinities are beyond our comprehension.

至乃辰開日朗，
太清無靄。
靈眼揚精以麗煥，
狀鼓崩天而砰磕。
陵雉訇隱以待傾，
方地嶪嶷其若敗。
蒼生非悟而喪魂，
龍鬼失據以顛沛。
光驚於泉底，
聲動於天外。
及其灑北斗以誕聖，
震昆陽以伐違。
降枝鹿以命桀，
島雙漬而橫屍。
驚倒檜於霄際，
摧騰龍於雲湄。
烈大地以繞映，
惟六合以動威。
在靈德而卷舒，
謝神艷之難追。

The poem's structure in temporal sequence is comparable to that of the *Lo-shen fu*; similarly its use of onomatopœic words, of literary similes and metaphors. Is it hindsight that causes us to see in it a richer display of observed and natural detail? Is there not a richer texture of direct physical impact, depending less upon abstruse vocabulary, and more upon sensual stimulation?

We may conjecture that literature achieved effects beyond the representational artist's powers, certainly in Ku K'ai-chih's time, and probably in all the pre-Sung dynasty periods. In the third quarter of the 20th century, when the converse is steadily becoming more and more evident, might we not pause to consider what might have been and what might be if both literary and pictorial creativity proceeded in equality?

---

[28]For the Yellow Emperor allusion, see the *Sung Shih* 宋史 "Fu-jui pien 符瑞篇"; the Wang Meng allusion, see Chang Heng 張衡's *Tung-ching fu* 東京賦; T'ien Heng's followers, see the *Shih Chi* 史記 biography; the Duke of Chou's death, see the *Shang Shu* 尚書 "Chin-t'eng pien" 金縢篇. Two allusions have not been identified.

The Artist and the Landscape:

Changing Views of Nature in Chinese Painting

By **Richard Edwards**

SOMETIMES IT IS necessary to re-examine the long view and in doing so learn to understand more exactly what is close. This is particularly true when the long view apparently reveals a continuous unchallenged tradition and seems therefore to assert a kind of changeless truth for which the next step must be unquestioned acceptance. In respect to the civilization of China, who is there to challenge the fact that the Chinese love nature? Who is there when we turn to the arts to quarrel with the proposition that as a reflection of this "love" the Chinese century after century painted landscapes?

What is perhaps obvious, and yet not always remembered, is that in the world of the painted landscape there is truly no Nature. There are only natures, if we drive the point to the limit, as many as there are paintings of those natures. Certainly there may be types and for convenience and understanding one may assemble many under a single heading, but at heart the story of the painting of the landscape is a very personal encounter and is linked to the fact that an almost infinite number of separate "natures" were painted down through the centuries. The broad generality of nature is only to be realized through the separate individual realizations of it.

To state that there are as many natures—or in this case landscapes—as there are individuals perceiving nature is not far from the truth. At the least the proposition makes us aware of the person that is painting the landscape, and that person at a given time. It places our understanding of the "love of nature" on the foundation of a particular perception. It establishes a basis for an acceptance of variety and change so that in our view of history and of individual artists we are pressed to constantly refocus "nature" whenever we confront it anew. Each painting presses upon us a multi-, rather than uni-, form sense of what we are trying to understand.

All this compels us to realize that "nature" is not something just to be accepted. Nor is it easy to define. When we return to the long view of Chinese civilization we cannot now be surprised to discover not only many landscapes but indeed the very opposite: that the nature-landscape was not always present. For centuries, if it was there at all, it was concealed in the abstractions of ornament and symbol, or the symbols of ornament, so that the understanding of streams and mountains can only come to us through the reading of a strange language which indeed may be saying something entirely different. (Pl. 15) Certainly the artist's "love of nature", which I take here to be revealed in love of the visible forms of nature, is not apparent. And this is a matter of no brief time.

From the high sophistication of early neolithic pottery as early as the fourth

Plate 15 CHINESE BRONZE, ceremonial vessel of the type *p'an*, Anyang, 12th-11th centuries B.C. Freer Gallery of Art. Courtesy of the Smithsonian Institution, Freer Gallery of Art, Washington, D.C.

millenium B.C. down through the varied refinements of bronze culture embellishment there is, exactly, no landscape. At the very outset "love of nature" in China is suspect and as in any other culture is in need of definition. It is questionable that we should translate this seemingly inward view into "fear of nature", but we cannot in these early centuries speak of "normal" nature at all, that is nature in an objective sense. However, knowing when it did not exist we can, perhaps, understand when it began. The one necessity, since objective perception is inconceivable without it, is the simple yet extremely complex ingredient of space. We must begin to find that love of nature, which is exactly to be seen in the painted landscape, where space begins.

HISTORICALLY IT MIGHT be argued that there are earlier intimations, but it is with the Western Han (206 B.C.-9 A.D.) that we can be sure of it, and here one is drawn to one of the most extraordinary of early Chinese paintings, the banner excavated in 1972 from the second century B.C. tomb Ma-wang Tui no. 1 at Chang-sha. It is painted in ink and colors on silk and was found in the tomb of an aristocratic lady, most famous because her body, in the flesh, was so completely preserved within its layers of coffins. Before being draped over the coffin this object was presumably carried as a banner in the funeral procession. What is painted clearly had a direct relation to the deceased and the final rites performed on her behalf.

BANNER FROM MA-WANG TUI, Changsha, Tomb No. 1. Ink and color on silk.
Plate 16   (*left*): Detail, upper centre.
Plate 17   (*right*): Detail, top.

For our purposes let us isolate a section and start close to the center (Pl. 16). At this center is a slab-like platform on which are human figures—the slab somewhat mysteriously suspended and ultimately framed on either side by two symmetrically arranged dragons and cloud forms—and on the top a canopy beneath which facing us hovers a bat-like form—while above the canopy is a central medallion flanked by long-tailed birds.

These forms—beasts, birds, dragons—come directly from earlier notions of rather mysterious forms, but they have quite literally stepped aside to allow a kind of cave of space in which the human figure can perform. The human figures here are six. The central one in profile, slightly bowed, hunched of shoulder, leaning on a staff, is indeed important enough in her position and scale, specific enough in her depiction, to be rightly interpreted as a portrait of the deceased. Two figures in smaller scale kneel in allegiance, or service, before her. Three tall, slender yet lesser scale figures stand in attendance behind. These three attendants are arranged in such a way as to overlap each other and thereby to create the illusion of a recession in space. There is thus, clearly, an ambient *around* the central figure and that ambient extends to an even more spacious extent above her. The spaces above have in turn their own depth, as is affirmed by the bat-like figure who in a kind of elemental foreshortening moves directly at us, certainly out of somewhere.

The nature of that somewhere is more importantly revealed at the next level of the banner (Pl. 17) where indeed we are confronted by a whole panoply of figures, animals, dragons, circular symbols, birds. That somehow we as humans relate to them is affirmed by the presence, in the lower part of this scene, of two symmetrically arranged persons, precisely robed in cap and gown. These two figures seated in a formal space—even at a kind of gate—beneath a large bell have most imaginatively and possibly rightly been interpreted as officials connected with an important part of the rites of death as practised in the south of China in the ancient Kingdom of

Ch'u, whose center was Chang-sha. These figures may have been responsible for what was known as the Summons of the Soul, Chao-hun 招魂.[1]

Here poetry comes to our aid, for poems which are that very summons have survived in the most famous collection of early southern poetry, the *Ch'u Tz'ŭ* 楚辭. "The Great Summons", Ta Chao 大招, was an effort to bring back the soul of the departed after it had passed that seemingly final barrier of death:

> *Green spring follows the old year and the bright sun shines,*
> *And the breath of spring stirs, quickening all creation.*
> *Dark winter's frosts melt away. O soul, do not flee!*
> *O soul, come back! Do not go far away!*
>
> *O soul, go not to the east!...*
> *In the east is the great sea, where the swelling waters billow*
> *   endlessly,*
> *And water-dragons swim side by side, swiftly darting above*
> *   and below.*
>
> *It is clammy with rain and fog, that glister white and heavy.*
> *O soul, go not to the east, to the desolate Valley of Morning!*
>
> *O soul, go not to the south! In the south is burning fire*
> *   (for a hundred leagues), and coiling cobras;*

[1]See "Tso-t'an Ch'ang-sha Ma-wang-tui i-hao Han mu" 座談長沙馬王堆一號漢墓, *Wen-wu* 文物, 1972, no. 9, pp. 52-73. Inevitably there are varied explanations of the complex imagery of the banner. The close connection with the Summons of the Soul is argued by Yu Wei-ch'ao 俞偉超, pp. 60-61. For a discussion in English see, Fong Chow, "Ma-wang-tui. A Treasure-trove from the Western Han Dynasty", *Artibus Asiae*, XXXV (1973), pp. 5-24.

The mountains rise sheer and steep; tigers and leopards slink;
The cow-fish is there, and the spit-sand, and the rearing
            python:
O soul, go not to the south! There are monsters there that
            will harm you.

O soul, go not to the west! In the west are the Moving Sands
            stretching endlessly on and on,
And beasts with heads like swine, slanting eyes and shaggy
            hair,
Long claws and serrated teeth, and wild, mad laughter.
O soul, go not to the west! In the west are many dangers.
. . . .

O soul, go not to the north! There is no bourn there to your
            journeying.
. . . .

O soul, come back to leisure and quietness![2]

The poem then goes on to describe the delights of living in the land of Ch'u. The parallelism to the painting is rather exact in the sense that there is a "safe" area, a limited part of the world where there is space for humans to move freely, to indulge in all variety of human delights, of food and wine, music and dancing, beautiful women, night revels, hunting parks and elegant courts. And indeed such themes are vital to much that has survived of Han art. But just beyond the gateway, where at least in hindsight we think we might find what we could affirm as *real* nature, we only encounter mystery as in the "unnatural" forms at the top of this banner and as in the east, south, west and north of "The Great Summons".

This, then, is nature: seemingly of vast extension, grasped as encompassing fixed directions, something separated from us, something other than us, something out there that can only be represented as symbol. It is connected with mysteries that affect us directly, but since they are mysteries they are involved with us most exactly when our own existence must face what we do not understand.

THEN AS HISTORY unfolds begins a process in which man becomes more confident in himself. His own image is more clear, and quite literally, with confidence he becomes more able to move in space. In being not only more sure of himself, he becomes as well more aware of what is around him.

It is an oversimplification to claim that the stages are exact, but as one looks at imagery from about the second century on one can see what is happening, and the drive toward the "classic" Chinese view of man and nature is apparent.

Fascinating as it may be, it is not the purpose of this essay to trace these steps but rather to establish the goal—an end which places us securely within a landscape that is most exactly that classic view—the image that can confidently be evoked in praise of China's most secure love of nature. Fan K'uan's 范寬 Travelling among Mountains and Streams is such a view and it brings us close to a readily remembered date of about 1000 A.D. (Pl. 18). Whatever else it may tell us it is a painting in praise

[2]David Hawkes, *Ch'u Tz'u, The Songs of the   South*, Oxford, 1953, pp. 109-110.

Plate 18 TRAVELLING AMONG MOUN-
TAINS AND STREAMS, by Fan K'uan.
Hanging scroll, ink on silk. National Palace
Museum, Taipei.

Plate 19   FISHING IN A MOUNTAIN STREAM,
by Hsü Tao-ning. Handscroll, ink on silk. Section.
William Rockhill Nelson Gallery, Kansas City.

of the great mountain. Indeed it is the very daring of the artist's conception that allows two thirds of its close to seven feet of silk to be devoted solely to the great peak itself. This is nature's substance in its largest most massive realization. True form is not a statue or an ornament. It is the visible structure of what stands most firmly in the world around us.

But as has already been suggested, it is space which is the true proof of the landscape. To exist the landscape must be "out there". The landscape rejects the spaceless "within" and establishes its truth, the statement of that which can be "loved", by its extension beyond the point where we stand. Thus to the form that is ultimately mountain is linked the space that is ultimately far distance. When Fan K'uan saw nature as mountain, others saw the greatness of nature more surely as extension. Hsü Tao-ning's 許道寧 Fishing in a Mountain Stream (Pl. 19), probably painted very close to the time of Fan K'uan's masterpiece, reveals that love of distance. It is an extraordinary accomplishment: the taking of a flat surface of wall or paper or silk and transforming that flat matter into the reality of infinite distance. ". . . with one small brush I can draw the vast universe."[3]

The notion of great mountains and far distances can, however, be expressed in another way. Our experience of mountains is in fact of something massive, powerful and high, and when in nature we are able to gain a physical vantage point and look out upon that nature, we do in fact see great distances. Despite the temptation to evoke mystic incantations of the *tao* 道 or dwell on the oft repeated wonders of "spirit-rhythm and life-movement" *ch'i-yun sheng-tung* 氣韻生動, philosophical and

---

[3]Attributed to Wang Wei (415-43) as quoted in   Shio Sakanishi, *The Spirit of the Brush*, London, 1939,
p. 44.

aesthetic ideals established when landscape either did not exist at all or was in its infancy, it may be that at heart the Chinese artist was trying to convey something quite simple and direct. This is the way mountains *look* to the eye. This is the way distances *are*. What power is there in distance if it does not extend forever? Or in a mountain that does not stand staunch and tall? In a word, landscape was caught in the realistic intent. The old symbols were rejected. Instead, the artist used newly discovered artistic conventions—a process of invention which took several centuries —to convey the immediate reality of moving over broad areas of water or of deep valleys, of capturing the rugged fractured rocks of lofty summits to which might cling the growth of strong persistent trees.

Hsia Kuei 夏珪 (act. c. 1190-1225) insofar as we know him was perhaps the greatest master of the broad view of nature (Pl. 20). Painting in the late twelfth or early thirteenth century he leads us persistently and always from statements of physical fact into the relation of those facts to a broad continuum—visually, space —and because of the vast extension of that space, into the reaches of time.

But it is the persistence of a respect for physical reality that within the Chinese tradition sets aside Hsia Kuei and his contemporaries and which gives their art, in what is now the late Sung, a special meaning within a tradition that has generally thought to have been more concerned with the arbitrariness of the romantic and inward imagination. Only as we accept this can we understand the Sung landscape. Realism in the visual arts is, inevitably, the visually real. Hence it is most persistently affirmed by those artists who are concerned with the look of solid shapes and the appearance of exact surfaces. But what shape looks like and what texture appears to be depends on light. Hence the true realist in the art of painting is he who seeks to

Plate 20   A PURE AND REMOTE VIEW OF STREAMS AND MOUNTAINS, by Hsia Kuei. Handscroll, ink on paper. Section showing near and far distance. National Palace Museum, Taipei.

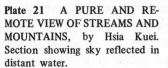

Plate 21 A PURE AND RE-
MOTE VIEW OF STREAMS AND
MOUNTAINS, by Hsia Kuei.
Section showing sky reflected in
distant water.

Plate 22 A PURE AND RE-
MOTE VIEW OF STREAMS AND
MOUNTAINS, by Hsia Kuei.
Section showing piled-up cliffs,
temples and figures.

place those shapes and textures, not in some generalized ambient but in the specific
context of specific light—which inevitably must also mean specific time. Following
this logic, the great realist in the modern western tradition is Claude Monet, for he
sought to affirm that to see a thing as it really is one must see it as exact light reveals
it to us.

To move further along the Hsia Kuei scroll (Pl. 21) it is indeed the subtle
presence of light that reveals his rather special visually realistic intent. For in a vast
space of water and sky we are looking not just at white paper, or paper generally
washed with light ink, but at a rather specific wash of ink in the sky which is
distinctly caught again in an echoing wash across the water below. It is the reflection
of thin clouds in the sky upon the mirror-like surface of the lake—a phenomenon
to which any one can attest who has seen the glassy sea or lake beneath a sky
touched with thin flat stretches of clouds.

This desire to fill one's eyes with "things", even as fragile a "thing" as light, is
further affirmed as we move to a suddenly emerging rocky section of the scroll
(Pl. 22). Not only is rock, as compared to water and sky, a sharply contrasting
substance, but the substance itself is filled and seemingly the deeper we go, the more
we find. Ultimately, hidden caves (left center) reveal men deep in the heart of a
powerfully structured nature.

Ma Lin 馬麟, an artist of the next generation from Hsia Kuei, painted his well-known Evening Landscape close to the date of 1254. It is now in the Nezu collection in Tokyo.[4] Seemingly reduced as are the elements, it is an extremely concrete—if you will, real—landscape. Our view-point is high but it is direct, and we catch on the far horizon the rose of a sunset glow. It is the light of an exact time of day. And the notion of the reality of the moment is made certain by the foreground where we catch the darting shapes of swallows skimming the water, possible only because the artist has made a moment when he has stopped the movement of a wing, arrested at a single time the arrow of flight.

Over and over again one catches in the painting of the twelfth and thirteenth centuries in China the love of physical reality—often made more intense by a concentration on a moment of that reality's existence. This is true of the landscape; it is true even more precisely of the loving care with which little things may be lifted out of the landscape, or at least from living nature, for our inspection. Thus there is constant delight at this time in painting a flower, an animal, a bird or even an insect. Ma Lin shared those interests. In a beautiful small album leaf attributed to him (Pl. 23) we are taken close to the selected subject and see not only an angled branch, the impeccable downward thrusting spears of bamboo, the star-like rosettes of plum-blossom, but in the lower part of the painting their answering shapes from reflection in the water. The fleeting facts of light are once again an integral part of what the artist wishes to convey.

Even though it has not been generally so interpreted, Mu Ch'i 牧谿's famous Six Persimmons[5] may only be six pieces of fruit sitting on an imaginary table in

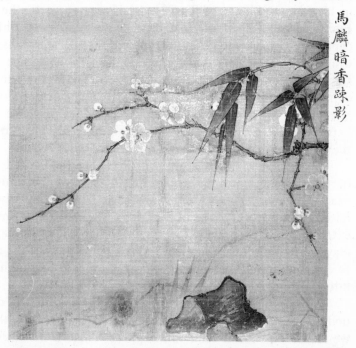

Plate 23
DARK FRAGRANCE AND SCATTERED SHADOWS, by Ma Lin. Album-leaf, ink and color on silk. National Palace Museum, Taipei.

馬麟暗香疎影

---

[4]Osvald Sirén, *Chinese Painting, Leading Masters and Principles,* London, 1956, vol. III, pl. 294.

[5]Reproduced in Laurence Sickman and Alexander Soper, *The Art and Architecture of China*, Baltimore, 1968, pl. 107B.

閣
次
于

Plate 24 HOSTELRY IN
THE MOUNTAINS, by Yen
Tzu-yu. Album-leaf, ink and
light color on silk. Freer Gal-
lery of Art. Courtesy of the
Smithsonian Institution, Freer
Gallery of Art, Washington,
D.C.

front of us. There are in fact both square and round persimmons which you can
purchase in the Chinese market.

STILL THERE IS a limit to the preciseness of this reality. The Chinese artist does
not stop the growth of his nature, does not freeze his grasses as does Albrecht Dürer
in his famous Clump of Turf.[6] And if we return to the view, the landscape, the
European artist does not seem to exactly match his Chinese counterpart. We can
capture a similar intent, however, within the late realistic landscape tradition of
China—the late Sung—and the late realistic landscape tradition in Europe. Constable's Waterloo Bridge of around 1823-24 in the Cincinnati museum is worth
comparing with Yen Tzu-yü 閣次于's Hostelry in the Mountains, a painting of the
second half of the twelfth century (Plates 24, 25). Once one gets over the contrast
between the colors of oil paint and the more subdued colors of ink and light wash,
the two paintings show remarkable similarities.

The frame of the western painting is like the limited, squared-off album format
of the Chinese painting—something to suggest the limited and, in one case, the
exactly framed view. We approach each from a similarly direct, eye-level (slightly
raised) point-of-view. The rise of land at one side against which can be seen the
extension of great spaces toward the other side is similar in both. In both, clouds
play across those spaces and add to our perception of the depth of that view. Darker
foreground definition across the bottom of each picture helps project our view back
into the contrasting lightness behind it.

It is only when we look closely into the very matrix of the painting that we can
understand what is the major difference. When we look thus at Constable's painting
we realize that forms tend to disappear. There is no outline, only rather irregularly
placed daubs of paint, an illusion which the eye fuses into the reality of human

[6]See Benjamin Rowland, Jr., *Art in East and West,*   Cambridge (Mass.), 1965, pp. 108-109 and plate 45.

Plate 25
WATERLOO BRIDGE, by
John Constable. Cincinnati Art
Museum, Cincinnati. Gift of
Miss Mary Hanna.

figures (Pl. 26). It is a kind of magician's trick: "It's the mind: the mind is fooled first and then the eye accepts what the mind believes, and it doesn't see what it really did see."[7]

With Yen Tzu-yü's painting, no matter how tiny, no matter how small, somehow the form still holds and it holds in a very special way. It holds because the Chinese artist will not surrender the notion of line. For example, behind the clusters of pine needles are fused areas of wash, but the needles—as tiny individual separate lines—are still there. Nor do the minute figures (two) become areas of ink or color. They are still exactly and precisely defined travellers carrying their burdens to the mountain village (Pl. 27).

Plate 26   (*left*): WATERLOO BRIDGE,
by John Constable. Detail.
Plate 27   (*right*): HOSTELRY IN THE
MOUNTAINS, by Yen Tzu-yü. Detail.

[7]A modern card-sharp, Frank Garcia, explaining his art as noted in the Detroit Free Press, Friday, April 11, 1975, p. 1-C.

Taken right into the heart of things, the Chinese artist will not let go of what we can define as basic structure. The fundamental idea—in this case the pine needle, the man—cannot be abandoned. The *concept* lies at the core of reality. In contrast, the nineteenth century European artist surrenders idea to experience. Everything is sacrificed to the view, indeed, the immediate view, and for a specific pair of eyes. It works if the interaction of particles of paint and the psychology of the eye and mind make it work. Indeed the whole process in the recent history of western art has been defined by Ernst Gombrich as a process of "making and matching".[8] You try combinations of paint. If they work in capturing the reality of the view, you go on. In this process the studio is inevitable anathema, for the studio is a return to the abstraction of the idea. Only as nature is before the eye can one find what it truly is.

In this exact surrender to what a direct view of the environment will bring, it would seem that the end result can only lie in beautiful dissolution. Any who know of the work of Claude Monet will realize that many of his canvasses are just that. What was left was to begin again. One had to return to the idea. After (indeed, still contemporary with) Monet came Cézanne.

The Chinese, having never surrendered the idea, presumably never had this problem. But they were clearly uncomfortable with the extent to which they had carried their realistic endeavors. The mainstream of Chinese painting in the late thirteenth and early fourteenth centuries shows that discomfort. This can often be seen in the way a painter of that time paints a flower or a bird or an animal. And when we turn to the landscape, the landscape clearly has a different look from the Sung.

In Huang Kung-wang 黃公望's famous Fu-ch'un Mountains 富春山居 of 1350 (Pl. 28) the definition of "things"—rocks, landspits, architecture or boats, trees,

Plate 28   DWELLING IN THE FU-CH'UN MOUNTAINS, by Huang Kung-wang. Handscroll, ink on paper. Section. National Palace Museum, Taipei.

[8]E. H. Gombrich, *Art and Illusion*, New York,   1960. See, for example, p. 183 ff. and pp. 296-297.

hillsides—is nowhere near as precise as the standard Sung view, and space is distinctly limited. Space does not stretch seemingly forever. Thus a flat curtain of wash suffices to define a mountain peak. And the sky is not so much the receding sky as the flat paper of the scroll. But mostly the difference is seen when one goes close, quite exactly, bores into the very heart of the painting to see how it is constructed. Here one picks up an extraordinary overlay and interweave of brushstrokes—lines, touches of ink, washes, overlapping darks and lights, movement in seemingly endless varied directions; ink bleeds into paper; paper seems to invade areas of ink; the architecture is lop-sided; there are no exact boundaries; one form overlaps another form; form is seen through form.

What, then, has happened to our clearly conceived idea? Where has the inviolable concept vanished? One cannot preserve what is not there. No longer primarily concerned with the optics of a view, the kind of idea that made that view a viable reality is no longer to be found. Instead, the whole painting has become an idea. Huang Kung-wang tells us that he took three years to complete this painting. He was not during all this time sitting (either in fact or imagination) in front of his view. Most of the time the scroll lay rolled up, unfinished. Then from time to time, as ideas came to him, he brought it back, unrolled it, worked on it a little, then rolled it up again. The patron grew impatient. He wondered if he would ever get his scroll.

The controlling factor in what is being created here is no longer the view, is no longer objective nature. The controlling factor is the artist himself. We have moved from the objective to the subjective. It is the idea in the artist's mind that determines the nature he reveals. To discover the world—as had the Sung—is, somewhat paradoxically to open the door to a rejection of that world. Or more positively, since it is clear that the Chinese are still painting landscapes, it is to rescue the landscape from the fragile existence of the moment and imbue it with notions of permanence —in this case the assurance of the artist's experience of that nature, a nature which because it is transformed into the vision of art is lifted out of time and can go on forever. This is no less than Cézanne's efforts to make impressionism permanent "like art in the museums" or to "revive Poussin in contact with nature".[9] For China this transformation was accomplished more than 500 years before the French experience.

The result in the fourteenth century was the flowering of the beauty of a new idea, or series of ideas about nature. This is what Yuan landscape is about, and the most valued of these ideas have been enshrined in Chinese critical appraisal in the distinctly definable styles of the so-called four great masters: Huang Kung-wang, Wu Chen 吳鎮, Ni Tsan 倪瓚 and Wang Meng 王蒙.

IT IS ONE OF the lessons of history that forms, somehow, will not remain the same. After the Yuan—it only lasted seventy years—came the Ming (1368-1644). Still, views of nature persist. The noble mountain is there. Level distances may stretch out before our eyes. Flowers, animals, bamboo, the little things drawn out of the land-

[9]These observations are found respectively in: Maurice Denis, *Théories 1890-1910*, Paris, 1920,   p. 250. and Paul Rewald, *Cézanne*, New York, (1948) 1968, p. 135.

scape may still fascinate the painter. However, there is a difference. Of course there
are currents and cross-currents, copies and new inventions, details and generalities.
But one does not normally confuse a Ming painting with a Yuan painting.

One inescapable fact is a return to what might be called an objectification of
nature. In painting an album of flowers in 1533 Wen Cheng-ming 文徵明 speaks of
sitting in a pavilion with flowers all around him. . . .[10] Hsü Wei 徐渭, also painting in
the sixteenth century, applies the ink on stalks of bamboo with a conscious sense of
light and dark so that the brushstroke becomes the vehicle not just for expressiveness
but for a clear revelation of the illusion of unmistakable three-dimensional roundness.[11] The great Ming painter, Shen Chou 沈周, says he painted a famous album of
flowers, animals and birds—in 1494—as they looked.[12] And if we extend his view
into a landscape setting we are in a well-known painting, Watching the Mid-autumn
Moon, presented with scholars gathered in the night at an open, rustic pavilion to
feast bathed in the light of the full moon at that specific time of seasonal fulfillment
and remembrance.[13] Only the time is even more specifically recorded in the writing
that follows the scene as being not the fifteenth, but the fourteenth, for only then
can one catch the festival at its precise fresh purity before it has been tainted by the
observance of others on the proper but very ordinary day itself. And certainly this
notion of being in direct contact with the facts of one's surroundings—the facts of
nature—persists so that the great independent painter, Tao-chi 道濟, working in the
late seventeenth and early eighteenth centuries of the Ch'ing period, is, in his grand
and towering landscape of Mount Lu, now in the Sumitomo collection in Japan,
declaring that such a mountain is not the result of his dependence on somewhat
similar mountainscapes of the Sung but of his own direct perception. Why, he com-
plains rhetorically, can one not do them as one ordinarily sees them?[14]

That Ming painters were concerned with a direct confrontation of their surroundings is further indicated by a favorite Ming compositional device whereby
forms in the top and bottom of a picture may be sharply cut by the edge eliminating
the possibility of further extension both higher and lower and thereby quite literally
thrusting us directly into the subject: the rocks and trees and hills and cliffs and
water of nature herself. That such devices are proof of a realistic intent is indicated
by their use in western art as well when the artist seeks direct confrontation with
what he paints. Thus the early seventeenth century realist Caravaggio may cut off
parts of his powerfully realized figures. And we know it in our own time in the
close-up of the camera.

We can thus find innumerable examples in Ming China of what after the intro-
spection of the Yuan might be described as a return to the realistic purpose. But
still a Ming painting is not a Sung painting. How can we account for what is usually a
clearly visible difference? What king of realism is Ming realism?

In Ming landscapes, as we have suggested, the great mountains do indeed return,

[10]*Ku-kung shu-hua lu* 故宮書錄, Taipei, 1965,   ton, D.C., 1962, p. 77.
ch. 6/p. 47.

[11]James Cahill, *Chinese Painting* (Skira), Geneva,   [13]Edwards, op. cit., p. 27.
1960, p. 154.
[14]University of Michigan, *The Painting of Tao-chi*,
[12]Richard Edwards, *The Field of Stones*, Washing-   Ann Arbor, 1967, p. 23.

but over and over again in a very special way. Paintings are so numerous as to allow generalization. Often we climb the heights and with our eye and mind travel both up and back. But when we get to the top, we are often confronted with strong black areas which in the rather deep value of the ink are as dark as those in the lower foreground. Even when we had thought we were travelling far we are brought back to the front plane of the picture—to the same forward plane at which we began our journey.

Certainly some Ming artists can come very close to the kind of exact precision that marks classical Sung painting. Such an artist was T'ang Yin 唐寅 (1470-1523). Looking at his Clearing after Snow in a Mountain Pass (Pl. 29) and particularly a

Plate 29 CLEARING AFTER SNOW IN A MOUNTAIN PASS, by T'ang Yin. Hanging scroll, ink and light color on silk. National Palace Museum, Taipei.

Plate 30
CLEARING AFTER SNOW
IN A MOUNTAIN PASS, by
T'ang Yin. Detail.

detail from it (Pl. 30) we see the tight substance of the mists, the exactness with which the trees melt into this surrounding ambient. But again we see how a dark accent—here an evergreen—jumps out at us. It is the kind of arbitrary variation that for the Ming artist inevitably added an element of vitality to his painting.

This might, perhaps, be interpreted as a new twist to the realistic purpose, whereby the artist is unwilling to let things disappear into a normal space and thus uses such a device to bring them back into our consciousness. But the more we examine the "things" that are so depicted, the more we realize that they are not shown as exactly convincing natural objects. The foreground rock of a painting by Wang E 王諤 of the late fifteenth and early sixteenth centuries is certainly strong enough and exact enough in terms of the sureness of the black ink that describes its shape. But what we see is a brilliant sharp pattern (Pl. 31) echoing in its tense aliveness the taut shape of the figure that approaches it. The artist is not interested in conveying the rock-like qualitites of the rock. Generally speaking a similar contrast could be found if one were to compare Ming flowers to Sung flowers, Ming birds or animals to Sung birds or animals.

WHAT THEN HAS happened to our return to realism? Despite the boldness of Ming forms, they are not unaffected by the subjective view of the Yuan. Insofar as looseness, or an arbitrary treatment of ink-values, is a product of personal choice as opposed to objective recording, we seem to be confronted with a kind of hyphenated view of nature—a subjective-objective approach to reality. But there is another factor—a major factor—that is an inevitable part of later Chinese painting. It is a factor well-known to anyone who has considered at all this period of Chinese art. It is the factor of style: the degree to which, from the Yüan dynasty on a painter was bound to paint not according to his direct perception of nature, but according to how someone else had seen nature.

There is not time here to give clear illustrations of how a series of varied styles of the past may have operated on a later artist. Max Loehr has expressed the situation in complete, perhaps over-complete, terms: "All art of significance, all true art from now on is an intellectual art."[15]

Plate 31 CROSSING A BRIDGE TO VISIT A FRIEND, by Wang E. Hanging scroll, ink on silk. National Palace Museum, Taipei.

[15]Laurence Sickman (ed.), *Chinese Calligraphy and Painting from the John M. Crawford Collection,* New York, 1962, p. 37.

I want, however, to deal with one painting. This is a very impressive, a rather large, a very strong mountain landscape painted by Shen Chou (1527-1509). From the single figure in the lower center the landscape carries the title of the Staff-bearing wanderer, *Tz'u-chiang t'u* 持杖圖 (Pl. 32). It is a landscape in the style of the fourteenth century artist, Ni Tsan, and behind that it reflects an adherence to the styles of the great tenth-century southern masters: Tung Yüan 董源 and Chü-jan 巨然.

Plate 32 THE STAFF-BEARING WANDERER, by Shen Chou. Hanging scroll, ink on paper. National Palace Museum, Taipei.

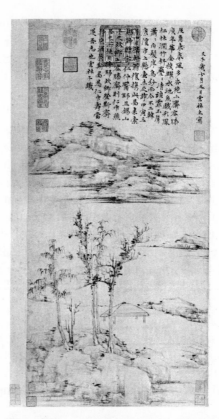

Plate 33 JUNG-HSI STUDIO, by Ni Tsan. Hanging scroll, ink on paper. National Palace Museum, Taipei.

As for dependence on Ni Tsan, Shen Chou has caught Ni's interest (Pl. 33) in a vertical composition ranging from bottom to top, his care in isolating a few select elements (Shen Chou, for example, has only eight trees) and in the rather spare manipulation of ink—brushstrokes and washes—which allows a great deal of the untouched paper to remain untouched. But the painting is completely Shen Chou in the firmness with which each piece or part of the landscape is rendered, in the way in which those surely conceived parts are fitted together and in the ultimate message of the powers of nature which this—somewhat paradoxically—creatively *new* landscape has revealed.

If we start with the foreground we are aware of the firmness of riverside path, the dike, the bridge, the rounded mounds of land, the exactness of those eight trees. At the same time that these elements are individually exact, their relation to each other is precisely structured. This is particularly true of the way a central foreground tree reaches up to exactly fill—or be precisely framed by—the valley space in the middle distance. And then we move on to tight knots of form which despite their blurred outlines or rather freely textured surfaces build up to the sure mountain masses at the top of the picture.

But to understand the painting one has to return again to the tiny single figure in the center foreground and having seen the shape of the top-most mountains one realizes that there is an unmistakable correspondence between the shape of this full-grown firmly based scholar and the ovoid flat-based shapes that tower layer on layer into the great heights above. The figure leans slightly to the left and it is exactly in such a slightly leaning cave-like space that he is framed by the two trees that immediately surround him. In turn, the background picks up this leftward tilt. We are led there by the left-hand tree. For in the upper middle distance the largest land-mass is to the left. The lesser cliff-like land to the right picks up, however, with the angled line of its plateau the same angle as the staff that the scholar far below holds in his concealed hand. And this plateau in turn directs us to the furthest range of hills, capped—as the scholar himself is hatted—with the dark flat wash of hill. This, it might be added, in characteristic Ming fashion limits our extension into distance.

The scholar, the man, inevitably becomes a vital core—a seed—from which grows and radiates the whole dynamic life of the painting; and from this focal firmly placed center the shapes which define Shen Chou's natural scene move upward toward the left, back to the right and ultimately are centered so that the furthest hills remain firm. But it is a center that is not an exact center, rather an implied axial line whose sureness rests on the dynamics of shape reacting with shape. Thus there is always the strong subtle quality of movement. This is a mountainscape that grows upward and also expands outward so that the mountain is not just there as a shape but as a force. It is the spirit, if you will, the "breath" of the mountain that makes it live.

I have spent some time in analyzing this painting because not only is it a Ming painting by an important artist, not only is it, I think, a great painting, but it stands as a kind of symbol of what painting in China from the post-Sung period—from the end of the thirteenth century—is about. Here, of course, the emphasis is on what happened to that post-Sung change in the Ming period.

NOW I MIGHT turn directly to the symbols of words. The Chinese experience clarifies three major factors in the creation of a painting: the artist, that is the individual creator; nature, that is the objective world around the subjective self, the world upon which the artist draws for his visual materials; and style, that element in any artistic tradition which tells us how other artists have recreated nature, or, as the tradition becomes more complex, recreated a combination of nature and style. Thus we have, quite simply:

          Artist   Nature   Style

Our problem is, at a given time, to appropriately grasp their relationship. In the Sung view the relation between artist and nature is direct. Style, always important in any art, is however incidental to one's commitment to use it to record the substance of nature. We can thus arrange our three verbal symbols as follows:

          Nature   Artist
                                        Style

In the later, or post-Sung view, it is the artist's withdrawal to a deliberately chosen position that establishes the uniqueness of the situation:

          Nature   Style
                    Artist

He affirms a special kind of freedom. Here he remains unfettered by a direct attachment to visible nature—unfettered, but not unrelated. Nature has not been rejected. The landscape still remains. But always the artist is free to move. He is not only free in his direct commitment to nature but in his commitment to the new and conscious factor of style which he has now elevated to a position which at the very least is of an importance equal to nature itself. It must be remembered, however, that in the Chinese landscape tradition style is not so much a rejection of nature as it is a further adjustment in the artist's involvement with nature itself—nature, as it were, once removed but at the same time further refined by the creation of another artist's brush.

The result may best be seen as a kind of free artistic wandering. The artist may be close to objective nature, or he may be closest to a dependence on style, or he may be far removed from both, creating almost totally his own notions of what nature and style should be:

Nature   Style
   Artist

Nature   Style
                          Artist

Nature   Style
              Artist

The artist can withdraw, but he never breaks—completely. That is why the Chinese artist never was able to paint a painting that could be said to be related to the modern western movement of cubism. For so much of what is "modern" in western art (Pl. 34) depends on a break with one's direct attachment to observe

Plate 34   NIGHT FISHING AT ANTIBES, by Pablo Picasso. Museum of Modern Art, New York. Mrs. Simon Guggenheim Fund.

physical reality. It is a realignment, no doubt, in terms of the complex realities of
the modern industrial-scientific world, but whatever the causes, a direct reading of
painting affirms that it is a break that the Chinese have never been willing to consider. Nor can we relate it to some kind of "time-lag" caused by China's failure to
enter the world of the contemporary West with proper speed and enthusiasm producing thereby the necessary conditions that could result almost automatically in
creating "modern" art. Time can hardly be the problem, since we have already seen
that centuries ago Chinese artists were creating paintings analogous to those of one
of the most modern of western artists, namely Cézanne, who himself was on the
very threshold of cubism. No, it is rather the exact reluctance of the Chinese artist
to desert nature in the name of style and personal independence that creates the gap.
For what happens in cubism is that the artist *makes* his own picture. There may be
suggestions of physical reality, but such a picture is essentially what the artist has
made out of the things of his craft: his line, his color, his forms. This is why, for
example, collage can be a serious art-form in the modern west. Thus, through his
own making, his own art, the artist creates what is real. It is the artist making form
rather than repeating form from nature; or to put it another way, much of contemporary western art places the locus of meaning in physical matter itself which, as
in a laboratory, is no longer permitted to rest unchallenged in nature's quiet ambient.

THE COURSE I have tried to chart here in Chinese painting has moved us from a
world in which distances and the realities they embraced were looked upon with
apprehension and dread to a time of their complete acceptance as areas of con-
templation, visual wandering and delight—an established source of enduring truth
and beauty. And then came a rejection of those self-evident and accepted truths in
favor of the individual's right to accept them only in terms of a conscious personal
relationship.

But always there has been one consistent fact in this changing landscape—the
balanced approach of an idea, or ideas, firmly related to man's necessary comprehension. Early it was the idea as symbol. In Sung painting it was the retention of the
clarity of the idea that prevented a surrender to total reliance on immediate experience. Thus the idea of object, of man, was preserved inviolate at the heart of
great nature. Finally the idea, firmly caged in the consciousness of the artist himself,
was expanded to embrace that unique combination of self, nature and style that
accounts for the later Chinese landscape. This is another way of saying that the
landscape, far from suggesting a departure from, is closely tied to the basic humanism
of Chinese civilization.

Since death is by definition the cessation of vital activity, and life the persistence
of those activities, can we not attribute the endurance of the landscape tradition
in China to its ability to change and ultimately to establish itself on a basis of
dynamic relationships that would not permit an easy end?

志 工：略談北魏的屏風漆畫

A Brief Note on the
Lacquer Screen Painting of Northern Wei

By **Chih Kung**

Translated by **Kao Mayching**

I

IN 1965 the twin burial of a Northern Wei nobleman, Ssu-ma Chin-lung 司馬金龍, and his wife was discovered in Ta-t'ung 大同, Shansi, and a large quantity of cultural relics excavated. The findings have been extensively reported in *Wen Wu* 文物, No. 3, 1972. Among the many relics unearthed from the tomb, a lacquer screen, on which are painted scenes depicting wellknown characters from history, has aroused the attention of the reading public, because it yields not only visible data on the living habits of the ancients, but also a considerable amount of important historical evidence concerning handicrafts and painting in the past.

As a result of the extensive and penetrating drive of archaeological work in China in recent decades, a number of ancient paintings have been discovered, including the painting on silk from the State of Ch'u in the period of the Warring States, many paintings on lacquerware, down to a large number of T'ang paintings on wall, paper and silk. These are enough to give the history of Chinese painting a rich treasury of material evidence (even greater in quantity are paintings which have survived from the Sung dynasty onwards). Under comparison, the only period which cannot boast of so much archaeological evidence is the Southern and Northern Dynasties. Even though the wall paintings of Northern Wei at Tun-huang 敦煌 may be said to be rather rich and centralized, their subject matter is limited to Buddhism and the majority of them suffer from the deterioration of the surface paints. Therefore the appearance of the present lacquer painting, with its depiction of historical and genre themes popular since the Eastern Han dynasty, conveniently fills the gap in this period of the history of Chinese painting.

Where lacquer handicraft is concerned, there has been a wealth of excellent examples unearthed, dating from the Warring Stages period down to T'ang and Sung. This lacquer screen of Northern Wei, therefore, serves an equally important role as historical data in the study of the development of lacquer technique.

In view of the fact that paintings done on silk and paper stand poor chances of preservation, those who do research on the paintings of the past often have to resort to tile, stone and wood carvings,

Plate 35
RUBBING,
Tomb of
Ssu-ma Chin-lung.

Plate 36   LACQUER SCREEN PAINTING,
Northern Wei. From the Tomb of Ssu-ma
Chin-lung, Ta-t'ung, Shansi.

lacquerware, woven stuff, embroidery etc. which, though engraved by knife, painted by brush or embroidered by needle and thread, can yet reflect the styles and characteristics of the original sketches on which they were based. Furthermore, the effect produced by painting in lacquer is closely approximate to that of painting with a brush on paper, silk, bamboo or wood. Therefore, this lacquer screen, in addition to being a product of ancient handicraft, is also an authentic work of ancient painting.

II

THE IMPERIAL clan of Northern Wei came from the upper class of the Hsien-pei Toba tribe. As they reached Central China, they teamed up with the landlord class of the native Han people to form the ruling clique of Northern Wei. That Ssu-ma Chin-lung, originally a descendant of the nobility of the Chin dynasty, should become a prominent figure in Northern Wei politics illustrates a characteristic of the ruling party of Northern Wei.

The Hsien-pei ruling class of Northern Wei maintained traces of the Hsien-nei tradition in their military organization and language habits, but in their culture and art almost all evidences that have survived or have been excavated belonged exclusively to the Han-Wei tradition. Taking painting and calligraphy as examples, a comparison of works of Northern Wei with those of the Southern Dynasties shows that the differences, if there were any, lie in the minor distinctions of regional styles, rather than in any major racial discrepancy. This reflects, in the formative process of the great Chinese race, the historical situation of an amalgamation of minority tribes with the Central Chinese, and the state of culture and art in which the joint efforts of these peoples brought into being a magnificent China.

Our great leader Chairman Mao Tse-tung teaches that, in feudal societies, "peasants and the handicraft workers were the basic classes which created wealth and culture." Painting, for example, was originated from actual production and practical use. The original creators, ranging from painters of simple animal motifs and geometric patterns on the pottery of primitive societies, the makers of what Lu Hsün described as "profound and monumental" sculpture in the Han dynasty, to those who painted historical and genre themes on Han and Wei screens, were none but the labouring people. The emergence of the painting of scholar-officials was a development founded on the basis of craftsmen painting, for obviously its techniques were first learnt from the latter. Of course, as Chinese painting developed, scholar-official painters of the ruling class had continued to make improvements and innovations in technique, and had exerted definite influences on craftsmen painting; still, in viewing technique, we cannot sever the history of painting's development. Painting was born from the hands of labourers who were directly engaged in production. Without the more archaic art of earlier painting, there could never have issued the rich and refined painting of later ages. In this, of course, is involved the differentiation between the low-development stage and the high-development stage, nevertheless it is true that all scholar-official painters who had made innovations in art had invariably drawn inspiration or borrowed from the paintings of craftsmen.

Whether judged by technique or by quantity, folk painting done by craftsmen is the main stream of Chinese painting, and forms a distinct system of its own. Histories of painting written by scholar-officials of the past tend to ignore craftsmen painting and cast it outside the realm of art. That, as we understand, is a distorted view of the history of painting. The present lacquer screen painting testifies by its bright colours and vivid images the achievements of folk art and exposes the prejudice and falsity of painting histories written by the ruling class.

III

LET US TAKE a look at the artistic origin and the style of this lacquer screen painting. Stylistically speaking, the figures on it are quite lively. Painted in few lines, they do not have complicated ornamental strokes, but the essential movements of the figures are captured in brief and concise brushwork. What has often been praised of the rock-cut sculptures of Northern Wei found at Yün-kang 雲崗 and Lung-men 龍門 —that their carving technique is "simple and archaic", or in other words that their style is plain, robust and powerful—has been thought to come from the effect of the chisel. Now that the same kind of simplicity, robustness and power is discerned in the way the figures are painted on this lacquer screen, we come to understand that this basically was the painting style of the time.

Comparing this lacquer screen painting with earlier paintings such as the Han dynasty wall paintings found at Lo-yang 洛陽, Liao-yang 遼陽, Wang-tu 望都 and An-p'ing 安平,[1] we find blood and flesh ties in their brush strokes, treatment of lines and methods of representation. They share certain similarities even in the basic tone of their colours.

Comparing this lacquer screen painting with a contemporary work, a scene of *The Seven Sages of the Bamboo Grove* 竹林七賢圖 engraved on a tomb the excavated in Nanking,[2] we find little difference between them in the liveliness of their figural images and the conciseness

[1]"On the Structure of the Burial Chamber and the Wall Paintings from a Han Tomb in Wang-tu County, Ho-pei" 河北望都縣漢墓的墓室結構和壁畫, *Wen Wu Ts'an K'ao Tzu Liao* 文物參攷資料, No. 12, 1954;

Wang-tu Han mu pi-hua 望都漢墓壁畫 (Wall Paintings from a Han Tomb at Wang-tu), Chinese Classical Art Press;

"Three Ancient Tombs with Wall Paintings Discovered at Liao-yang" 遼陽發現的三座壁畫古墓, *Wen Wu Ts'an K'ao Tzu Liao*, No. 5, 1955;

"Excavations of a Western Han Tomb with Wall Paintings at Lo-yang" 洛陽西漢壁畫墓發掘報告, *Kaogu Xuebao* 考古學報, No. 2, 1964.

[2]"A South Dynasties Tomb and Its Wall Paintings of Inscribed Bricks Found at Hsi-Shan Bridge, Nanking" 南京西善橋南朝墓及其磚刻壁畫, *Wen Wu* 文物, Nos. 8 & 9, 1960.

and forcefulness of their lines, despite the absence of brush manner and colour on the tile engraving. Although some minor details had to be different because of the larger size of the tile and the difference in subject matter, in both the overall painting style is the same.

This lacquer screen painting can also be compared with later paintings such as the extant *Admonitions of the Court Instructress* scroll 女史箴圖 and the Sung copy of the *Benevolent and Wise Women* scroll 列女仁智圖. The former, originally a masterpiece by an anonymous painter, was inscribed with a signature written in four small characters *"Ku K'ai-chih hua"* 顧愷之畫 ("painted by Ku K'ai-chih") at some unknown point of time, making it a standard authentic work by Ku. Sections of calligraphy had been written on the scroll, in a style obviously later than the Northern Wei period; also, they were written by a hand different from the four-character signature, whose calligraphic style should be even later in date. Therefore, the work can only be attributed to the T'ang dynasty or slightly earlier. The latter scroll,

WEI LING-KUNG
AND HIS WIFE

Plate 37
Section from
lacquer screen
painting.

Plate 38
Section from
the Benevolent and
Wise Women scroll,
Sung copy
based on an
original work
by Ku K'ai-chih.

PORTRAIT OF AN EMPEROR

Plate 39 (*left*):
Section from the
Thirteen Emperors scroll,
attributed to
Yen Li-pen.

Plate 40 (*top*):
Section from
lacquer screen painting.

Benevolent and Wise Women, has also been attributed to Ku K'ai-chih, its one surviving copy having been proven by the quality of its silk, its particular use of brush and ink, its inscription and other characteristics to be obviously not a work of the Eastern Chin dynasty. This has led some to acknowledge that it is a copy made in the Sung dynasty, but based on an original work by Ku K'ai-chih. Viewing the Northern Wei lacquer screen painting against these two scrolls soon makes it evident that throughout these works there is a similarity in narrative content and even closer resemblance in the treatment of subject matter, the costumes and ornaments of the figures and the daily utensils depicted. Of course, as paintings done on scroll, the *Admonitions* and the *Benevolent and Wise Women* are more finely and intricately executed than the decorative painting done on lacquerware, and, being later in date, they were naturally more advanced in painting technique. From the above comparison we derive this understanding: that the painting style of the two scrolls came from folk art and folk craft, and that the scrolls were made upon an elaboration on the fundamentals of craftsmen painting.

We may refer to two more painting scrolls bearing the attribution of Yen Li-pen 閻立本 of the T'ang dynasty, namely the scroll of *Emperor T'ai-tsung in a Sedan Chair* 步輦圖 and the *Thirteen Emperors* scroll 帝王圖. They are painted in more refined technique, while many figures, costumes and utensils depicted on them are similar to those found on the lacquer painting. This shows that in artistic technique the same historical tradition is shared by the historical figure paintings of T'ang and the lacquer craftsmen's painting of the earlier age.

The fact that since T'ang and Sung times the above-mentioned scrolls have been attributed to Ku K'ai-chih and Yen Li-pen can be explained by the possibility that these scrolls might have been based on original sketches by those two masters, or that their style and technique were adopted from Ku and Yen. But the discovery of the Northern Wei lacquer screen painting has supplied us with strong material evidence which confirms the heritage of the art of certain famous scholar-official painters. The masters of these painters were in fact the anonymous craftsmen of previous generations and the works which those craftsmen had left behind them.

THE LADY PAN
DECLINED TO
ACCOMPANY THE
EMPEROR IN
HIS PALANQUIN

Plate 41 (*top left*)
Plate 42 (*top right*):
Sections from the
Admonitions scroll,
attributed to Ku K'ai-chih.

Plate 43 (*below*):
Section from lacquer
screen painting.

IV

THE CALLIGRAPHY found on this lacquer screen also deserves our attention. The world-famous Chinese art of calligraphy, with its long history and rich variety of scripts such as the seal script, the clerical script, the cursive script, the running script and the regular script, has enjoyed uninterrupted development for several thousand years and formed a complete system. The Six Dynasties, which saw the flourishing of numerous calligraphy artists, was a glorious age for calligraphy into which the great Chin calligrapher, Wang Hsi-chih 王羲之, was born. The calligraphy of the Six Dynasties as seen on the tile and stone engravings, Buddhist manuscripts and letters of the time appear as either dense and heavy, or untrammelled and vigorous, or archaic and wonderful, or powerful and spontaneous. Among these various stylistic characteristics, they yet illustrate one thing in common: calligraphy's gradual evolution from clerical script to regular script. We need only to compare the following examples to see this similarity in all of them: the inscribed tile of Chiang Miao-yang 江妙養記磚 (dated the 7th year of T'ien-pao 天保 of Northern Ch'i); the scroll fragment of Buddhist manuscript of Northern Liang, now in the collection of the Museum of Chinese Revolutionary History; the Buddhist stele excavated at Hsiang-yang 襄陽, Hupei (dated the 5th year of T'ien-t'ung 天統 of Northern Ch'i); the ink inscription (dating from the Southern Dynasties) written on the side of the tile decorated with armoured horses, excavated at Teng-hsien 鄧縣, Honan; and the document by Hou Fu 侯馥 and others requesting weapon and armour (dated the 6th year of Chien-ch'u 建初 of Western Liang).

Plate 44
RUBBING,
Tomb of
Ssu-ma Chin-lung.

It is the same with the inscription on the lacquer painting from the tomb of Ssu-ma Chin-lung. The calligraphy is extremely firm, graceful and spontaneous. Its form and construction belong neither to the clerical script of Han nor to the regular script of T'ang, but falls between the clerical and the regular, bearing resemblances as well as dissimilarities to both, and at the same time it imbibes the calligraphic style found on Wei stelae. It is a kind of script which has both flesh and bone, with slender yet rounded brush strokes. Its manner, spacious and clear, imparts to the viewer a feeling of beauty.

Though every individual calligraphy artist may have his own habits and characteristics with regards to strokes and forms, works that are produced in the same period are bound to show common stylistic traits. If comparison is made between some famous stelae of the Six Dynasties and the present lacquer painting and its inscription, it will be seen that the calligraphy on the Stele of Kao Chen 高貞碑 and the Commemorative Stele of Ts'ao Wang-hsi 曹望憘題象記, both of the Northern Wei dynasty, bear close affinity to the inscription on the lacquer painting, except for the fact that characters after being transcribed on to stone are largely affected by the chiselling process, and thus their strokes no longer possess the clarity of those written with brush and ink. Most Buddhist sutras of Northern Wei were executed in the format of books or scrolls, and their calligraphy unavoidably differ from the characters on stone stelae, whereas the calligraphic style of the lacquer painting inscription is close to the style and manner of stelae calligraphy. Before our archaeological workers discover those Northern Wei stelae originals that were written in red and black ink, this inscription on the lacquer painting should be very important

**Plate 45
CALLIGRAPHY
FRAGMENTS,**
lacquer screen painting.

reference material for verifying the calligraphic style of Northern Wei stelae.

We may also refer to the Ch'iao-tan Stele 肖憺碑 of Prince Shih-hsing 始興 of Southern Liang, written by the calligrapher Pei I-yuan 貝義淵 of the Southern Dynasties, which is quite refined in both its calligraphic style and its manner of engraving. The general characteristics of its brush strokes and character formation display close affinity to the Kao Chen Stele and the Ts'ao Wang-hsi Stele of Northern Wei, which is to say that it may also be compared to the inscription on the present lacquer painting. These are factors worth paying attention to in our study of the art of calligraphy.

Plate 46   KAO CHEN STELE, section.

Plate 47   CH'IAO-TAN STELE, section.

(For Chinese text see page 207)

A Question of Choice, a Matter of Rendition

By **Hin-cheung Lovell**

IN THE RAREFIED world of Chinese painting scholarship, the translation of titles of paintings into English is of decidedly peripheral interest compared to such weighty concerns as analyzing styles, defining schools and trends, isolating individualism from traditionalism, establishing authenticity, reconstructing transmission and searching for corroborating textual evidence. . . . Perhaps because it is so peripheral, the matter has been somewhat overlooked. The following are some random thoughts on the subject in the time-honoured *pi-chi* 筆記 tradition which absolves one from cogent reasoning and penetrating analysis.

Grammatical Infidelity

Broadly speaking, titles of Chinese paintings fall into two grammatical categories: the noun construction and the verb construction. Examples of the former category are legion: *Tsao ch'un t'u* 早春圖 ("Early Spring"); *Liu-yin kao-shih t'u* 柳陰高士圖 ("Scholar under a Willow"); *Wen-hui t'u* 文會圖 ("Literary Gathering"); and so on. They are simple noun phrases and present no problem in translation. Less numerous, but still considerable by proportion, is the latter category, titles with a verb construction. These have on the whole been less well served by translators. When rendering these titles into English, there is a tendency on the part of the translator to turn what is grammatically a verb construction into a noun phrase or noun clause. Examples which come readily to mind are Kuan T'ung 關同's *Kuan-shan hsing-lü t'u* 關山行旅圖, which is usually rendered as "Travellers in the Mountains" instead of "Travelling in the Mountains", and Fan K'uan 范寬's *Ch'i-shan hsing-lü t'u* 谿山行旅圖, usually rendered as "Travellers among Mountains and Streams" instead of "Travelling among Mountains and Streams". It is evident that along with the grammatical alteration from verb to noun, something of the sense of movement in the original title is lost, and the emphasis shifts from travelling to the traveller.

The sense of movement is important because the image of travelling is a pervading one throughout the history of Chinese painting. It is a reflection of an important facet of life, almost a way of life, of the Chinese literati in medieval times, from the Six Dynasties period to the Ch'ing. Indeed, it would be difficult to think of a society in history in which travel played as significant a role in the life of a certain social caste as it did to the educated Chinese. The Chinese scholar travelled for official reasons, taking up appointments a long distance from home and undertaking numerous trips in the course of duty. He also travelled for family reasons. Above all, he travelled for spiritual reasons, to meetings with friends, to secluded mountain retreats, to regions of scenic beauty, and to locations hallowed by historical and literary associations. In a life not infrequently touched by disappointments, sad partings and sudden deaths, his imagination found solace in the cosmic imagery of man as traveller through the journey of life.

T'ang Yin 唐寅's (1470-1523) *Nan-yu t'u* 南遊圖 provides an excellent example of a painting on the theme of travel as a source of spiritual renewal, and as a means of communion with kindred spirits of the past.[1] The short handscroll presents a close-up view of a path which winds along the rocky bank of a river. At the right is a young scholar astride a donkey, followed by an attendant carrying a *ch'in* 琴 on his back, and preceded by wheelbarrows loaded with boxes and bundles of scrolls. There is no dedication on the painting, but on the same piece of paper, immediately following the painting, T'ang Yin has written a poem of farewell with an obvious musical reference.

> *"In the old days, Chi K'ang composed the Kuang-ling-san.*   嵇康舊日廣陵散,
> *Its melodies are lost in the silence of a thousand years.*   寂寞千年音調亡;
> *Today I travel here with you and perchance we can*   今日送君遊此地,
> *Rediscover the music according to the score."*   可能按譜覓宮商。

Chi K'ang 嵇康 (Hsi K'ang 奚康, 223-262 A.D.), poet, philosopher and musician, was one of the Seven Sages of the Bamboo Grove, the famous coterie of literary figures of the Three Kingdoms period. He fell out of favour with the Wei 魏 emperor and was executed in 262 A.D.. Just before his execution, he sang the *Kuang-ling-san* 廣陵散, accompanying himself on the *ch'in*. When he finished the melody, he said, "Yüan Hsiao-ni 袁孝尼 [his brother-in-law] used to ask me to teach him this tune, but I persistently refused. The melody *Kuang-ling* now dies with me."[2] Over the centuries, the name Chi K'ang evoked the poet's tragic fate and the *Kuang-ling-san* became the symbol of something beautiful that had been irretrievably lost. Although most of his life was spent in the Loyang 洛陽 area in Honan, Chi K'ang was a native of Ch'ü 滁 in eastern Anhui which adjoins Nanking. Moreover, the Kuang-ling of the title of the lost melody refers to the region of T'ai-hsing 泰興 east of Nanking in modern Kiangsu. Thus, Nanking became a place of pilgrimage to generations of musicians, as well as to the literati to whom such an association conveyed a special poignancy.

The identity of the person for whom T'ang Yin painted the *Nan-yu t'u* as well as composed and wrote the poem is revealed elsewhere in the handscroll: in the inscription which accompanies the title and in some of the colophons which follow the painting. He was Yang Chi-ching 楊季靜 (ca. 1477-after 1530),[3] a young and distinguished *ch'in* master, apparently much esteemed by his contemporaries, as evidenced by the praise of his musical virtuosity expressed in the nine colophons appended to the painting. These were by Wen Cheng-ming 文徵明, Hsü Shang-te

---

[1] Freer Gallery of Art, acc. no. 53.78. Discussed and fully illustrated by Thomas Lawton in "Notes on Five Paintings from a Ch'ing Dynasty Collection", in *Ars Orientalis*, vol. VIII (1970), pp. 191-215; figs. 9-14.

[2] *Shih-shuo hsin-yü* 世說新語, 中 A/24a-b.

[3] There is no biography of Yang Chi-ching in the official history, but Chiang Chao-shen 江兆申, in his "Yang Chi-ching and the Wu School of Painters" (*National Palace Museum Bulletin*, vol. VIII, no. 3 [July-August, 1973]), has reconstructed an outline of Yang's life by culling all the information from the *Nan-yu t'u*, as well as from Wen Po-jen 文伯仁's "Portrait of Yang Chi-ching" and T'ang Yin's "The Lutist", both in the National Palace Museum, Taipei.

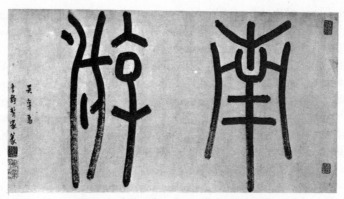

Plate 48 TITLE OF NAN-YU T'U, seal script
by Wu I. Freer Gallery of Art, Washington, D.C.

徐尙德, Wang Huan 王渙, Liu Pu 劉布, P'eng Fang 彭昉, Huang Yün 黃雲, Chu Yün-ming 祝允明, Ch'ien T'ung-ai 錢同愛, and Hsing Ts'an-fu 邢參復. Serving as a preface to the other contributions, P'eng Fang's colophon provides the most explicit background information on the event which brought about the handscroll.

> " . . . Chi-ching is troubled that he rarely meets anyone who understands [his music]. Therefore he takes all his possessions and, thinking nothing of travelling 1,000 *li*, he will in the second month of *i-ch'ou* [1505] carry his *ch'in* in a sack to the top of Chung-shan at Chin-ling. [Nanking] and to the banks of the Ch'in-huai River. There he will loosen his clothes and play a melody on his *ch'in*. So ancient is the melody and so pure and resounding are the notes that no one who hears him will not be moved or exhilarated. His trip will not be in vain. For his journey, the poet Ch'ien K'ung-chou [Ch'ien T'ung-ai] composed an eight-line poem and presented it to him. Several others followed the example. Their poems and essays are abundant and harmonious as a string of pearls. I humbly place my coarse words at the beginning. . . . "[4]

> ...季靜慨知者之罕遇，以故挾其所有，不遠千里而遊。乙丑之二月携琴一囊復上金陵鍾山秦淮之畔。解衣盤礡試一鼓焉。渾渾古調，琅琅清響，其無感而興者乎，非徒行也。于其行，詩人錢孔周賦一律以贈，繼而作者凡若干篇。倡和盈帙，鏗如貫珠，而猥以鄙言在首...

It is evident that the colophons, abounding in references to Chi K'ang and the *Kuang-ling-san*, were written by Yang Chi-ching's friends before his departure for Nanking. They were then assembled and appended to the *Nan-yu t'u*, which can be firmly dated to the year 1505 on the basis of the cyclical year *i-ch'ou* in P'ang Fang's preface.

The title of the painting is of singular interest (Pl. 48). *Nan-yu*, two perfectly formed characters in seal script, are followed by the calligrapher's signature and

[4]By virtue of its role as the preface, P'eng Fang's colophon should occupy the first rather than the fifth place in the sequence of the nine colophons. The order was re-arranged at the time of the mounting or re-mounting probably in deference to the seniority or eminence of some of the writers.

dedication: *Wu I wei Chi-ching ch'i-chia chuan* 吳奕爲季靜契家篆, "seal-script [calligraphy] for my sworn relative Chi-ching by Wu I". He was the nephew of Wu K'uan 吳寬 (1435-1504), the famous connoisseur and one of the leading spirits of the Suchou literati circle at the time of Shen Chou 沈周 (1427-1509). Although Wu I (1472-1519) was an active member of the same circle in his generation, little is known about his life and only three specimens of his seal-script calligraphy seem to have survived.[5] The year of his birth, 1472, is ascertained from the seal at the lower right corner of the title which reads *jen-ch'en sheng* 壬辰生, and the year of his death, 1519, is computed from Wang Ch'ung 王寵's (1494-1533) eulogy which laments Wu I's untimely death at 48 *sui*.[6]

The profusion of documentary material contained in Wu I's title, in T'ang Yin's poem, in P'eng Fang's preface as well as in the other eight colophons leaves not the slightest doubt as to the exact nature of the painting's subject matter. The painting depicts not any trip undertaken by a scholar, but one particular trip undertaken by Yang Chi-ching from Suchou to Nanking in the spring of 1505, and the beardless young man riding the donkey is none other than the *ch'in* master himself. Such specificity demands an equal measure of exactitude in the comprehension and translation of the title. *Nan-yu t'u* is perhaps best translated as "Journeying to Nanking", a rendition which retains the sense of movement in the original verb construction, states the specific destination and conveys the spiritual *raison d'être* of the journey.

In the context of verb construction versus noun construction, one might take passing note of Huang Kung-wang 黃公望's *Fu-ch'un shan-chü t'u* 富春山居圖, where the seeming ambiguity of *"shan-chü"* in the original title is fortuitously matched by a similar ambiguity of "dwelling" in the generally accepted English title, "Dwelling in the Fu-ch'un Mountains". While "dwelling" triumphantly straddles the fence which separates the verb from the noun, and while "travellers" and "journey" can be painlessly changed to "travelling" and "journeying", the life of the translator is bedevilled by innumerable words which defy translation. One such is the character *hsing* (in the title *Ming-huang hsing Shu* 明皇幸蜀), denoting "to bestow one's imperial presence on", of which there is no succinct English equivalent. "Ming-huang Bestowing His Imperial Presence on Szechwan" is indeed a cumbersome title, one which a translator, however brave, would hesitate to advocate in preference to the much simpler "Ming-huang's Journey to Shu". The subject of the two versions of this composition in the National Palace Museum, Taipei, has been identified as the flight of T'ang Ming-huang from Ch'ang-an 長安 to Szechwan 四川 in 756 A.D..[7] The journey was no glorious imperial tour, but an ignominious flight from the rebel forces of An Lu-shan 安祿山, a flight made more catastrophic by the death of Yang Kuei-fei 楊貴妃. The translator is fortunately spared the dilemma of having to choose between an awkward translation and an abbreviated one by two pertinent points.

---

[5]The other two, in the collection of John M. Crawford, Jr., are illustrated and discussed by Marc F. Wilson and Kwan S. Wong in *Friends of Wen Cheng-ming*, nos. 12 and 17.

[6]Wang Ch'ung, *Ya-i-shan-jen chi* 雅宜山人集 [facsimile reprint] (Taipei, 1968), p. 432.

[7]*Ku-kung ming-hua san-pai-chung* 故宮名畫三百種 (Taipei, 1959), vol. I, nos. 4 and 35.

Firstly, the subject matter of the two paintings in question is still uncertain, and the attachment of the title to the paintings occurred in very recent times. Secondly, even if the subject matter is correctly identified, the unmistakable note of irony in the title is entirely unintentional, and to render *Ming-huang hsing Shu* faithfully would be to perpetuate a nuance of meaning which is absent from the original.

Literary Allusions

In the cases of those paintings which illustrate specific literary works, their titles present a special problem in translation. The problem is exemplified by a painting by Lu Chih 陸治 (1496-1576) in the Freer Gallery of Art.[8] The handscroll depicts a wide expanse of river, with horizontal spits of land in the background, another projecting from the right in middle ground, and a promontory at the left foreground. Skirting the promontory is a path by which host and departing guest had travelled to the boat which is moored along the riverbank. The painting bears an inscription by the artist: *Chia-ching chia-yin chiu-yueh Pao-shan Lu Chih tso* 嘉靖甲寅九月包山陸治作, "Painted by Lu Chih, [*hao*] Pao-shan, in the ninth month of the *chia-yin* year in the reign of Chia-ching [1554]".

The title preceding the painting, written in *hsing-shu* 行書 by P'eng Nien 彭年 (1505-1565), reads: *Hsün-yang ch'iu se* 潯陽穐色, "Autumn Colours at Hsün-yang" (Pl. 49). The allusion is to Po Chü-i 白居易's (772-846 A.D.) famous poem, the *P'i-p'a hsing* 琵琶行, which narrates an encounter on the Hsün-yang River in the Chiu-chiang 九江 district of Kiangsi province.

> "One night by the Hsün-yang River, I was bidding a guest
>   farewell.
> Maple leaves and rushes rustled in autumn's desolate chill.
> I, the host, dismounted and the guest had boarded the boat.
> We raised our wine cups, but alas there was no music. . . ."

潯陽江頭夜送客，
楓葉荻花秋瑟瑟。
主人下馬客在船，
舉酒欲飲無管絃。

The allusion is confirmed by the transcription of the poem in *chuan-shu* 篆書 by Wen P'eng 文彭 (1498-1573) which is appended to the painting. Both P'eng Nien's title and Wen P'eng's transcription of the poem were probably executed immediately or very soon after the painting. There is no doubt that Lu Chih's painting was intended to illustrate Po Chü-i's poem. Within the simple composition of the painting are contained all the details in the first four lines of the poem—the riverbank, the maple trees, the reeds, the host and departing guest, the boat—as well as the virtuoso *p'i-p'a* player who is about to make her appearance. With a dry brush, a sparing use of *ts'un* 皴, and washes of pale colours accented only by touches of red for the maple leaves, the artist evokes to perfection the profoundly melancholic, almost elegaic, quality of Po Chü-i's poem.

Several choices present themselves as possible renditions of the title. A straight-forward translation of *Hsün-yang ch'iu-se* into "Autumn Colours at Hsün-yang" has

[8]Acc. no. 39.3. For illustration, see *The Freer Gallery of Art, I: China* (Kodansha, Tokyo, [1972?]), p. 171, top. For a colour illustration of a portion of the painting, see James F. Cahill, *Chinese Painting* (Skira, 1960), p. 133.

the virtues of being faithful to the original as well as being descriptive of the painting. However, to those unfamiliar with the opening passage of Po Chü-i's poem, the allusion is obscure. That translation is, however, preferable to the adoption of the poem's title *P'i-p'a hsing* for the painting. A third possibility is the rather unfortunate "The Lute Girl's Lament", to be mentioned only to be immediately rejected. It is a title less recondite than either of the other two and is meaningful to the generation familiar with Giles' translation of Po Chü-i's poem into English. It would appear that the ideal translated title of this type of painting should retain the allusion, and at the same time be not too abstruse for the English reader; further, it should not lose sight of its function as the title of a painting. By these criteria, "Autumn Colours at Hsün-yang" does seem to be the most satisfactory.

Amplification and Overamplification

Amplification of the original title may be justifiable, even desirable, in cases where the information is otherwise too terse to be meaningful to the English reader. There exists a number of handscrolls entitled *Wang-ch'uan t'u* 輞川圖 by various artists which illustrate the twenty stanzas of the poem *Wang-ch'uan chi* 輞川集, written by Wang Wei 王維 (699-759 A.D.) and his friend P'ei Ti 裴迪 (active 740's). The poem describes Wang Wei's country villa at Wang-ch'uan and its surroundings. Wang-ch'uan is in the southern part of Lan-t'ien 藍田 in Shensi province, an area of scenic beauty traversed by the Wang River 輞川. Not only did Wang Wei immortalize the locality in the poem, but he is also said to have created a pictorial record of Wang-ch'uan in the form of a long handscroll, thus bringing into play the two sides of his creative genius. All the paintings bearing the title of *Wang-ch'uan t'u* do claim descent from Wang Wei's lost painting. Artists who are recorded as having worked in this tradition include Kuo Chung-shu 郭忠恕 (latter half of the tenth century), and Chao Meng-fu 趙孟頫 (1254-1322).[9] There are two extant versions of the *Wang-ch'uan t'u* by Sung Hsü 宋旭 (1525-ca.1605). One of these, dated in correspondence to 1574, was formerly in the Victoria Contag collection and is now in the Asian

[9]For various versions attributed to these and other   文人畫粹編第一卷：王維 (Chuo Koron, Tokyo, 1975).
artists, see *Bunjinga suihen, vol. I: O Ui* (Wang Wei)

Plate 49 TITLE OF HSÜN-YANG CH'IU SE, *hsing-shu* by P'eng Nien. Freer Gallery of Art, Washington, D.C.

Art Museum of San Francisco.[10] The other, which is in the Freer Gallery of Art (acc. no. 09.207), bears a spurious Wang Meng 王蒙 signature, and is now attributed to Sung Hsü because of its close stylistic affinity to the San Francisco painting.[11]

A mere romanization of the title into *Wang-ch'uan t'u* is unsatisfactory, as the name *Wang-ch'uan* carries little meaning to those unfamiliar with the background of this group of paintings. It is an impoverished version of the Chinese original; an arrangement of eleven letters of the alphabet simply does not convey the wealth of literary, pictorial and pictographic associations inherent in the three Chinese characters. This seems to be a case in which the translator is entitled to a certain licence to expand. "The Poet Wang Wei's Country Retreat at Wang-ch'uan" may be quite acceptable as it both retains the name Wang-ch'uan and provides enough information to make it immediately intelligible.

The licence to expand should be tempered with discretion. Sometimes it is advisable to refrain from using it even though additional information seems to warrant an amplification of the title to make it more precise. "The Hangchow Bore in Moonlight" for Li Sung 李嵩's (ca. 1190-1230) *Yüeh-yeh kuan-ch'ao t'u* 月夜觀潮圖 [12] may serve as an admonition to leave well alone.

ONE OR TWO conclusions may be drawn from the above random observations. By their very nature, titles which are contemporaneous with the paintings and are therefore more true to the artists' intent, as distinct from titles acquired in relatively recent times, deserve closer attention paid to their identification, interpretation and rendition. The ideal translation of a painting title combines correct information, precision, fidelity to grammar and quintessential meaning, and, not least, elegance of language. These are qualities so diverse as to be almost impossible for any one translated title to possess. It is perhaps inevitable that any translation would in the end be a compromise. But in arriving at that compromise, one might do worse than to bring to the process a measure of the attention accorded to the major aspects of the study of Chinese painting.

[10]*Ibid.*, pl. 27.

[11]*Ibid.*, pls. 37-39.

[12]*Chinese Art Treasures*, no. 51.

王方宇：朱耷世說新語詩

Chu Ta's "Shih Shuo Hsin Yu" Poems

By **Wang Fang-yu**

Translated by **Aileen Huang Wei and Wang Fang-yu**

Not explainable, then do not explain it.
Not explaining, then resolve it without explanation.*
不可解，則可不解。不解，以不解解之。

I. What kind of a book is Shih Shuo Hsin Yü?

Shih Shuo Hsin Yü is a fascinating book about life and conversation among the Chinese upper classes during the period from the last years of the later Han dynasty to the end of Chin (A.D. 200-419). Most of the stories in this book are based on contemporary records, written in a style and vocabulary that was largely derived from the colloquial of the time. This collection of lively anecdotes can help us understand the life and thought of the people of the period. It is a rare document, unique in Chinese literature. The editor of this book was Liu I-ch'ing 劉義慶 (403-444), himself nearly contemporaneous with the persons whose stories he compiled.

The language of *Shih Shuo Hsin Yü* is not easy to understand, and there are misprints in the book. Also, the stories themselves are not entirely reliable. Therefore, when the book first appeared many tried their hands at annotating it. Most notable of these was Liu Hsiao-piao 劉孝標 (462-521), who was born 59 years after the birth of

This is an abbreviated translation of the original article which appeared in the Hong Kong magazine *Ta Ch'eng* 大成, September 1975.

*This quotation, source unknown, epitomizes the difficulty of rendering into English the artist's cryptic poems, which were based in turn on some of the more obscure stories found in the book *Shih Shuo Hsin Yü*.

the editor Liu I-ch'ing. In his detailed notes he quoted profusely from books which are now lost, without adding much commentary of his own. He simply used quotations from other books to reveal the mistakes in the text. For this reason bibliographers and other scholars who have studied *Shih Shuo Hsin Yü* have high praise for Liu Hsiao-piao's annotations.

II. Why was Chu Ta an avid reader of Shih Shuo Hsin Yü?

It is easy to see the reason why the artist Chu Ta 朱耷 (Pa-ta-shan-jen 八大山人) was fond of reading *Shih Shuo Hsin Yü*. The life and art of the people in the Chin dynasty, such as the celebrated "Seven Sages of the Bamboo Grove", are held in high esteem by later scholars. They are impressed by the independent way of life of the recluse. Chu Ta admired the calligraphy of Wang Hsi-chih 王羲之 and Wang Hsien-chih 王獻之, the paintings by Ku K'ai-chih 顧愷之, the poetry and prose of Ts'ao Ts'ao 曹操, Ts'ao Chih 曹植 and others of the Chien-an school, and the eloquence of the Buddhist-Taoist Chih Tun 支遁 and the drunkard Liu Ling 劉伶, and he found himself a kindred spirit to all the eccentric persons who could not fit into society. It follows that he liked reading about them in this book. He would memorize many passages in *Shih Shuo Hsin Yü* and readily use phrases from them in his own poetry. Sometimes,

Plate 50 STONE PAINTING by Chu Ta. *An Wan Album.* The inscription: *"I heard you can play the flute well...."*

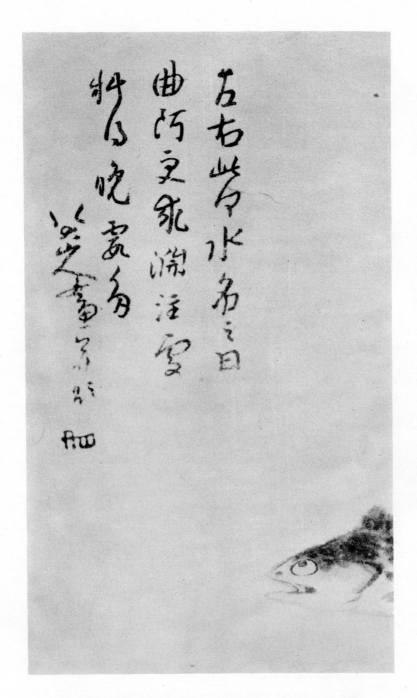

Plate 51   FISH PAINTING by Chu Ta. *An Wan Album.* The
inscription: " *'Gentlemen! What lake is this?'....*"

in composing his poems, one such allusion would lead to another, and he would often by association refer to personal incidents that could not be discussed openly for political reasons. He had already formed the habit of using cryptic, metaphorical expressions in all his works; his poetry was no exception. This makes the meaning of his poems very obscure. Trying to understand them is like doing detective work. Some of these poems contain clues which help us get a very clear idea of what he was talking about. With others, we can at best achieve only a partial understanding.

III. An attempt to explain Chu Ta's Shih Shuo Hsin Yü poems

The eight poems and one colophon discussed in this article are all concerned with stories found in *Shih Shuo Hsin Yü*. Some of them are quite obvious in meaning, while others are not so clear. Some of the references are difficult to understand because when Chu Ta was writing he associated them with other matters on his mind. Others are difficult because Chu Ta misinterpreted the meaning of the text in *Shih Shuo Hsin Yü*.

(1) A poem inscribed on a stone painting on one of the leaves in the An Wan album 安晚册, collection of Sumitomo, reads—

聞 君 善 吹 邃 (笛)
wen chǔn shan ch'ui ti
[hear/you/well/blow/flute]

已 是 無 蹤 跡
yi shih wu tsung chi
[already/be/no/trace]

乘 舟 上 車 去
ch'eng chou shang ch'e ch'ü
[board/boat/mount/carriage/leave]

一 聽 主 與 客
yi t'ing chu yǔ k'e
[one/listen/host/and/guest]

This poem is based on a story about Wang Hui-chih 王徽之 (the son of Wang Hsi-chih) and Huan Yi 桓伊. Huan Yi was a famous flute-player who later rose to be a general. The story appeared in *Shih Shuo Hsin Yü*, Section 23—

Wang Hui-chih was leaving the capital, and was

still in his boat moored by the riverside. Formerly he had heard that Huan Yi played the flute well, but had never met him. It happened that Huan passed by along the bank of the river while Wang was in his boat. Someone who knew Huan reported to Wang that it was Huan Yi. So Wang sent a man to Huan, saying: "Wang Hui-chih has heard that you are a good flute player. Will you play for him?" Huan Yi, who was already a high official at the time, had heard about Wang Hui-chih also. So he came down from his carriage, sat on his couch and played three tunes. When he had finished playing he got on his carriage and left. Throughout the host and the guest exchanged not a word.

王子猷出都，尚在渚下，舊聞桓子野吹笛，而不相識。遇桓於岸上過，王在船中，客有識之者云：「是桓子野。」王便令人與相問云：「聞君善吹笛，試爲我一奏。」桓時已顯貴，素聞王名，即便廻下車，踞胡牀，爲作三調；弄畢，便上車去。客主不交一言。

This poem may be rendered as follows:

I heard you can play the flute well,
But there was no trace of you anywhere.
You boarded the boat, then left by carriage.
Just listening—the host and the guest.

(2) A second poem, inscribed on a fish painting in the An Wan album, collection of Sumitomo, reads—

左 右 此 河 水
tso yu ts'i he shui
[left/right/this/river/water]

名 之 曰 曲 阿
ming chih yueh ch'ü ah
[name/it/say/Ch'ü-/ah]

更 求 淵 注 處
keng ch'iu yüan chu ch'u
[even more/seek/water/flow into/place]

料 得 晚 霞 多
liao te wan hsia tuo
[suppose/get/evening/clouds/much]

This poem is based upon a story concerning Hsieh Wan 謝萬. When he was at Yunyang, he saw the Ch'ü-ah (crooked) Lake and had a conversation with his subordinates about it. This story appears in *Shih Shuo Hsin Yü*, Section 2—

Hsieh Wan passed the crooked Ch'u-ah Lake and asked his subordinates: "What lake is this?" They answered: "Ch'ü-ah Lake." Hsieh said: "So the water can stay here and will not flow away."

謝中郎經曲阿後湖，問左右：「此是何水？」答曰：「曲阿湖。」謝曰：「故當淵注亭箸，納而不流。」

"Gentlemen! What lake is this?"
"It's named Ch'ü-ah (crooked)."
"Where then does it lead?"
There are probably many clouds at sun-down.

(3) Inscribed on a dog painting in the An Wan album, collection of Sumitomo, there is this poem—

林 公 不 二 門
lin kung pu erh men
[Lin/Kung/no/second/door]

出 入 王 與 許
ch'u ju wang yü hsü
[exit/enter/Wang/and/Hsü]

如 上 法 華 疏
ju shang fa hua su
[resemble/present/Saddharma-/Pumdarika/commentary]

象 喻 者 籠 虎
hsiang yü che lung hu
[look like/illustrate/that which/cage/tiger]

This poem involves a number of stories in *Shih Shuo Hsin Yü*. The association is rather complicated. In the first place, the picture is that of a dog. The pronunciation of the Chinese character for dog 狗 is *kou*. In Section 4 of the book there is a story about Wang Kou-tzu 王茍子 whose other name is Wang Hsiu 王修. Immediately before and after this passage there are several stories about discussions on Buddhism and Taoism logic, most of which demonstrate the eloquence and intelligence of Chih Tun 支遁 (314-366). Having read these stories, and having associated them in his mind with the dog that he painted, he then composed this poem.

In the first line, 林公不二門 *lin kung pu-erh men*, Lin Kung is another name of Chih Tun. A priest of both Buddhism and Taoism, Chih Tun, sometimes called Chih Tao-lin 支道林, was much

admired by his contemporaries for his intelligence and wisdom. He was very good at clarifying vague points of metaphysics and was also a skilled debator.

Pu-erh-men is a Buddhist term, meaning the "one undivided truth", "the Buddha-truth", "the unity of the Buddha-nature". In Section 4 of *Shih Shuo Hsin Yü* there is this story—

Chih Tun established the "Theory of Rupanisunyata". He showed his work to Wang T'an-chih, but Wang didn't say anything. Chih Tun asked: "Do you accept it by silence?" Wang T'an-chih said: "Since Manjusri isn't here, who can appreciate my silence?"

支道林造即色論，論成，示王中郎；中郎都無言。支曰：「默而識之乎？」王曰：「既無文殊，誰能見賞？」

The meaning of the conversation is clarified by a paragraph of *Vimalakirti Sutra* which was quoted by Liu Hsiao-piao—

Manjusri asked Vimalakirti: "When is the Bodhisattva said to attain the Buddha-truth?" Vimalakirti kept silent. Then Manjusri said with a sigh, "This must indeed be the true state of having entered the 'door of the Buddha-truth!' "

What Wang T'an-chih meant was: "Look, when Vimalakirti kept silent, Manjusri understood him. But now that there isn't a Manjusri here, who could understand my silence?" He was a little sarcastic toward Chih Tun. This passage is the origin of the first line of this poem.

The second line is 出入王與許 *ch'u ju wang yü hsü*. Wang is Wang Hsiu 王修, or Wang Kou-tzu 王茍子, who liked to debate; Hsü is Hsü Hsun 許詢. The two of them discussed and debated with Chih Tun frequently. There is a very interesting story in *Shih Shuo Hsin Yü* about their debating—

When Hsü Hsun was young, people compared him with Wang Hsiu. Hsü Hsun felt it was unfair and became very disturbed. At that time Chih Tun and many other people were gathered in the Western Temple for a discussion. Wang Hsiu was also there. Hsü Hsun was very angry and went to the Western Temple to debate with Wang Hsiu, wanting to see who could do better. Hsü Hsun gave Wang Hsiu a hard time, and Wang Hsiu eventually lost. Hsü Hsun then challenged Wang Hsiu to switch positions and debate again, but again Wang Hsiu lost. After that, Hsü Hsun asked Chih Tun: "What do you think of my argument?"

Chih Tun very casually said: "Your statements were good all right, but why must they be so harsh? How could those kind of remarks be considered logical criticism?"

許掾詢年少時，人以比王茍子，許大不平。時諸人士及林法師，並在會稽西寺講，王亦在焉。許意甚忿，便往西寺與王論理，共決優劣；苦相折挫，王遂大屈。許復執王理，王執許理，更相覆疏，王復屈。許謂支法師曰：「弟子向語何似？」支從容曰：「君語，佳則佳矣，何至相苦邪！豈是求理中之談哉！」

In the third line, 如上法華疏 *ju shang fa hua su, fa-hua* is Saddharma-pumdarika or the Lotus Sutra. In this line, I presume that Chu Ta particularly referred to the "three vehicles" in the Lotus Sutra. In Section 4 of *Shih Shuo Hsin Yü*, there is this story—

To explain the "three vehicles" is not an easy job. Once, when Chih Tun was at the altar, he explained them very clearly. It seemed everybody understood them. But after he had finished, the people in the audience started discussing them, and they could only understand two vehicles. When they talked about the third one, they became confused again.

三乘佛家滯義，支道林分判，使三乘炳然；諸人在下坐聽，皆云可通。支下坐，自共說，正當得兩，入三便亂。

Plate 52 DOG PAINTING by Chu Ta. *An Wan Album.* The inscription: *"Chih Tun's supreme theory...."*

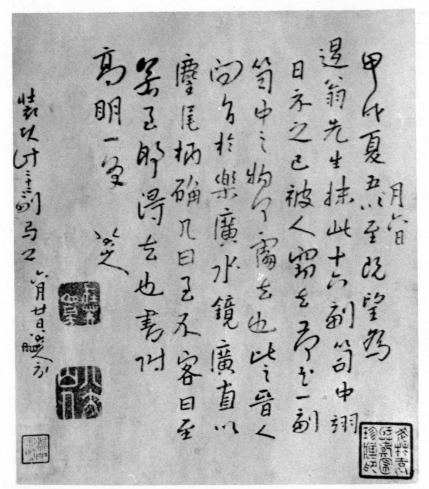

Plate 53   COLOPHON by Chu Ta. *An Wan Album. "Between the sixth and fifteenth of the fifth month in the summer of the year Chia-hsu [1694], I painted these sixteen leaves for T'ui Weng...."*

"Vehicle" is an instrument for reaching a goal. The so-called "three vehicles" means there are three ways to reach Nirvana. If we try to explain it as two vehicles, "great vehicle" (Mahayana) and "small vehicle" (Hinayana), it would be easier to understand. "Small vehicle" means to acknowledge the misery of human life and to try to suppress one's desires. In order to reach Nirvana, he may be enlightened by Sravaka or by Pratyekabuddha. These two, although they are thoroughly different channels, are both "small vehicles". The "great vehicle" means not only to save oneself but also to save others; the purpose is to have all people reach Nirvana. If one has this intention, he must go through the path of Manjusri. In other words, basically there are "two vehicles". But the "small vehicle" may be subdivided into two more vehicles, Sravaka and Pratyekabuddha. The results are: great vehicle, middle vehicle and small vehicle.

The fourth line is 象喩者籠虎 *hsiang yü che lung hu*. It is possible that Chu Ta, at this moment, because of seeing the "dog" which he had painted, thought of another story.

There is a story in Section 6 of *Shih Shuo Hsin Yü* that goes—

Emperor Wei Ming-ti had a tiger. He had the tiger's teeth and claws removed, and displayed the beast to the people in a field. Wang Jung who was only seven years old was among those who went to look. The tiger grabbed the railings of his cage and roared very loudly. The spectators were all frightened and fell over one another backwards. But Wang Jung stood there, motionless and not afraid.

魏明帝於宣武場上，斷虎爪牙，縱百姓觀之。王戎七歲，亦往看，虎承間攀欄而吼，其聲震地，觀者無不辟易顛仆，戎湛然不動，了無恐色。

Taking into account all the above references,

the poem can be rendered thus—

> *Chih Tun's supreme theory,*
> *Concurs with Wang Hsiu and Hsü Hsun.*
> *As mystical as explaining the Lotus Sutra,*
> *This puppy resembles the caged tiger.*

In the colophon of the An Wan album, there are also a number of lines relating to a story in *Shih Shuo Hsin Yü*. The colophon may be translated as follows—

> Between the sixth and fifteenth of the fifth month in the summer of the year Chia-hsü [1694], I painted these sixteen leaves for T'ui Weng. I put them in the cabinet, but one painting of lotus flowers was stolen by someone the next day. Where did it go, that has been put away in the cabinet? I may compare this instance with the Chin person asking the "water-and-mirror" (lucid) Yueh Kuang concerning the meaning. Yueh Kuang used the handle of his fly whisp to touch the table, and asked: "Has it arrived?" The person answered: "Yes." If it has "arrived", how come it has "gone?" I write this anecdote for you to get a laugh. (Signed) Pa-ta-shan-jen.

> 甲戌夏，五月六日以至旣望，爲
> 退翁先生抹此十六副，笥中。翌日示之，已被人竊去
> 荷花一副，笥中之物，何處去也？比之晉人問旨於樂
> 廣水鏡，廣直以麈尾柄確几，曰：「至不？」客曰
> 「至。」若至，那得去也？
> 書附
> 高明一笑   八大山人

Yueh Kuang was known for his ability to use very few words to clarify a point. All his contemporaries praised him for this.

In Section 8 of *Shih Shuo Hsin Yü*, there is this incident—

> Wang Yi-fu had said: "I have always felt that I was too wordy when I talked with Yueh Kuang.

> 王夷甫自嘆：「我與樂令談，未賞不覺我言爲煩。」

As to addressing Yueh Kuang as "lucid," a story also appears in Section 8 to the following effect—

> When Wei Po-yü was in the position of minister, he saw Yueh Kuang in a discourse with the scholars. Wei Po-yü was amazed, and said: "I have always been afraid that the good words would be extinguished after the ancient people were gone. But now I can hear them from you." He commanded his students to visit Yueh Kuang and said to them: "This person is a person of "water-and-mirror" (lucid). When you see him, you will feel that the misty cloud is erased and you can see the blue sky."

> 衛伯玉爲尚書令，見樂廣與中朝名士談議，奇之曰：
> 「自昔諸人沒已來，常恐微言將絕，今乃復聞斯言於
> 君矣！」命子弟造之，曰：「此人人之水鏡也，見之
> 若披雲霧覩靑天！」

The story which Chu Ta referred to in his colophon is in Section 4 of *Shih Shuo Hsin Yü*—

> There was a guest of Yueh Kuang who asked him about the meaning of "*chih pu chih*". Yueh Kuang did not analyze the sentence. He directly used the handle of his fly whisp to touch the table and said: "Has it arrived?" The guest said: "Yes." Yueh Kuang then lifted the handle and said: "If it has arrived, how come it has gone?" Then the guest understood and admired his method of explanation. Yueh Kuang can use few words, but he makes his meaning clear. There are other instances like this.

> 客問樂令「旨不至」者。樂亦不復剖析文句，直以麈
> 尾柄確几曰：「至不？」客曰：「至。」樂因又舉麈尾
> 曰：「若至者，那得去？」於是客乃悟服。樂辭約而旨
> 達，皆此類。

The important point in this story lies in the meaning of the phrase "*chih pu chih*". It seems that Chu Ta did not understand it, although Liu Hsiao-piao indicated the origin of this statement. Chu Ta wrote in his colophon:

> 晉 人 問 旨 於 樂 廣 水 鏡
> *chin jen wen chih yü yueh kuang shui ching*

In this sentence, the character 旨 *chih* stands for "meaning".

It is true that 旨 may be used in this sense, and there are many instances in *Shih Shuo Hsin Yü* in which 旨 is used to mean "meaning". But in the original text of *Shih Shuo Hsin Yü*, the first line reads:

> 客 問 樂 令 旨 不 至 者
> *k'e wen yueh ling chih pu chih che*
> [guest/ask/Yueh/Kuang/"chih/pu/chih"/one that]
> *There was a guest of Yueh Kuang who asked him about "chih pu chih".*

Chu Ta punctuated this line thusly:

客　問　樂　令　旨，　不　至　者

k'e wen yüeh ling chih , pu chih che

[guest/ask/Yueh/Kuang/the meaning/pu/chih/one that]

There was a guest of Yueh Kuang who asked him about the meaning of "pu chih".

The problem is with the character 旨 *chih*, which is used as a variation of 指 *chih*.

In the texts of *Chuang Tzu* and *Lieh Tzu*, the written forms of this phrase appear as 指不至, not 旨不至. However, in *Shih Shuo Hsin Yü*, it is 旨不至.

The meaning of the phrase 指不至 may be explained as follows:

The 指 *chih* in 指不至 *chih pu chih* means: "to have a definite and unchangeable concept". Since all things constantly change, then a permanent concept of objective reality (physical universe) is impossible. If one has a definite and unchangeable concept, then that concept will never reflect objective reality 不至. That is why Yueh Kuang asked when the handle of his fly whisp touched the table: "Has it arrived 至不?" After the guest answered: "Yes 至", he moved the handle away from the table and asked again: "If it has arrived, how come it has left now?" The implication is that everything is continuously changing.

This argument was raised by Kung-sun Lung 公孫龍 and appeared in several philosophical texts of the Warring States period. In *Chuang Tzu* and *Lieh Tzu* this parable is discussed at length. Since Liu Hsiao-piao used excerpts from both *Chuang Tzu* and *Lieh Tzu* in his annotation, he apparently knew that the 旨不至 in *Shih Shuo Hsin Yü* is the

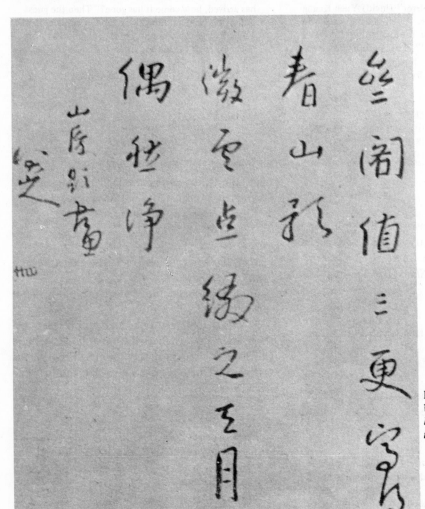

Plate 54 **CALLIGRAPHY** by Chu Ta. *Authentic Works by Pa-ta-shan-jen. "Midnight in the studio, . . ."*

same thing as the 指不至 in *Chuang Tzu* and *Lieh Tzu*. However, it seems that Chu Ta did not know that 旨 is a variation of 指. He thus wrote in his colophon 比之晉人問旨於樂廣水鏡 *"I may compare this instance with the Chin person asking the 'water-and mirror' (lucid) Yueh Kuang concerning the meaning* 旨*."*

Actually, the Chin person did not ask about 旨 *chih* but asked about 指不至 *chih pu chih*.

(4) The following poem appeared on two different album leaves: *Ta Feng T'ang Ming Chi* 大風堂名蹟, Vol. III, and *Authentic Works by Pa-ta-shan-jen* 八大山人眞蹟, Vol. I—

齋 閣 值 三 更
chai ko chih san keng
[studio/pavilion/happen/third/beat]

寫 得 春 山 影
hsieh te ch'un shan ying
[paint/obtain/spring/mountain/shadow]

微 雲 點 綴 之
wei yün tien chui chih
[little/cloud/decorate/it]

天 月 偶 然 淨
tien yueh ou jan ching
[sky/moon/occasionally/clear]

The origin of the poem is in Section 2 of *Shih Shuo Hsin Yü*.

Ssuma sat in his studio at night. At that time the sky was very clear, and there were no clouds. He commented admiringly on the beautiful clear sky. Hsieh Ching-chung, who was sitting with him, said: "I feel it would be better if there were some spots of clouds." Ssuma joked with Hsieh, saying: "Is it just because you have a dirty mind that you want to smear the clear sky?"

司馬太傅齋中夜坐，于時天月明淨，都無纖翳；太傅歎以爲佳。謝景重在坐，答曰：「意謂乃不如微雲點綴。」太傅因戲謝曰：「卿居心不淨，乃復强欲滓穢太淸邪？」

This poem may be rendered as:

Midnight in the studio,
Painting the spring hills.
It would be prettier with spots of clouds,
In the clear moonlit sky.

(5) In *Authentic Works by Pa-ta-shan-jen*, Vol. I, there is one leaf of calligraphy with a poem after a *Shih Shuo Hsin Yü* story—

亦 可 揚 州 賦
yi k'e yang chou fu
[also/may/Yang-/chou/prose-poetry]

翻 思 山 海 人
fan ssu shan hai jen
[turn/think/mountain/sea/people]

羣 公 未 霑 接
ch'ün kung wei chan chieh
[group/gentlemen/not yet/entertain]

蘭 闍 已 回 春
lan she yi hui ch'un
[Lan/She/already/return/spring]

The story behind this poem concerns the diplomatic talent of Wang Tao 王導 (276-339). The story is in Section 3 of *Shih Shuo Hsin Yü*—

When Wang Tao was the Governor of Yangchou, he gave a party. Several hundred guests were there. He went around and talked with everybody except a certain Mr. Jen from Linhai and several foreigners. Later on he casually went over to Mr. Jen and said: "Now that you have left Linhai, there are no talented people in Linhai anymore". This made Jen very happy. Then he went over to the foreigners, snapped his fingers and said: "Lan She, Lan She." The foreigners all laughed. All the guests were very happy.

王丞相拜揚州，賓客數百人並加霑接，人人有悅色；唯有臨海一客姓任，及數胡人爲未洽。公因便還，到過任邊云：「君出，臨海便無復人。」任大喜悅。因過胡人前彈指云：「蘭闍，蘭闍。」羣胡同笑，四坐並懽。

What does "Lan She" mean?

In *Chu-tzu Yü Lu* 朱子語錄 by Chu Hsi 朱熹, the two characters were written as 蘭奢. Definitely it is a transliteration of a foreign word. Chu Hsi's explanation is: "It is a foreign term used for praising." This fits the situation perfectly. But what is the origin of this word?

In *K'un Hsueh Chi Wen* 困學紀聞 by Wang Ying-lin 王應麟 of the Sung dynasty, the author tried to connect the sound with a Sanskrit word, "aranya". Therefore, he explained it as a variation of 蘭若. In Chinese text 蘭若 usually refers to "a

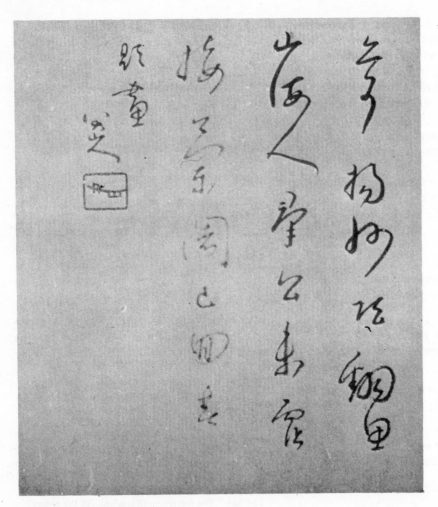

Plate 55 CALLI-
GRAPHY by Chu Ta.
*Authentic Works by
Pa-ta-shan-jen.* "This
may also be in the
Yangchou Lyric. . . ."

temple", but "aranya" may mean "a quiet place."

The passage may be more understandable if we adopt the meaning of "praising." If we can imagine a kind of situation in which Wang Tao said something in a foreign tongue and everybody was laughing, he must have sounded like an American host speaking to a group of Chinese, saying: "*Ding-hao, ding-hao.*"

This poem may be rendered as follows:

> *This may also be in the Yangchou Lyric,*
> *Thinking of the strangers at the gathering.*
> *Just as the gentlemen felt somewhat neglected,*
> *The words "Lan She" brought them a touch of spring.*

(6) In a hanging scroll of calligraphy by Chu Ta collected in the *Authentic Works by Pa-ta-shan-jen*, Vol. I, this poem is carried with illustration—

漢 去 昇 平 樂
han ch'ü sheng p'ing yueh
[Han dynasty/go/peace/music]

柏 梁 臺 上 人
po liang t'ai shang jen
[Po-/liang/Terrace/on/people]

六 花 誰 受 簡
liu hua shuei shou chien
[snow/who/receive/slip of number]

七 字 總 宜 春
ch'i tzu tsung yi ch'un
[seven/words/always/suitable/spring]

This poem cannot be fully understood. But we found a story in Section 2 of *Shih Shuo Hsin Yü* which might have some relationship with it —

> When Yü Chih-kung was the governor of Chingchou, he presented a feather fan to the Emperor Wu-ti. The Emperor suspected that it was a used one. One of the Emperor's close attendants, Lin Shao, said: "When Po-liang Terrace was constructed in the Han dynasty, it wasn't the Emperor who was there first, it was the workers. When the music was rehearsed, it was not the Emperor who heard it first, but Chung and Kuei. When Yü Chih-kung presented the fan to Your Majesty it is because it is good, not because it is a new one." Later on, Yü Chih-kung heard this story and said: "This person should be kept near the Emperor."

（庾稚恭）〔庾叔預〕爲（荆州）〔豫州〕，以毛扇上（武帝）〔成帝〕，（武帝）〔成帝〕疑是故物。侍中劉劭曰：「柏梁雲構，工匠先居其下；管弦繁奏，鍾夔先聽其音；（稚恭）〔叔預〕上扇，以好不以新。」庾後聞之曰：「此人宜在帝左右！」

This poem may be rendered as:

Music of the peace of Han,
People on the Po-liang terrace.
Receiving favors in snow and ice,
Seven words established spring.

(7) In the book *Pa-ta-shan-jen and his Art* 八大山人及其藝術 by Chou Shih-hsin 周士心, one poem by the artist is cited without illustration. It reads—

西 南 畫 史 丹 還 轉
hsi nan hua shih tan huan chuan
[south/west/painter/pills/change/turn]

二 子 廬 山 一 片 心
erh tzu lu shan yi p'ien hsin
[two/gentlemen/Lu/Shan/one/stretch/heart]

畢 竟 阿 瓜 稱 法 護
pi ching ah kua ch'eng fa hu
[after/all/ah/kua/call/fa/hu]

黃 冠 莫 定 老 元 琳
huang kuan mo ting lao yüan lin
[taoist/not/decide/old/yüan/lin]

A colophon reads:

"The Taoist Mu-kua-yen brought a painting of Mukua by Wang Ching-pi for me."

木瓜曇道人携王荆璧先生所畫木瓜見遺老夫。

西南畫史 *hsi-nan hua-shih* (the artist from the Southwest) refers to Wang Ching-pi. 二子廬山 *erh-tzu Lu Shan*, the two gentlemen who came to Lu Shan (which is close to Nanchang), refers to the Taoist Mu-kua-yen who had the good will to come to Lu Shan with a painting by Wang Ching-pi. Ah-kua, Fa-hu and Yüan-lin are all names of Wang Hsün 王珣 (349-400), a calligrapher.

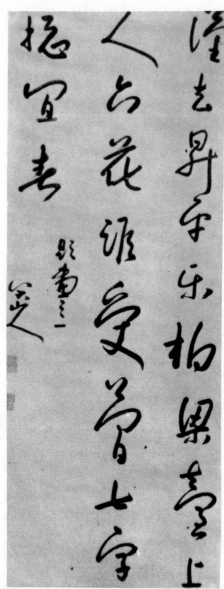

Plate 56 CALLIGRAPHY by Chu Ta. *Authentic Works by Pa-ta-shan-jen. "Music of the peace of Han. . . ."*

The poem does not describe nor is it directly concerned with any story in *Shih Shuo Hsin Yü*. Chu Ta is merely using the names to make a play on words in order to write some ambiguous lines. The third line of the poem may mean that, "After all, Ah-Kua is named Fa-hu, (both are names of Wang Hsün)". Since "hu" 護 means "to protect, to take care of" and "kua" 瓜 may also refer to the Taoist Mu-kua-yen, then, the same line may also mean, "The Taoist Mu-kua-yen brought a painting to me. He could be called a caretaker of the painting." The last line may be interpreted this

way: Since Yüan-lin's surname is Wang, and the painter's surname is also Wang, then this Yüan-lin really refers to the painter Wang and his work. The poem may be rendered like this:

The southwest artist has become active again,
Two gentlemen whole-heartedly visited Lu Shan.
After all Ah-kua served as the protector,
A Taoist cannot judge the work of old Wang.

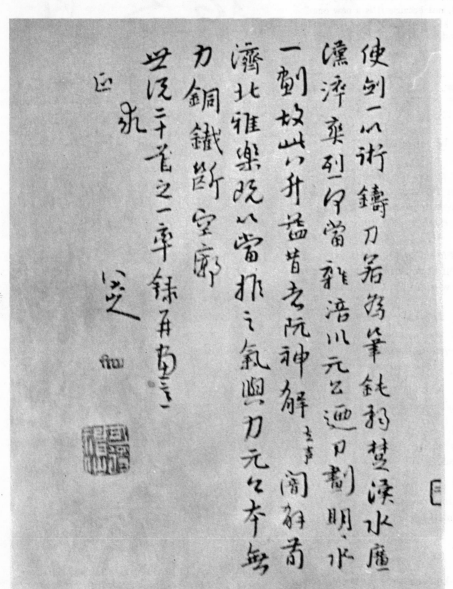

Plate 57
CALLIGRAPHY
by Chu Ta.
Authentic Works by Pa-ta-shan-jen.
"The trick in forging a sword is skill...."

(8) An album leaf of calligraphy in the *Authentic Works by Pa-ta-shan-jen*, Vol. II contains this statement: "This is one of the twenty poems concerning *Shih Shuo Hsin Yü*." The poem reads—

使 劍 一 以 術
Shih chien yi yi shu
[make/sword/one/use/skill]

鑄 刀 若 爲 筆
chu tao jo wei pi
[cast/knife/like/use/brush]

鈍 弱 楚 漢 水
tun jo ch'u han shui
[dull/weak/Ch'u-/Han/water]

廣 漢 淬 爽 烈
kuang han ts'ui shuang lieh
[Kuang-/Han/temper/lively/violent]

何 當 雜 涪 川
ho tang tsa fu ch'uan
[how/should/mix/Fu/River]

元 公 迺 刀 劃
yuan kung nai tao hua
[Yuan/Mr./then/sword/strike]

明 明 水 一 劃
ming ming shui yi hua
[clear/clear/water/one/strike]

故 此 八 升 益
ku ts'i pa sheng yi
[reason/this/eight/liter/add]

昔 者 阮 神 解 (去聲)
hsi che juan shen chieh
[formerly/Juan/spirit/understand]

闇 解 荀 濟 北
an chieh hsün chi pei
[clear/understand/Hsun/Chi-/pei]

雅 樂 旣 以 當
ya yüeh chi yi tang
[ceremonial classical/music/already/proper]

推 之 氣 與 力
t'ui chih ch'i yü li
[apply/it/air/and/force]

元 公 本 無 力
yuan kung pen wu li
[Yuan/Mr./originally/have no/force]

銅 鐵 斷 空 廓
t'ung t'ieh tuan k'ung kuo
[brass/iron/broken/emptiness]

This poem is very difficult. I tried to unravel it by starting with the name Yuan Kung 元公. There is a person named Ku Jung 顧榮 in *Shih Shuo Hsin Yü*. He is also called Yuan Kung. There are four stories concerning Ku Jung in *Shih Shuo Hsin Yü*, but none of them has anything to do with this poem. I also found another Yuan Kung in *Ming History*. Huang Tuan-po 黃端伯 in the Ming dynasty was also called Yuan Kung because—

1. He was a contemporary of Chu Ta.
2. He was from Chianghsi, same as Chu Ta.
3. At the end of the Ming dynasty he didn't surrender to the Ch'ing and was executed.
4. He was once a monk and then came back to society.

Therefore, I thought that he was probably the one Chu Ta was talking about. I sent my draft to Mr. Jao Tsung-i 饒宗頤 and received a long letter from him. In his letter he pointed out that Yuan Kung was P'u Yuan 蒲元 who lived in the Three Kingdoms period. He generously gave me all the materials he found. After I read the biography of P'u Yuan in *Yi Wen Lei Chü* 藝文類聚, Vol. 60, I realized that P'u Yuan is the very person that Chu Ta was talking about. The passage reads—

> P'u Yuan has a lot of imagination. He made three thousand swords at Hsieh K'ou for Chuke Liang. After they were finished, he said that the Water of the Han River (which is close to Hsieh K'ou) was weak and that it could not be used for tempering iron. The water in the rivers of Szechuan was strong and it had the spirit of metal. Nature made it that way. So he ordered his men to go to Chengtu to fetch water from the river there. He dipped the sword in the water, and said that the water had been mixed with some water from the Fu River, Thus it could not be used. The men who fetched the water insisted that it was not mixed. P'u Yuan struck the water with the sword and pronounced that there were eight liters of water from the Fu. Then the men knocked their heads on the ground and admitted that while they were at the Fu River, some water had spilled, and so they added eight liters of water from the Fu. The swords P'u Yuan made were very sharp. He put iron balls in a bamboo container and used his sword to cut it. It broke immediately. They were called "spiritual swords".

君性多奇思，于斜口爲諸葛亮鑄刀三千口。刀成，自
言漢水鈍弱，不任淬用，蜀江淬烈，是謂大金之元精，
天分其野，乃命人于成都取江水，君以淬刀，言雜涪
水，不可用。取水者捍言不雜，君以刀畫水，言雜八
升。取水者叩頭云：「於涪津覆水，遂以涪水八升益
之。」以竹筒納鐵珠滿中，舉刀斷之，應手虛落，因
曰神刀。

There is no information about the author of
the biography of P'u Yuan. This anecdote does not
appear in Chen Shou 陳壽's *San Kuo Chih* 三國志
(History of the Three Kingdoms), but it does
appear in both the encyclopedias. There is no
doubt that the Yuan Kung whom Pa-ta-shan-jen
referred to is P'u Yuan, and I am deeply indebted
to Mr. Jao for this discovery.

Two lines in this poem concern Hsun Hsü 荀勗,
also known as Hsun Chi-pei 荀濟北 . A story in
Section 20 of *Shih Shuo Hsin Yü* says—

> Hsun Hsü was a connoisseur of music. People
> called him "an-chieh" (clear understanding). He
> corrected the musical scales and scores of cer-
> emonial classical music. Whenever there were court
> gatherings he would perform and produce fine
> harmony. Juan Hsien also understood music well,
> and people called him "shen-chieh" (spiritual
> understanding). Whenever Hsun Hsü performed,
> Juan Hsien would feel that something was not
> right. He never commented favorably on Hsun Hsü's
> performance. Disliking this, Hsun Hsü ousted Juan
> Hsien and made him the Prefect of Shih-p'ing.
> Later, a farmer found some jade measurements in
> his field. They dated from the Chou dynasty and
> were the final standard for all musical instruments.
> Hsun Hsü used them to check the percussive, brass
> and string instruments that he was working on, and
> realized they were all a little bit shorter than they
> were supposed to be. He then surrendered to Juan
> Hsien's superior judgement.

荀勗善解音聲，時論謂之闇解。遂調律呂，正雅樂。
每至正會，殿庭作樂，自調宮商，無不諧韻。阮威妙
賞，時謂神解。每公會作樂，而心謂之不調。既無一
言直勗，意忌之，遂出阮爲始平太守。後有一田父耕
於野，得周時玉尺，便是天下正尺。荀試以校己所治
鐘鼓，金石，絲竹，皆覺短一黍。於是伏阮神識。

Hsun Hsü is mentioned in another story, in
Section 21 of *Shih Shuo Hsin Yü*—

> Chung Hui is an uncle of Hsun Hsü. They did

not get along very well. Hsun had a very good
sword, which was worth a million dollars. It was in
the custody of his mother (Chung's sister). Chung
Hui was a good calligrapher and could imitate other
people's hand-writing. He wrote a letter to Hsun's
mother asking for the sword, imitating Hsun's style
of writing and signature. After he got the sword, he
did not return it.

鍾會是荀濟北從舅，二人情好不協。荀有寶劍，可直
百萬金，常在母鍾太夫人許。會善書，學荀手跡，作
書與母取劍，仍竊去不還。

Now that we know the references to Yuan
Kung, Hsun Hsü and Juan Hsien, we can understand what this poem is trying to say.

Chu Ta connected the story of music and the
story of tempering the sword, both of which
revolve around the point that there is a subtle
difference between the perfect and the imperfect.
In Chu Ta's mind this subtle difference is also
associated with brushwork. When one uses a brush
in calligraphy or painting, one must seek to catch
this subtlety. It is just like tempering an iron sword
and making musical instruments. The important
thing is to catch the subtlety through "spiritual
understanding".

The poem may be rendered as follows:

> *The trick in forging a sword is skill,*
> *Forging a knife is like making a brush.*
> *The water in Ch'u-Han is dull and weak,*
> *The water in Kuang-Han is strong and*
>   *sharp.*
> *How can it be mixed with the water of*
>   *Fu?*
> *So struck P'u Yuan with his sword.*
> *Everything is made clear with one stroke*
>   *of the sword,*
> *Thus revealing the eight added liters.*
> *In the past Juan Hsien had spiritual*
>   *understanding of music,*
> *Hsun Hsü also clearly understood.*
> *The scores of ceremonial classical music*
>   *were righted,*
> *Air and strength must be applied.*
> *P'u Yuan at first didn't have any strength,*
> *Brass and iron broke the thin air.*

Some Relationships between Poetry and Painting in China

By **Jonathan Chaves**

SU TUNG-P'O 蘇東坡 (1037-1101) once said of Wang Wei 王維 (701-761) that "there is poetry in his painting and painting in his poetry." This has become the most frequently repeated quotation on the relationship of Chinese poetry and painting, a relationship which has often been discussed by students of these subjects.

There are many ways in which the two arts relate to each other in China—in this paper I would like to call attention to several which would be fruitful areas for more intensive study.

To begin with, poems often can be used as sources by art historians. For example, the important Northern Sung poet Mei Yao-ch'en 梅堯臣 (1002-1060) wrote a great many poems that deal with painting and calligraphy. Some of these are useful for determining contemporary attitudes toward the art of painting. Here is part of a poem by Mei on a picture by the monk Chü-ning 居寧:[1]

On Seeing a Painting of Plants and Insects by Chü-ning

When the ancients painted swans and tigers
They turned out looking like ducks and dogs.
But now I see these painted insects
Successful both in feeling and in form.
The walkers truly seem to move,
The fliers truly seem to soar,
The fighters seem to raise their limbs,
The chirpers seem to swell their chests,
The jumpers really move their legs,
The starers really fix their eyes!
And so I learn that the Creator's power
Cannot match the agility of the artist's brush.

観居寧畫草蟲

古人畫虎鵠，
尚類狗與鶩。
今看畫羽蟲，
形意兩俱足。
行者勢若去，
飛者翻若逐。
拒者如舉臂，
鳴者如動腹。
躍者趯其股，
顧者注其目。
乃知造物靈，
未抵毫端速。

It is evident that Mei considers realism to be a primary criterion for evaluating painting. In addition, he expresses the idea that modern artists, such as Chü-ning, surpass the ancients in the field of "flower and bird" painting. Kuo Jo-hsü 郭若虛, an important eleventh century writer on painting, also felt that "in landscape, forests and rocks, flowers and bamboo, and creatures and fish, the ancients are not as good as the moderns."[2]

Another poem by Mei[3] illustrates other ways in which poetry may be of use to the art historian. Here, Mei describes some of the paintings in the collection of a certain Ho Chün-pao 何君寶. The poem begins with a long discursus on water-buffalo painting. Mei explains that it is much harder to paint water-buffaloes than to paint horses, as the fine hairs of a horse can be suggested by an overall hazy treatment, while the sparse hairs of a water-buffalo must be painstakingly depicted. All of this is by way of introduction to a scroll by the famous T'ang water-buffalo painter

[1] *Wan-ling chi* 宛陵集 (in *Ssu-pu ts'ung-k'an*), 10/13a.

[2] Kuo Jo-hsü, *T'u-hua chien-wen chih* 圖畫見聞誌 (in *Mei-shu ts'ung-k'an* 美術叢刊, Vol. II, Taipei, 1964), p. 56.

[3] *Wan-ling chi*, 15/1a-2a.

Tai Sung 戴嵩, which Mei saw at Mr. Ho's house. He proceeds to describe a scene of two water-buffaloes fighting, and his description, although written in the difficult medium of verse, is considerably more detailed than the brief entries often found in the better-known painting catalogues. Toward the end of the scroll, Mei continues, is a red seal with characters which read, "Secretary T'ao." Mei relates how the Secretary, who lived "early in the dynasty", collected many paintings, "not sparing cash or silk." But his descendants, not faring as well financially as their illustrious ancestor, were forced to sell his collection in the market place. In this way the Tai Sung work came into Mr. Ho's hands. This section of the poem would be of invaluable aid to students of T'ang painting, as there are no extant authentic works by Tai Sung, to my knowledge.

Mei goes on to describe in detail a scroll of famous legendary and historical scenes by the famous T'ang figure painter, Yen Li-pen 閻立本 (d. 673), including such episodes as the Dark Lady 玄女, a goddess, handing a magic military talisman to the Yellow Emperor, the last emperor of the Shang dynasty indulging in various perversions, and King Fu-ch'ai 夫差 of Wu entertaining the great beauty, Hsi-shih 西施. As a whole, the poem provides us with a fascinating account of an eleventh century collection of paintings, as well as with detailed descriptions of individual works.

MEI YAO-CH'EN was a poet who was interested in painting. With poets who were also painters, we come closer to the heart of our theme. In the West, such a combination of talents was rare—one thinks of Michelangelo, best known as a painter but an excellent poet as well. But only in William Blake do we find a figure who corresponds somewhat to the Chinese conception of the poet-painter. Blake too, in addition to being adept in both arts, combined them in integral works, particularly in his illuminated books, such as *Jerusalem*. And in Blake, as in Chinese art, the relationship between text and picture was often complex, each offering a counterpoint to the other.

Poet-painters are more frequently encountered in China. Perhaps the most famous are Wang Wei and Su Tung-p'o. To their names should be added those of an important circle of Ming poet-painters who flourished in the late fifteenth and early

sixteenth centuries—Shen Chou 沈周 (1427-1509), his pupil Wen Cheng-ming 文徵明 (1470-1559), and Wen's friend, T'ang Yin 唐寅 (1470-1523). All three men are best known as painters, but all were fine poets as well, in particular Shen Chou. In fact, one Chinese writer complained that "although Shen has written some outstanding poems, they have been obscured by his fame as a painter."[4] Because no authentic paintings by Wang Wei survive, and few if any by Su Tung-p'o, the works of these Ming artists, who form the core of the so-called "Wu" school 吳派, provide more accessible sources for the study of our subject.

Su Tung-p'o was the central figure in the first circle of true *wen-jen* 文人, or literati poet-painters. Other members of the circle were the poet and calligrapher, Huang T'ing-chien 黃庭堅 (1045-1105), the painter Li Kung-lin 李公麟 (c. 1040-1106), and the painter, calligrapher and critic, Mi Fu 米芾 (1051-1107). Something of the spirit which prevailed among these men is suggested by a poem written by Huang T'ing-chien about a picture entitled *Herdboy with Bamboo and Rock*, jointly painted by Su Tung-p'o and Li Kung-lin. The poem is preceded by a brief prose preface:[5]

Su Tung-p'o painted a clump of bamboo and a fantastic rock. Li Kung-lin added a slope in the foreground and a herdboy riding a water-buffalo. The picture, full of life, has inspired these playful verses:

題竹石牧牛 并引

子瞻畫叢竹怪石。伯時增前坡牧兒騎牛，甚有意態。戲詠。

Here's a little craggy rock in a wild place, shadowed by green bamboo.
A herdboy, wielding a three-foot stick, drives his lumbering old water-buffalo.
I love the rock! Don't let the buffalo rub his horns on it!
Well, all right, let him rub his horns—but if he gets too rough he'll break the bamboo!

[4]Quoted in *Ming shih tsung* 明詩綜, 26/1a.

[5]P'an Po-ying 潘伯鷹, *Huang T'ing-chien shih hsüan* 黃庭堅詩選 (Hong Kong, 1958), p. 31.

野次小崢嶸，
幽篁相倚綠；
阿童三尺箠，
御此老觳觫。
石吾甚爱之，
勿遣牛礪角！
牛礪角尚可，
牛鬥殘我竹！

Here we have another aspect of the poetry-painting relationship in China—a poem inspired by a painting. Such poems often went beyond mere description of the painting in question, and became vehicles for the expression of the poet's own feelings. Another example would be Su Tung-p'o's own superb poem about a painting by his contemporary, the landscapist Wang Shen 王詵:[6]

Inscribed on the Painting "Misty River and Tiered Mountains" in the Collection of Wang Ting-kuo

Saddening my heart, a thousand tiers of
    mountains along the river
Shimmer with blue-green colors across the
    sky like clouds or mist.
Are they mountains? Are they clouds?
    It's hard to tell,
But when mist opens and clouds disperse,
    the mountains remain.
Here I see two verdant cliffs, shadowing
    a deep valley,
And a hundred cascades that fly down
    the cliffs,
Twist through forests, coil around rocks,
    hide and reappear,
Then rush down to the valley mouth to
    form a stream.
The stream grows calm, the mountains
    open, and the foothill forests end;
A tiny bridge and rustic shops lean against
    the mountain.
Travelers pass beyond the tall trees;
A fishing boat floats, light as a leaf;
The river swallows the sky.
Where did the Governor find this painting,
Its limpid beauties brushed by such a
    sensitive hand?

[6]Ch'en Erh-tung 陳邇東, *Su Tung-p'o shih hsüan* 蘇東坡詩選 (Hong Kong, 1965), pp. 212-213.

Where in our world is there such a place?
I'd go there now, and buy myself an acre
    or two of land!
But I remember an isolated spot at Fan-
    k'ou, near Wu-ch'ang,
Where the Gentleman of the Eastern
    Slope resided for five years.
Spring breezes rippled the river; the sky
    was vast.
Summer rain clouds curled up at dusk;
    the mountain glowed.
Crows shook branches of red maple leaves
    before my river home;
Winter snows, dropping from towering
    pines, woke me from my drunken
    sleep.
The flowing waters of Peach Blossom
    Spring are in this world;
Why insist that the Wu-ling story was
    only a fairy tale?

But the rivers and mountains are fresh
    and pure, while I am covered with
    dust;
There may be a path that leads to them,
    but it's hard to find.
With many a sigh, I return the scroll,
And wait for a friend who lives in these
    mountains to send me a poem, "Come
    Back!"

書王定國所藏
烟江疊嶂圖

江上愁心千疊山，
浮空積翠如雲煙，
山耶雲耶遠莫知，
煙空雲散山依然，
但見兩崖蒼蒼暗絕谷，
中有百道飛來泉，
縈林絡石隱復見，
下赴谷口爲奔川。
川平山開林麓斷，
小橋野店依山前，
行人稍度喬木外，
漁舟一葉江吞天，
使君何從得此本？
點綴毫末分清妍。
不知人間何處有此境？
徑欲往買二頃田。
君不見武昌樊口幽絕處，

東坡先生留五年。
春風搖江天漠漠，
暮雲卷雨山娟娟，
丹楓翻鴉伴水宿，
長松落雪驚晝眠。
桃花流水在人世，
武陵豈必皆神僊？
江山清空我塵土，
雖有去路尋無緣。
還君此畫三嘆息，
山中古人應有招我歸來篇。

The opposite phenomenon also occurred—that is, painting might be inspired by poems. To take another example from the Su Tung-p'o circle, the second of Su's famous pair of prose-poems on the Red Cliff inspired a superb handscroll by the little-known painter, Ch'iao Chung-ch'ang 喬仲常 (active first half twelfth century), a follower and possible relative of Li Kung-lin. In this work, now in the John M. Crawford, Jr. collection,[7] Ch'iao has been faithful to the text in such details as the shadows of Su and his friends which appear at the beginning of the scroll, possibly the only known depictions of human shadows in Chinese painting, but has added details which do not appear in the poem, such as the horse and the sleeping groom in the stable. The text of the poem is divided into sections which are inscribed at various stages along the scroll, possibly by someone other than the painter himself. Thus painting, poetry and calligraphy are brought together in a single work of art.

[7] *Chinese Calligraphy and Painting In the Collection of John M. Crawford, Jr.* (New York, 1962), pp. 72-75 and plates 15, 16.

Plate 58   ON THE RED CLIFF. Handscroll by Ch'iao Chung-ch'ang, illustrating Su Tung-p'o's second prose-poem by this name. John M. Crawford, Jr.'s collection. Beginning section.

Plate 59   ON THE RED CLIFF, by Ch'iao Chung-ch'ang. Section.

Plate 60   ON THE RED CLIFF, by Ch'iao Chung-ch'ang. Section.

THE PRACTICE OF inscribing poems on paintings, or on special sections of paper or silk attached to the paintings for this purpose, was another aspect of the poetry-painting relationship. The poem might be a work by a poet of the past, or by the artist himself, and the calligraphy might be written by the artist, a friend of his, or a later owner or connoisseur. When painter, poet and calligrapher were the same person, the result was that unique product of Chinese literati culture, the work of art in which three forms of expression perfectly complement each other and create a whole which is more than the sum of its parts.

A perfect example of this is a small handscroll by Wu Chen 吳鎮 (1280-1354), one of the Four Masters of Yuan painting, in the John M. Crawford, Jr. collection.[8] Wu has inscribed a poem of his own composition in the upper right-hand corner or the picture. The poem may be translated,

> West of the village, evening rays linger on
>   red leaves
> As the moon rises over yellow reeds on
>   the sandbank.
> The fisherman moves his paddle, thinking
>   of home—
> His pole, lying in its rack, will catch no
>   more fish today.

漁父圖

紅葉村西夕照餘，
黃蘆灘畔月痕初；
輕撥棹，且歸與，
掛起漁竿不釣魚。

The poem adds two images which are entirely absent from the painting—those of the village and the moon ("moon shadows" in the original text), —and colors the leaves and reeds red and yellow, although in the picture they are done in shades of gray ink. We learn that it is sunset, and that the fisherman is thinking of returning home. Because these imagistic and psychological enhancements of the picture are expressed in words, they affect the viewer on a subtler level than the purely visual, and deepen his experience of the total work of art.

Another work of this kind is the hanging scroll, *Drunken Fisherman by a Reed Bank*, also in the Crawford collection,[9] by T'ang Yin, one of the Wu school painters referred to earlier. The poem in the upper right-hand corner of the picture is again by the artist himself, and reads,

> Punting pole stuck in the reeds, he ties up
>   his boat;
> Late at night, the moon climbs to the top
>   of the pole.
> The old fisherman is dead drunk—call
>   him, he won't wake up—
> In the morning he rises, frost-prints on
>   the shadow of his raincoat.

釣題魚翁畫

插篙葦渚繫舴艋，
夜深月上當竿頂；
老漁爛醉喚不醒，
滿船霜印簑衣影。

Here again, the poem contains images which are not seen in the painting—the frost and the shadow of the fisherman's raincoat—and refers to the psychological state of the fisherman; in this case, he is drunk! In addition, the slightly off-balance, spiky calligraphy echoes the swaying, sharp-leaved reeds below, and also, perhaps, hints at the fisherman's inebriation. Obviously, the poem is not merely a description of the painting, nor the painting an illustration to the poem—the poem, the painting and the calligraphy are complementary elements of an aesthetically integrated creation.

STILL ANOTHER aspect of the relationship between poetry and painting in China is the fact that the two arts share the same images, and that these tend to be traditional, or conventional. An excellent example is the fisherman as an exemplar of Taoist freedom, an image which occurred in the poems and paintings of Wu Chen and T'ang Yin just discussed. In painting, the image can be traced back to a T'ang catalogue, the *Chen-kuan kung-ssu hua-shih* 貞觀公私畫史 by P'ei Hsiao-yuan 裴孝源 (preface dated 639), where a painting of a fisher-

[8]*Ibid.*, pp. 107-108 and plate 29.

[9]*Ibid.*, pp. 138-139 and plate 39.

man is attributed to a Six Dynasties painter.[10] The image then continues to occur throughout the history of Chinese painting. In poetry, the *locus classicus* is the poem on the fisherman in the *Ch'u Tz'u* 楚詞 anthology, the poem in question being dated by David Hawkes to the third century B.C.[11]

The standard images of both arts were, in fact, catalogued in two important encyclopedias, both published in the early eighteenth century. One, the famous *Mustard Seed Garden Manual of Painting* (*Chieh tzu yuan hua chuan* 芥子園畫傳, translated as *The Tao of Painting* by Mai-mai Sze, Bollingen, 1956), appeared in its final form in 1701. This work is a collection of all the traditional images of Chinese painting—mountains and rocks, painted in various styles, trees and flowers of many kinds, birds and insects, temples, villas, and scholars and fishermen in boats.

The other encyclopedia is the *P'ei-wen yün-fu* 佩文韻府, the *P'ei-wen Treasury of Rhymes,* published in 1711, but using material going back to the Yuan dynasty. This is a compendium of poetic images and phrases, each of which is quoted in chronologically arranged passages. Every image in the *Mustard Seed Garden Manual of Painting* can be found here as well. Under the heading "fisherman" (*yü-fu* 漁父), the passages quoted range from the *Ch'u tz'u* poem to a couplet by Su Tung-p'o:

I should meet the old fisherman here,
Winding his way through the reeds.

應逢古漁父，
葦間自延緣。

That poetry and painting shared the same traditional images suggests a similarity in the creative process of both arts. The point also gives rise to an important question: how does the artist express his individuality in an essentially conservative artistic milieu? An interesting passage from the writings of the late Sung thinker and poet, Ho Ching 郝經 (1223-1275) may help to throw some light on this problem. "The writers of past and present," he states, "have not necessarily sought to make the style (*fa* 法) of another person their own style. They have only comprehended the basic patterns (*li* 理). When one has fully comprehended the basic patterns of Heaven and Earth, then creativity will inhere in the Self (*wo* 我)."[12] The idea appears to be that mere imitation of others is not creativity—intense personal experience must precede any form of artistic creation. But the stuff of that experience will ultimately consist of the essential truths which the great artists of the past have also discovered. Thus the poet and the painter will reach a point where the expression of an individual perception and the expression of the Absolute are one and the same.

---

[10]In *Mei-shu ts'ung-k'an*, Vol. I (Taipei, 1963), p. 45. The painter's name is Shih I 史藝.

[11]David Hawkes, *Ch'u Tz'u: The Songs of the South* (Oxford, 1959), p. 88.

[12]Quoted in Kuo Shao-yü 郭紹虞, *Chung-kuo wen-hsüeh p'i-p'ing shih* 中國文學批評史 (Hong Kong, *Hung-chih shu-tien* 宏智書店), p. 271.

From the Chinese of Wang Wei

Translated by Albert Faurot

A FARM BY THE WEI RIVER

Slanting sun across the land,
    Cows and sheep in crooked lanes;
Aged farmers, propped on canes,
    Watching for their shepherd lads—
Pheasants whirr in the heavy wheat;
    In sparse mulberry, the silk worms sleep.
Homeward trudging with their hoes
    Workmen murmur when they meet.
This life I long for makes me hum
    That ancient folk-song, "Going Home".

渭川田家

斜光照墟落。
窮巷牛羊歸。
野老念牧童。
倚杖候荊扉。
雉雊麥苗秀。
蠶眠桑葉稀。
田夫荷鋤至。
相見語依依。
即此羨閑逸。
悵然吟式微。

The six poems by Wang Wei 王維 *printed here are selected from a portion of his works written in* wu-yen *form, i.e., lines each containing five characters. Ranging in length from four lines to above, they represent the poet's mastery in coining the most sensitive and inspired utterances within the confines of the short line, his best medium. With each poem, he depicts a scene of nature which he responds to, in that quiet, musing voice unmistakably his own.*

Born into the T'ang empire at the height of its power, Wang Wei (701-761) enjoyed a career of high officialdom, only shortly eclipsed during the period of recovery from An Lu-shan 安祿山's *rebellion. But, rather than write about the sweeping changes in the face of society, like his younger contemporaries Li Po and Tu Fu, he devoted himself to hermetic thoughts far removed from human want and woe. In artistic achievement, he was painter, poet, musician all in one, his cult being that of the Buddhist who sought pleasure in solitude and meditation. Unrivalled in landscape description, he has passed down to us a body of poetry that reveals his sharp observation and rich artistry. He is also recognized as one of the earliest masters of monochrome landscape painting, though only copies of his work exist today to justify it. Among the many judgements passed on him, the most famous came from Su Tung-p'o* 蘇東坡 *, himself a connoisseur of poetry and painting: "There is poetry in his painting and painting in his poetry."*

MOUNT CHUNG-NAN

Towering to celestial heights,
    Linking mountain range and sea,
Your white clouds behind me gather;
    Mists I enter seem to flee.
By your ridge the wilds are parted,
    Sun and shadow split in vales.
Needing shelter for the evening,
    Woodsmen o'er the stream I hail.

終南山

太乙近天都。
連山到海隅。
白雲迴望合。
青靄入看無。
分野中峯變。
陰晴衆壑殊。
欲投人處宿。
隔水問樵夫。

HUA-TZU HILL

Ceaselessly the birds fly by
    The range again is autumn-dyed.
Up-hill and down-hill, time on time—
    I grow ever sadder, with each climb.

華子崗

飛鳥去不窮。
連山復秋色。
上下華子岡。
惆悵情何極。

DEPARTURE

I dismount and pour refreshment.
    Friend, why go? And whither bent?
You say, I have not found contentment.
    Back to South Mountain I am bound.
So let me go, and do not press me.
    White clouds drift there, endlessly.

送別

下馬飲君酒。
問君何所之。
君言不得意。
歸臥南山陲。
但去莫復問。
白雲無盡時。

RETREAT IN MOUNT CHUNG-NAN

I followed, mid-way in life, the Way,
    And of late retired to Mount Chung-nan.
In solitude I roam all day
    Midst beauty known to me alone.
I stroll to where the stream begins,
    Then sit and watch the cloud banks turn.
Sometimes I meet an old woodsman
    And chat, and laugh—and not return.

談笑無還期。
偶然值林叟，
坐看雲起時。
行到水窮處，
勝事空自知。
興來每獨往，
晚家南山陲。
中歲頗好道，
終南別業

HOME TO SUNG MOUNTAIN

By grassy banks, the river lingers
    Like my carriage rolling on:
Man and stream, with birds together
    Homing in the setting sun.
Past the ford and ruined fortress,
    Now the whole fall mountain glows!
Far away, beneath its summit
    Latch the gate, and find repose.

歸來且閉關。
迢遞嵩高下，
落日滿秋山。
荒城臨古渡，
暮禽相與還。
流水如有意，
車馬去閑閑。
清川帶長薄，
歸嵩山作

王維五言詩

The Printer Emulates the Painter
—the Unique Chinese Water-and-ink Woodblock Print

By **Diana Yu**

中國的木版水印

THE MEANING of the term *mu-pan shui-yin* 木版水印, literally "wood plate, water print", is now confined to that type of woodblock printing specially devoted to the reproduction of traditional Chinese paintings, i.e., paintings executed in traditional method using the water-and-ink medium.

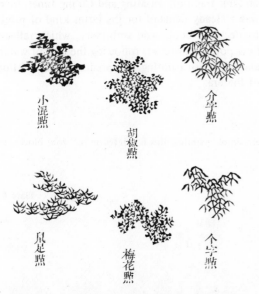

Plate 61 A PAGE FROM THE MUSTARD SEED GARDEN PAINTER'S ALBUM. Woodcut illustration of how different leaf-forms should appear when executed by brush. From an edition dated the 18th year of the Ch'ing Emperor K'ang-hsi.

By nature a handicraft, *mu-pan shui-yin* has nevertheless been called "an art of re-creation" for having reproduced extremely close likenesses of fine works of art. Its wonder and charm lie in its completely hand-made process of production, while its secret is in its altogether non-use of photography and oil, so essential to modern printing. In block-carving and printing, it is in fact an assemblage of indigenous techniques garnered from an age-old heritage.

Tracing its ancestry

The history of picture-printing in China can be traced back to the T'ang dynasty, when a lot of Buddhist scriptures printed in block-carving carried illustrations from the life of Buddha. The extant earliest example of this is the cover-picture of a version of the "Diamond" Sutra (金剛經 Vajrac-chedikā-prājnāpāramitā-sutra), discovered in Tun-huang 敦煌. The picture, depicting the Buddha giving a sermon in a garden, is dated the 9th year of Hsien-t'ung 咸通, corresponding to the year 868 in the late T'ang period. From then on, there has been no lack of carved illustrations in the Chinese book-making tradition, serving not only religious denominations in their widespread outreach for converts, but also architects, engineers, agricultur-alists, medical doctors, encyclopaedists and other compilers who commissioned book-carvers to publish the fruits of their studies.

A field in which book-carvers could exercise their skill as well as their imagination was literature, and excellent wood-carved editions of popular fiction and drama had been produced since Yuan and Ming, especially in the years *Wan-li* 萬曆 and

T'ien-ch'ih 天啟 (1573-1627, late Ming period). In this era, well-loved novels and dramas and the elegant illustrated editions in which they were printed reciprocated each other's influence, pushing both these genres of literature and woodblock prints into wider and wider popularity. Four places were specially noted for the production of woodblock prints—Peking (in Hopei), Chien-an (in Fukien), Chin-ling—today's Nanking (in Kiangsu) and Hsin-an (in Anhui). There emerged families of famous carvers, such as the Huang 黃 family in Hsin-an, and among the many wellknown artists who drew and illustrated for such books were Ch'en Lao-lien 陳老蓮, Ting Yün-peng 丁雲鵬 and Hsiao Yün-ts'ung 蕭雲從.

The popularity of wood-carved books continued into the Ch'ing dynasty, with its centre in Peking. In such representative works as the "Li-sao t'u" 離騷圖 and "Wan-hsiao-t'ang hua-chuan" 晚笑堂畫傳, the strong influence of the realistic style of Ming is apparent. Though some artists adopted western technique in creating their pictures, such as Chiao Ping-chen 焦秉貞, who painted the original pictures for the Kang-hsi 康熙 edition of the "Keng-chih t'u" 耕織圖, the majority of them held firm to the folk tradition. Beside the above-mentioned albums, there were mass-productions, printed in the millions, of copy-books for learners of painting, writing-paper printed with fine decorations, and festival pictures, the most widely sought after of which was the New Year picture. Before it lost its popularity to lithographic printing, introduced into China from the West after the years *Chia-ch'ing* 嘉慶 and *Tao-kuang* 道光 (1796-1850, mid Ch'ing dynasty), woodblock printing was the chief medium by which writing and art was known to the populace.

Line-cuts and Ink-tones

In developing the modern water-and-ink woodblock print, much inspiration was drawn from the experience of the past. We have seen the great variety of woodblock-printed material in China in the Ming and Ch'ing. Roughly speaking, they fall into two categories when analyzed from the point of view of visual effect. The first is the line-cut, which is produced by using a single block to print an area of ink, of uniform density, whose edges distinguish sharply from the paper. This method can be elaborated upon to form the second category, the multiple-block print which, by superimposing areas of different water-and-ink density on one another, produces a picture with gradations in ink-tone. While contour drawings are usually reproduced by the first method, there are many occasions which require the use of the second, to reproduce the subtle-ink-tones issued from the brushes of artists painting in the water-and-ink tradition. In Ming and Ch'ing times, there was a steady demand for the latter kind of prints to decorate books and stationery, which reflects how popular taste was following the lead of water-and-ink brush painting, the predominant tradition of the era.

A PLANT PAINTING TAKES SHAPE. A relatively simple painting, this is printed in just four blocks, in

Plate 63   Plate 64

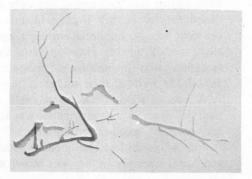

Plate 62
DESIGNING AND TRACING.
A print factory
in Peking.

These methods of woodblock printing are best demonstrated in old painter's albums, designed to define basic brushstrokes and painted forms for learners of water-and-ink painting. Of such albums, the *Ten Bamboos Studio Painter's Album* (*Shih-chu-chai hua-p'u* 十竹齋畫譜) and the *Mustard Seed Garden Painter's Album* (*Chieh-tzu-yuan hua-chuan* 芥子園畫傳) are still wellknown today. Carved in the year 1627 (late Ming dynasty) by Hu Cheng-yen 胡正言, a native of Anhui residing in Nanking, the *Ten Bamboos Studio Painter's Album* is divided into sections explaining how brushstrokes depicting bamboos, plum-blossoms, rocks, orchids, fruits, plumes and feathers etc. should be executed. It is the first book to have illustrations printed in five colours, using a method called *tou-pan*, 餖版, i.e., separate colour blocks, which very successfully brought out the variations in colour and ink-tone. In the *Mustard Seed Garden Painter's Album*, carved in 1679 (early Ch'ing dynasty) by Wang Kai 王概 and his brothers, exegeses on the the art of painting were printed to line-cut effect, while the

different shades of black and red—

Plate 65

Plate 66

Plate 67 CARVING.

profuse illustrations of how brushstrokes and painted forms should appear when executed by brush in water-and-ink were printed either in line-cut, or multiple-blocks in water-and-ink, or blocks of different colours.

Today, water-and-ink woodblock prints are produced by Peking's Jung-pao Chai 榮寶齋, The Calligraphy and Printing Company of Shanghai 上海書畫店 (formerly known as Tuo-yun Hsuan Studio 朵雲軒) and the Woodblock Printing Studio of Hangchow 杭州版畫店. Jung-pao Chai Studio, now China's leading printing-house for water-and-ink woodblock reproductions, was opened roughly some 77 years ago (1899), in the reign of the late Ch'ing Emperor Kuang-hsu 光緒. Situated in the Liu-li Ch'ang 琉璃廠, Peking's old market for *objets d'art*, it started off as a small paper shop and became wellknown for the multi-colour letter-paper produced by its small printing-house. In the troubled years of late Ch'ing and after, Jung-pao Chai Studio had preserved the knowledge of *tou-pan* printing until now, under the People's Re-public, its production was re-organized and much more ambitious programmes were introduced to make high-quality art reproductions more easily available to the public.

In the Print Factory

Water-and-ink woodblock reproductions of

Chinese paintings are loved for the same qualities possessed by their originals—the non-oily black ink (pine-smoke ink, *sung-yen mo* 松煙墨, as it is called), which when mixed with water can produce seemingly endless ink-tone variations; paper manu-factured in Hsuan 宣 county, Anhui, uniformly used by painters for its fine quality and particular receptivity to water-and-ink; and the versatile array of brushstrokes, forming the painting, backed by so much tradition and learning. Whenever possible, a reproduction is executed in exactly the same kind of ink and paper in which its original was made. It is in reproducing the look of the brushstrokes that the ingenious imitative skill of the carver and printer takes over the creativity of the painter's brush. Within this process, the craftsmen's expertise is put to challenge through an elaborate system of division of labour.

Designing and Tracing

An original painting must first be traced out, to enable blocks to be made from it. In fact, block-designing and tracing is the most im-portant step of all in the process of production, as those who undertake it must possess not only fine draughtsmanship but also a thorough understanding of the painting as a work of art. Sometimes, when the original is a mural or some other kind of painting that cannot be easily transported into the studio, detailed copies of it have to be made, before analysis can proceed. With a connoisseur's knowledge of art, the block-designer then analyses the painting's content and composition, and decides how it is to be separated into blocks which can best follow the artist's use of brushstrokes, colour-combination and varying degrees of ink-and-water density. His analysis must be fine and exact, at the same time practical for block-carving and printing.

Very often, a fine analysis of a complicated painting results in its separation into several tens of ink-tone variations, each of which requires a block to be carved. Some masterpieces require even more blocks, hence more impressions. The shapes of the blocks can range from lines thinner than human hair, if it is a *kung-pi* 工筆 painting, to large amorphous areas which correspond to the washes of the *i-pi* 意筆 painter. Jung-pao Chai has improved upon the old *tou-pan* method by increasing the number of blocks, thus enhancing the fineness of the reproductions. For instance, fine copies of the T'ang painter Chou Fang 周昉's "Ladies with Flowery Headdresses" scroll (*Tsan-hua shih-nü t'u* 簪花仕女圖) were completed by the collaborated efforts of Chang Yen-chou etc. 張延

洲等 (carve) and T'ien Yung-ch'ing 田永慶 (print), using 48 blocks. There have been cases where the number of blocks designed for one reproduction reached over a hundred.

Having settled on the separation of the blocks, the designer covers the surface of the painting with pieces of transparent plastic film, on each of which he traces out the outlines of one block. The films are in turn placed under pieces of extremely thin "wild goose skin paper" (*yen-p'i chih* 雁皮紙), on which the outlines are traced out a second time, with constant reference to the original painting. Then the carver's proofs are ready.

Carving

Usually, carvers use rosewood (*hua-li mu* 花梨木) to carve their blocks, and, for blocks representing particularly fine and complicated brushwork, they use boxwood (*huang-yang mu* 黃楊木). To prepare for carving, the reverse side of the paper carrying the block-outlines is smoothened over the wood plane. Some parts of the paper are carefully scraped off to make the outlines stand out more clearly, and to lessen the resisting force which the paper might exert against the carving-blade. When the carver applies his blade to the wood, in order to

Plate 68 COLORING.

Plate 69   PRINTING.

achieve the effect of "using his blade like a painter's brush", he must do more than just follow the lines drawn on the paper—he must carve with thorough understanding of the spirit of the original painting. He must bear in mind how the painter actually executed the painting —how the round, full look of a stroke was achieved by running the tip of the brush vertically on the paper, i.e., by using the *chung-feng* 中鋒 of the brush; how a vigorous, broken appearance of brushwork was achieved through "dry" brushstrokes (*k'u-pi* 枯筆); how the rapidity of brush movement created jerks and inuendos in the brushwork; and how clarity, beauty and liveliness of style was conveyed thereby . . . all this the carver aims to re-create, without exposing any traits of the touch of his carving-knife.

Printing

When an entire series of blocks has been carved, there must be very careful consideration as to the order of printing the blocks, which is decisive to the final look of the reproduction. In the working process of Jung-pao Chai Studio, the first blocks to be put to print are those carrying the lines which in the original painting are the black ink outlines defining the shapes of the painted forms. Then follow other blocks representing areas of different ink-tones. Where colour blocks are concerned, the general practice is for lighter colours to be printed first, but the order is sometimes changed to fit the actual situation.

The process of printing is as follows: The block is first run over with a wet brush, then dabbed with a painting-brush soaked to the same ink or colour concentration as the original painting. Then the printer lays the paper over the block, and rubs the reverse side of the paper strongly against the wood plane with a *pa-tzu* 耙子, a tool made of coir. One impression is thus completed.

As the paper is applied to more and more blocks, it gradually takes on the look of the original painting. The increasing likeness to the original is achieved in many ways. When printing parts of the brushwork where ink melts into water—typical of Chinese painting—the printer usually soaks his painting-brush to the right water-and-ink density and does an imitation painting on the block, then prints it. By this method, known as *t'an* 擤, he achieves a much closer proximity to the original. If the original brushwork has a heavily-inked and wet look, the block is run over with an additional layer of water, to ensure the effect of ink-play. If the original brushwork consists of dry brushstrokes,

Plate 70 LADIES WITH FLOWERY HEAD-DRESSES, woodblock print after the painting by Chou Fang. Section. Collaborators: Chang Yen-chou etc. (carve), T'ien Yung-ch'ing (print). 48 blocks.

tissue paper is applied to the block to soak away some of the water-and-ink painted on it. Thus, when the image is printed, it retains the dry, forceful appearance of the lines. The completion of the final impression yields a reproduction that bears very close resemblance to its original, almost indistinguishable from the original when mounted in the same way. It is an achievement in which the printer's skill successfully re-creates the technical mastery and imagination of the artist.

Where Its Value Lies

In China's local market as well as abroad, a water-and-ink woodblock reproduction is still priced many more times higher than its machine-printed counterpart. This is because by comparison its carving requires much more labour, and the easy wear of the woodblocks during the process of printing puts a limit on the quantity of output. But it is also treasured more as a piece of handicraft produced by extremely skilled labour. While all kinds of methods of plate-making by photographic process, whether they be metal plates, synthetic plates, collotype or lithography, reproduce various degrees of light and shade by varying degrees of image density, the water-ank-ink woodblock print, by directly applying water and ink onto paper through the use of carved blocks, captures the genuine shape, size and, most important of all, the tactile quality of an original Chinese painting.

Looking at the history of art in China, the development of the *mu-pan shui-yin* technique can be interpreted as a two-fold advancement. It represents a new level reached in the art of printing, by collective efforts. *Mu-pan shui-yin* craftsmen are so masterly in their methods of execution that even creative artists working on water-print woodcuts (*shui-yin mu-k'e* 水印木刻) have to learn from Jung-pao Chai. It also represents a liberation of the means of art appreciation from the monopoly of the élite. As increased production of these high-quality reproductions widen the circle of art-lovers who are able to enjoy them, art concepts conveyed in them also reach a wider public. In this respect, *mu-pan shui-yin* is also a useful tool for strengthening art education and education through art, a means by which more enlightenment can be brought to people on the meaning of art themes old and new.

Peasant Paintings from Hu-hsien

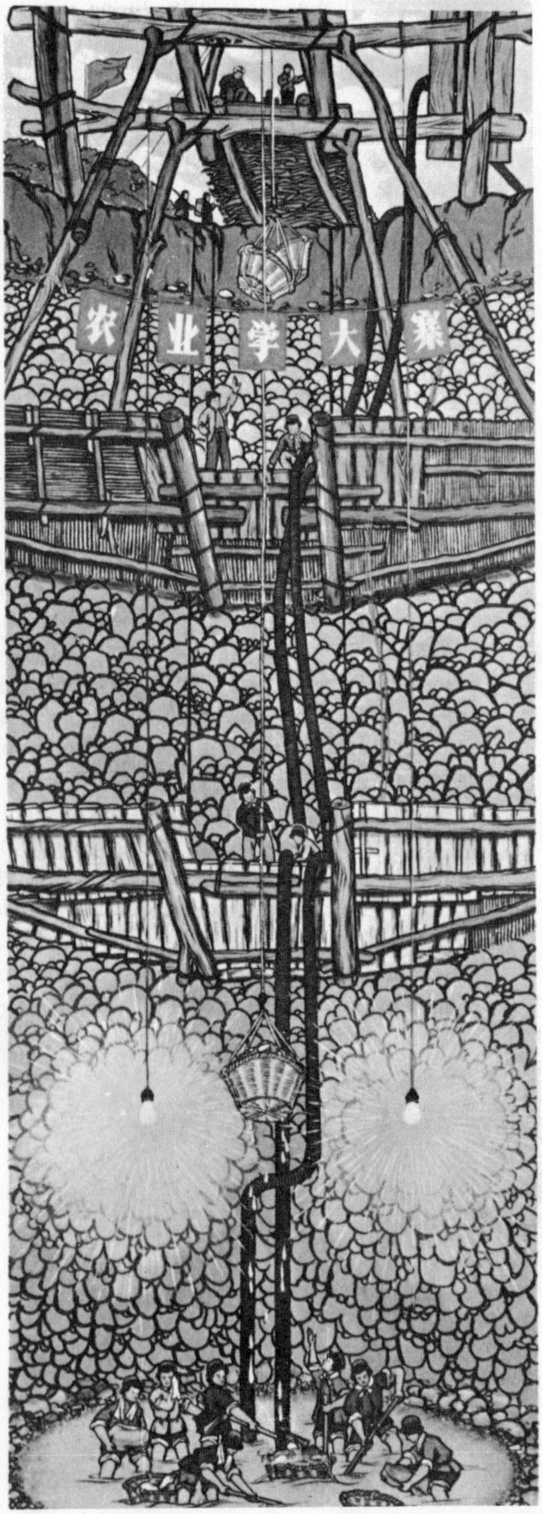

Plate 71 DIGGING A WELL ON THE PLATEAU, by Li Keh-min.

THE PEASANTS of Hu-hsien 戶縣, a model commune in Shensi near the ancient city of Sian 西安, have recently attracted much attention through their spare-time artistic efforts performed in the past two decades. At home, professional painters from Peking are travelling to Hu-hsien to learn from them, and abroad they have been exhibited in Paris and consequently aroused considerable discussion by historians of Chinese art as well as observers of modern China. Reactions from the outside world range from patronising praise to mildly denigration reflecting perhaps some uncertainty in the judgement of the critics.

Scepticism has been expressed on the spontaneity of the Hu-hsien paintings and the amateur states of the painters. There has been much speculation on how these paintings have been derived in the first place.

Uncertainty and scepticism perhaps are the results of excessive attention on the political content of the paintings. To be sure, the message of these paintings is plain, but the purely artistic roots are perhaps not too difficult to discern. First, there are the bold use of basic colours, the crowded effect and the schematised designs, all characteristic of the wholly or partially wood-block printed new year pic-

Plate 72   COMMUNE FISH POND, by Tung Cheng-yi.

tures (*nien hua* 年畫), popular throughout the Ch'ing period.
Indeed the Hu-hsien paintings lend themselves very well to
reproduction by wood-block printing—and to adaptation in
paper-cut, another popular art form in China. Secondly, there
is the most striking use of traditional perspective emphasizing
a feeling of distance rather than an illusion of three dimen-
sional space. Then there is the actual mechanics of the
creative process in which the picture is composed by juxtapos-
ing standardised elements most of which are to be found in
handbooks of drawing which are as readily available in China
today as the *Shih-chu-chai* 十竹齋 and *Chieh-tzu-yuan* 芥子園
were in the late Ming and early Ch'ing periods. This last
observation is by no means a criticism of the creativeness of
the peasant painters of Hu-hsien. A summary comparison
between the Hu-hsien paintings and those by the members of
another model commune, Hsi-yang Hsien 昔陽縣 in Shansi
Province, will convince any observer of the artistic superiority
of Hu-hsien. The paintings of Hu-hsien are just as valid as art
form as the wood-block prints and the decorative arts of the

Plate 73   NEVER STOP BEING INDUSTRIOUS AND THRIFTY, by Chang Lin.

late Ming and early Ch'ing—
which was perhaps the greatest
period in the history of "folk
art" in China. In common with
the best wood-block artists of
the 17th century, such as Chen
Hung-shou and Hsiao Yün-ch'ung,
the peasant painters of Hu-hsien
combine boldness and originality
(in the form of the unexpected)
with extreme stylisation. In this
way, Hu-hsien paintings may be
regarded as a true renaissance of
the art of the Chinese people.

J.W.

Plate 74
COMMUNE PERSIMMON GROVE,
by Wen Chih-chiang.

Plate 75 *(top)*: Children outside a house with wall-paintings, a common sight in this commune. Hu-hsien, 1976.

Plate 76 *(below)*: GATHERING THE COMMUNE'S LOTUS-ROOTS, by Tu Chien-jung.

The Use of Colour in Chinese Folk Art

FOLK ARTISTS in China have the knack of making their art products extremely attractive. Be they portraits, sculptures, new-year pictures or lanterns, these goods are all donned in bright, sharp colours which make them equally eye-catching whether viewed closely or at a distance. The maxims for colour treatment in Chinese folk art are "sharp" (*chien* 尖) and "bright" (*yang* 陽), and they stand for a style that has its peculiar merits.

Artists who manufacture new-year woodblock prints like to give their prints strong, bold colours to make them impressive and easy to sell. In their jargon, to make a colour "sharp" means to "bring it out"—"what is red should be made redder, and what is green greener." *Yang* is derived from *t'ai-yang* 太陽, the sun. Colours must be as bright as the sun, i.e. they should have a glaring and fiery quality that can catch anyone's eye from far or near. The colouring in new-year pictures is bold and daring, though there are plain ink pictures too.

Lanterns decorate all seasons of the Chinese calendar, and paintings on them can be very sophisticated. Very fine colouring is required of lantern-painting. Artists only use the lightest parts of colour solutions, while dense colours are usually avoided. There is a strong lean on vegetation-extracted pigments. Thus the colouring on lanterns is sharper and brighter than in traditional Chinese paintings, which may use bright colours but always

to a soft, calm and never glaring effect. Lanterns must look exciting enough to attract people even at a distance, hence the necessity to give them eye-dazzling glamour, no matter how superficial that may be.

The control of colouring is important because a lantern has different appearances by day and by night. In daylight, the viewer looking from one angle sees only one face of the lantern. At night, however, when the lantern is lit up from behind by a candle or electric bulb, the viewer also sees its back face. The silk lantern shade, which carries the painting, is alum-coated. Since illumination comes from behind it, and the viewer is looking from the front, a painting executed in dense colour will not look good, because it will appear as a vision of dark shadows rather than a variation of colour tones. Even if the colour density is alternately dense and thin, the viewer will only see dark, unattractive patches. Therefore, lantern-painters only use the lightest and purest parts of colour solutions, which yield bright and lovely hues alike in daylight and under illumination at night. Colouring on lanterns must first be thin, to enable light to shine through the shade. It must also be even, without any trace of brushwork or water-mark. The painting must have a smooth, even look without and within, and no viewer must detect any shadow on it.

Translated by D. Y.
From *A Study of Colour in Chinese Painting*
中國畫顏色的研究 by Yu Fei-an 于非闇

Plate 77 *Traditional Chinese new-year picture.*

Biographical Notes on Three Seventeenth Century Chinese Painters

By Ellen Johnston Laing

Today, most knowledge about secondary Chinese painters is derived from skimpy entries in a few standard biographical compendia; dwelling tersely on artistic style or subject matter, such notices are dryly laconic, often silent, on aspects of purely biographical import. It is small wonder, then, that when placed beside the richly documented careers of major masters, the lives of minor artists pale into thin abstractions seemingly devoid of human personality.

Rectifying this situation demands tremendous effort, for information, fragmentary and tenuous though it may be, about such minor painters' lives and activities, is recovered only by slogging through vast, uncharted seas of written material. The purpose of this paper is to present, after summarizing already readily available facts on each, some newly-discovered data concerning three seventeenth-century artists: Ch'en Kuan, Li Chao-heng and Tseng I.

Ch'en Kuan 陳裸

The following composite biography of Ch'en Kuan is drawn from the standard cyclopedias (omitting the strictly critical comments on his painting style). A native of Suchou, he was originally named Ch'en Tsan 陳瓚, *tzu*, Shu-kuan 叔裸; he later took Kuan as his personal name and adopted Ch'eng-chiang 誠將 as his *tzu* and Po-shih 白室 as his *hao*. His landscapes, which visitors to Suchou strove to acquire, were after those of Sung and Yuan masters; Chao Po-chü 趙伯駒 and Chao Meng-fu 趙孟頫 are specified as is Wen Cheng-ming 文徵明 of the Ming dynasty. As a calligrapher, Ch'en was noted for his running and standard scripts. Fond of reading the *Li Sao* ("On Encountering Sorrow") and the *Wen Hsüan* (Anthology of Literature), he was himself a poet. He finally retired to Tiger Hill, passing the time composing and chanting poems; a collection of his writings was entitled *Yü-chieh chi* 嫗解集.[1] This basically is all that can be learned about Ch'en from the usual sources. His *Yü-chieh chi* is apparently now lost, although couplets on his paintings preserve examples of his poetic achievement.[2]

[1] Chiang Shao-shu, *Wu-sheng shih-shih* 姜紹書, 無聲詩史, *Hua-shih ts'ung-shu* 畫史叢書 ed., 4.69; Hsü Ch'in, *Ming hua lu* 徐沁, 明畫錄, HSTS ed., 4.48; *Suchou fu-chih* 蘇州府志 (reprint ed., Taipei, 1970), 87:82b; Lu Chün, *Sung Yuan i-lai hua-jen hsing-shih lu* 魯駿, 宋元以來畫人姓氏錄 (n.p.), 7:23b-24a; Sun Ta-kung, *Chung-kuo hua-chia jen-ming ta-tz'u-tien* 孫鑅公, 中國畫家人名大辭典 (reprint ed., Taipei, 1962), p. 435.

[2] See P'an Cheng-wei, *T'ing-fan-lou shu-hua chi* 潘正煒, 聽颿樓書畫記, *Mei-shu ts'ung-shu* 美術叢書 ed., IV/7, ch. 3, p. 269; *Ku-kung chou-k'an* 故宮週刊, 151. Two poems have been translated, one in *The Restless Landscape: Chinese Painting of the Late Ming Period*, James Cahill, ed. (Berkeley, 1971), p. 162 and one in Chu-tsing Li, *A Thousand Peaks and Myriad Ravines: Chinese Paintings in the Charles A. Drenowatz Collection*, Artibus Asiae Supplementum XXX (Ascona, 1974), vol. I, p. 83.

A few of Ch'en's scrolls have been discussed by Osvald Sirén,[3] Marsha Smith,[4] and more recently by Chu-tsing Li. Sirén and Smith both give approximate dates for Ch'en's activity as between 1610 and 1640. Li, puzzling over a work dated only by the cyclical sign *hsin-wei*, which can be either 1571 or 1631, argues for the former, and thus extends Ch'en's period of activity from 1570 to 1640; he further proposes that Ch'en may have attained ninety or one hundred years of age.[5]

New information from Ch'en's own inscriptions on his paintings and from the writings of his contemporaries help illumine this painter's personal and artistic life.

Ch'en's inscriptions disclose that he, like many another artists, generously presented works to his comrades (most, unfortunately, as yet unidentified) and that he participated in making cooperative paintings with such partners as Ch'eng Chia-sui 程嘉燧 (1565-1634), Wen Ts'ung-chien 文從簡 (1574-1648), Sheng Mao-yeh 盛茂曄 (fl. c. 1625-1640), and Pien Wen-yü 卞文瑜 (fl. c. 1620-1670).[6] In Ch'en's circle of friends was the well-known literatus, artist and critic, Li Jih-hua 李日華 (1565-1635) to whom, in 1609, Ch'en sent a scroll by the Yuan master, Huang Kung-wang 黃公望.[7]

Still another acquaintance, Ch'en Chen-hui 陳貞慧 (1604-1656), wrote this sketch of Ch'en Kuan:

> "Po-shih when young roamed the famous mountains and great rivers. Wherever he went [people] sought him as a guest and to acquire his paintings [as if they were rarities] like the pearls [of the Marquis] of Sui or the brocades [described in the] *Yeh* [*-chung-chi* 鄴中記]. Often his purse was filled with thousands of gold-pieces which he spent recklessly. [In this] he was rather like [the T'ang poets] Chang Hu 張祜 with his meditation and wisdom and Li Po 李白 with his wine drinking. [Ch'en] saw the myriad forms of clouds and mists, strange mirage-like buildings, the jade-plaque peaks of the Yen [-tang Mountain 雁蕩山], of several myriad *li* [and presumably included these wonders in his paintings]. He traveled until old and his wrist [i.e. brushwork] became increasingly marvellous. Late in life he retired to Tiger Hill. His wealthy, influential in-laws lent him a place to live. [When] someone asked about this, he responded, 'I pay rent for it!' and never mentioned the names [of his in-laws]. From this, one knows he really was a man of principle [*tao*]. His landscapes were moist and wet, not inferior to the ancient masters'. He once did two paintings, 'Snow Scene' and 'Spring in Kiangnan' as well as a poem and sent them [to me] to see. Opening [them] by a clear window I always exclaim over these 'ink treasures.' Earlier I did not realize he wrote poetry, but

---

[3]*Chinese Painting: Leading Masters and Principles* (New York, 1956-58), vol. V, p. 28. Sirén mis-writes Ch'en's name as Ch'en Lo 陳祼.

[4]"The Wu School in Late Ming, I: Conservative Masters," in *Restless Landscape* p. 45.

[5]*Thousand Peaks and Myriad Ravines*, vol. I, pp. 77-79, 83-84.

[6]Yao Chi-heng, *Hao-ku-t'ang shu-hua chi* 姚際恆, 好古堂書畫記, *hsia*, MSTS III/8, pp. 75-76; Hu Chi-t'ang, *Pi-hsiao-hsüan shu-hua lu* 胡積堂, 筆嘯軒書畫錄 (n.p.), *hsia*, 49a.

[7]Li Jih-hua, *Wei-shui-hsüan jih-chi, Hsiao-yüan ts'ung-shu* 味水軒日記, 嘯園叢書 ed., 1:6b.

there were many things he did not let people know."[8]

白室先生。壯遊名山大川。所至爭客之。得其筆墨。如隋珠鄭錦。橐中
致千金裝者屢矣。輒散去不顧。張祜之禪智。李白之酒樓。庶幾似之。
所見雲煙萬狀。蜃樓海市。雁峯玉板。幾萬里。遊益老。腕益奇。晚乃
歸隱於虎丘也。貴人姻家。假屋以居之。或詢之。曰僦寓耳。絕不及貴
人姓氏。以此知先生眞有道人也。先生山水渲染。不愧古大家。曾作雪
景江南春二圖並一詩見寄。晴窗展對。每呼墨寶。蓋不知先生能詩。然
先生不使人知者多矣。

What could easily be the most significant discovery concerning Ch'en Kuan's life is also the most problematic. On his landscape album leaf dedicated to a certain Erh-ju 二如 the artist states that the work was done in 1632 when he was seventy years old.[9] Since this important painting is apparently no longer extant, its authenticity and the validity of the inscription can be only provisionally accepted. Nevertheless, all things considered, a birthdate of 1563 for Ch'en Kuan is entirely plausible.

Li Chao-heng 李肇亨

The son of Li Jih-hua, Chao-heng became a monk in the Ch'ao-kuo Temple 超果寺 in Sung-chiang and took the name Ch'ang-ying 常瑩. His other sobriquets were: Hui-chia 會嘉, K'o-hsüeh 珂雪, and Tsui-ou 醉鷗. In addition to grapevines, he depicted landscapes after Sung and Yuan masters; his fame equaled that of Chao Tso 趙左 (fl. c. 1610-1630); he was also a poet and a calligrapher.[10] A handful of his paintings survive, but have never been a subject of study. He is said to have worked between the Ch'ung-chen (1628-1644) and K'ang hsi (1662-1722) periods;[11] Sirén suggests from around 1630 until around 1647.[12] A recent finding, given below, however, perhaps resolves some of the uncertainty about Li's dates.

Tseng Ch'ing 曾鯨 (t. Po-ch'en 波臣, 1568-1650), the foremost portraitist of the times, made a likeness of Li Chao-heng on which the sitter wrote a colophon. The concluding passage of Li Chao-heng's inscription goes:

> "In the T'ien-ch'i [era], *ting-mao* [year, 1627] when Tseng Po-ch'en painted this portrait, I was thirty-six years old. Ten years later in the early spring of the Ch'ung-chen [era], *ping-tzu* [year, 1636] I unrolled and looked at it. Then, sighing, inscribed [it]."[13]

天啟丁卯。曾波臣寫此像時。我年卅有六。又十年爲崇禎丙子初春。展
視慨歎而書。

Presumably it was for this portrait that Li's father, Jih-hua, presented a "thank you" poem to Tseng Ch'ing.[14]

Again, however, confronted with a situation where the original document ap-

[8]Ch'en Chen-hui, *Shan-yang lu, Shuo-k'u* 山陽錄, 說庫 ed., (reprint ed., Taipei, 1963), 6b (p. 1324). I wish to thank Professor Chang Chün-shu of The University of Michigan and Nora Ling-yün Shih Liu for their assistance in translating this text.

[9]Li Tso-hsien, *Shu-hua chien-ying* 李佐賢, 書畫鑑影 (1871, reprint ed., Taipei, 1970), 15:13b.

[10]Chiang Shao-shu, *Wu-sheng shih-shih*, 6:103; Hsü Ch'in, *Ming hua lu*, 5:69; Ch'in Tsu-yung, *T'ung-yin lun-hua* 秦祖永, 桐陰論畫 (reprint ed., Taipei, 1967), II, *shang*, 6a; Sun Ta-kung, CKHCJMTTT,

p. 200.

[11]Shang Ch'eng-tso and Huang Hua, comp., *Chung-kuo li-tai shu-hua chuan-k'e chia tzu-hao so-yin* 商承祚, 黃華, 中國歷代書畫篆刻家字號索引 (Peking, 1960), I, p. 870.

[12]Sirén, *Chinese Painting*, vol. VII, p. 158.

[13]Lu Hsin-yuan, *Jang-li-kuan kuo-yen lu* 陸心源, 穰梨館過眼錄, (Wu-hsing, 1891), 27:16b-17a.

[14]Li Jih-hua, *T'ien-chih-t'ang chi* 恬致堂集 (reprint ed., Taipei, 1971), 1:18ab.

parently is lost, it can only be proposed that a possible date for Li Chao-heng's birth was the year 1592.

Tseng I 曾鯨

Tseng I, t. Shou-po 受伯, who excelled in painting figures, birds and flowers, and portraits, is claimed to be Tseng Ch'ing's grandson. It is asserted that he was active during the K'ang-hsi (1662-1722) and Ch'ien-lung (1736-1795) eras.[15] I am informed by Howard Rogers that a painting by Tseng is in the Lin Po-shou collection in the National Palace Museum, Taipei.

Actually Tseng I must have made his livelihood as a portrait painter and the following anecdote related by Kuei Chuang 歸莊 (1613-1673) is included here because it not only conveys a sense of the constant productivity demanded of a successful professional artist, but also highlights certain relationships between patron and portraitist.

"Written on a Fan for Portraitist Tseng

[The T'ang poet Tu Fu's 杜甫] poem to General Ts'ao Pa 曹霸 [says]: 'Your excellency as a painter is divinely inspired. You used also to paint portraits, though only if you met an unusual person. Today drifting about in an age of violence, you often make likenesses of quite ordinary people.'[16] Mr. Tseng Shou-po from Min [Fukien] is skilled at portraiture; he has been in my district for more than a month and has already painted thirty or forty [portraits] for people. I asked his age: sixty-three; [he] does not know how many myriads of 'ordinary people's' portraits he has done over the decades. In the past I have altogether seven or eight times commissioned artisans to paint portraits, not one was successful; only Tseng's is a veritable likeness. In the difficult [task] of coming upon a good artist I have been definitely fortunate, so I asked [Tseng] how many people as handsome as this he has painted in his lifetime. A laugh! I know superficial, common-world people will consider my words foolish. Written in the tenth month of the *kuei-mao* [year, 1663]."[17]

書寫照曾君扇

杜少陵贈曹將軍詩。將軍善畫蓋有神。每逢佳士亦寫眞。只今飄泊干戈際。屢貌尋常行路人。閩中曾君受伯工寫眞。在吾邑月餘。已爲人寫三四十。問其年六十有三。不知數十年中。貌幾千萬尋常行路人矣。余嘗令畫工圖像凡七八。無一肖者。惟君乃酷肖。余固幸好手之難遇。更問君平生所畫如此佳士得幾人。一笑。吾知世俗皮相者。必以吾言爲妄也。癸卯十月。鏖鼕鉅山人歸莊書。

Assuming this document to be accurate, Tseng I was born in 1601; it is, then, impossible that he was still active during the Ch'ien-lung period. It is also difficult to believe that Tseng I was Tseng Ch'ing's grandson since Ch'ing would have become a grandfather at the unlikely age of thirty-three.

[15]Shang and Huang, *op. cit.*, I, p. 631; Sun Ta-kung CKHCJMTTT, p. 515.

[16]The translation of this quotation from Tu Fu is that of David Hawkes (*A Little Primer of Tu Fu* [Oxford, 1967], p. 144).

[17]Kuei Chuang, *Kuei Chuang chi* 歸莊集 (Shanghai, 1962), 4:295.

Problems Concerning the Life of Wang Mien, Painter of Plum Blossoms

By Chu-tsing Li

PREFACE

The following article grew out of a biography of Wang Mien first written for the Ming Biographical History Project, the result of which is being published by the Columbia University Press. It is an attempt to use the case of Wang Mien as a demonstration of the many problems surrounding the use of various records and documents concerning the life of an artist. As such, it is neither a translation of one particular biography nor a summary of a number of materials dealing with his life. Rather, it shows how one can attempt to use historical events and cultural traditions to interpret the life of a well-respected painter.

There is a considerable amount of material on the life of Wang Mien. Aside from some of the standard biographies mentioned in this article, there is also information from many other sources, such as local gazetteers, informal notes written by contemporaries and later writers, literary writings by friends and admirers, inscriptions by the artist himself on his own paintings or on other people's works, and colophons on his paintings by his friends and connoisseurs. In addition, there are more than twenty extant paintings attributed to him, and one volume of his poetry, *Chu-chai shih-chi* 竹齋詩集, in various editions, still available. These have been used by the author to write the biography of Wang Mien which will form part of a forthcoming book on biographies of Yuan painters.[1] The present article deals with one aspect of the methodology of using these materials.[2] No attempt is made here to discuss the problems concerning his paintings or his poetry, more thorough study of which will be made in the future.

—CHU-TSING LI

[1] Research on Wang Mien has been a part of my Yuan Art History Project, which has been supported by the University of Kansas General Research Fund.

[2] Materials for this article have all been drawn from traditional Chinese sources on Wang Mien, of which the most important ones are: Hsü Hsien 徐顯, *Pei-shih chi-chuan* 稗史集傳 (Collected biographies from unofficial history), *Li-tai hsiao-shih* 歷代小史 (A short history of the dynasties) ed., 9b-11a; Sung Lien 宋濂, *Sung Hsüeh-shih wen-chi* 宋學士文集 (Collected writings of Sung Lien), *Ssu-pu ts'ung-k'an* 四部叢刊 (Four Libraries Series) ed., 10/15a-16b; Hsü Mien 徐勉, *Pao Yueh lu* 保越錄 (Records on the defense of Yueh), *Ching-chia t'ang* ed., 16a-17b; Liu Chi 劉基, *Ch'eng-i-po wen-chi* 誠意伯文集 (Collected writings of Liu Chi), *Ssu-pu ts'ung-k'an* ed., 5/143-144; Ch'ien Ch'ien-i 錢謙益, *Lieh-ch'ao shih-chi hsiao-chuan* 歷朝詩集小傳 (Stories of poetry collections from various dynasties), Shanghai 1957, 16-17; Huang Tsung-hsi 黃宗羲, *Ming-i tai-fang lu* 明夷待訪錄 (Notes on Ming characters to be visited), Taipei 1956, 1; Chu I-tsun 朱彝尊, *Pao-shu-t'ing chi* 曝書亭集 (Collected writings from Pao-shu Pavilion), *Ssu-pu ts'ung-k'an* ed., 64/1a-2a; Wu Ching-tzu 吳敬梓, *Ju-lin wai-shih* 儒林外史 (Unofficial history of the literati), ch. 1; and Hung Jui 洪瑞, *Wang Mien* 王冕 (Story of Wang Mien), Shanghai 1962.

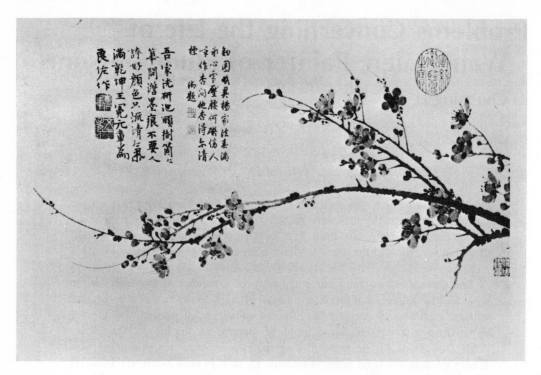

Plate 78   PLUM BLOSSOMS, by Wang Mien.

IN THE HISTORY of Chinese painting, Wang Mien 王冕 (1287-1359) is known as the greatest painter of ink plum blossoms, at least as far as extant works are concerned. Living in the middle of the fourteenth century, he stood at a pivotal juncture in the history of plum painting, which gave him the opportunity to summarize all the previous developments and to influence many of the later painters of the same subject. Perhaps because of his important position in painting, but perhaps more so because of the events of his life, his biographies have been shrouded in some colorful legends and fiction. While in recent years there have been some Chinese publications dealing with this problem, some of the issues remain. In this article, an attempt is made to render some of the basic facts of his life from Chinese sources and to explore the significance and meaning behind some of his biographies.

It is customary for the Chinese, because of their respect for their painters and poets, to idealize and romanticize them into legendary or semi-legendary figures. Sometimes this is done by dramatizing certain colorful facts of their lives; sometimes it is achieved by twisting some event into a supernatural act. Thus Ku K'ai-chih 顧愷之 is noted for the many eccentric stories of his life, especially how he managed to raise one million cash for a temple, and Wu Tao-tzu 吳道子 is said to have had such a superb power of depicting realistic horror in hell scenes that the butchers were frightened into leaving their profession. However, there are also some other interesting stories about painters which were fabricated for certain definite purposes. Stories concerning Cheng Ssu-hsiao 鄭思肖's expression of loyalty to Sung (he never sat with his face toward the north; he painted the orchid without the ground) are quite well known. In contrast, Chao Meng-fu 趙孟頫 is often depicted in various stories as betraying his own Sung imperial ancestry. One story, concerning how Chao was humiliated by his distant cousin, Chao Meng-chien 趙孟堅, has recently been proved totally wrong, for when Meng-chien died, Meng-fu was only a few years old, still under the Sung. In the case of Ni Tsan 倪瓚, again, recent research has found that many episodes of his life were given legendary treatment by later writers. Although his fastidious taste for cleanliness must have been based on some facts, his giving away of his fortune to his relatives and friends and living a wandering life in rivers and lakes has now been found to be the result of circumstances in late Yuan rather than of his own eccentricity. It is in this context that we can look upon some of the stories concerning Wang Mien's life.

TWO OF THE earliest biographies of Wang Mien are those by Hsü Hsien 徐顯 in his *Pei-shih chi-chuan* 稗史集傳 and by Sung Lien 宋濂 in his *Sung Hsueh-shih wen-chi* 宋學士文集, both written within a short period after Wang Mien's death. Of the two, Hsü's, which gave Wang's death date as 1359, was the earlier, while Sung's, which was written for the *Yuan-shih* 元史, must have been written around 1370. Both of these biographies were written from a strictly Confucian point of view, glorifying him as a great model of Confucian virtues. However, it is also interesting to see how they differ in their accounts of Wang's life.

Though there were some prominent officials in Wang Mien's family background, neither of these biographies mentioned it, but only indicated that he came from the family of a farmer. Hsü Hsien said only that "His father was a farmer, but Mien, though a farm boy, showed an interest in learning when young." Sung Lien, on the other hand, cited several vivid episodes of his early life to show the same idea. In one, when he was only seven or eight, he sat at the window of the village school to listen to the recitation of the classics by the pupils. He learned to memorize the classics, but completely forgot the water buffaloes he was supposed to be caring for, resulting in a beating from his father. In another, through the intercession of his mother, he was sent to a Buddhist temple to learn. During the nights, he often sat on the knees of the Buddhist statues to read by the lamp of the altar, often until day-break. Even though some of the statues showed ferocious and fearsome faces, he did not seem to care. No doubt, these stories were mentioned to dramatize his interest in learning, a Confucian virtue.

While Hsü only indicated Wang's thorough knowledge of the *Ch'un-ch'iu* 春秋 and other classics and his familiarity with ancient military texts in spite of his failure to place in the *chin-shih* examination, Sung especially told of how Han Hsing 韓性 (1266-1341), perhaps the greatest Confucian scholar in Chu-chi 諸暨 at that time, took an interest in Wang Mien. Later, after Han's death, all his pupils came to regard Wang as their teacher. Here, Sung Lien was trying to emphasize the importance of Wang's Confucian learning.

Both biographers wrote about Wang's eccentricity. Hsü Hsien said that he would wear a high-brimmed hat, a rain-coat made of green leaves and high wooden shoes, hold a wooden sword, and sing in the streets of K'uai-chi 會稽, or he would ride on a yellow ox reading the history of the Han dynasty. In Sung Lien's account, Wang once wore an ancient costume and walked behind his mother's ox-carriage as a filial son. Again, there is a stronger emphasis on his Confucian virtue.

Most colorful are the stories of how he treated some of the officials who came to pay him respect. As recorded by Hsü, Wang Yin 王艮 (1278-1348), a native of the same district, came to see him after being appointed censor for the Chiang-che Province. Finding Mien in poor clothes and broken, toeless shoes, the official became concerned and left him a pair of straw-shoes and tried to induce him to accept an appointment as a civil servant. But Wang refused. In the same account, two officials, Shen-t'u Chiung 申屠駉 and Sung Tzu-chang 宋子章, made a special effort to befriend him and insisted that he take the position of a school instructor. Reluctantly he accepted. But when other officials did not show the same respect for him, he resigned, having served a little over a year. Sung mentioned an episode involving an official, Li Hsiao-kuang 李孝光 (1297-1348), who wanted to recommend him to be a civil servant. Wang was furious, saying, "I have fields to farm and I have books to read. How can I let myself be a slave standing in front of the court day and night?"

The most interesting story, mentioned by both accounts, is the one involving the Chief Secretary of the Court in Peking, T'ai Pu-hua 泰不華 (1304-1352), who had achieved fame for his administration as prefect of Shao-hsing 紹興, Wang Mien's home prefecture, in the early 1340's. Hsü's biography mentions that, while staying in T'ai's home, he was offered many positions by Han-lin scholars. But in response, he wrote a poem on a painting of plum-blossoms with these lines:

> "The blossoms, all covered with ice to appear like jade,
> Cannot be blown down by the barbarian flutes."

> 花團冰玉，羌笛吹不下來。

Those who saw this were said to be very nervous and frightened. They turned away from him. However, in Sung's version, Wang Mien, after turning down T'ai Pu-hua's attempt to offer him a job, told his host:

> "How foolish you are! In less than ten years, all these people here will
> fight against each other like foxes and rabbits. What's this serving in the
> government good for?"

> 公誠愚人哉！不滿十年，此中狐兔游矣。何以祿仕爲。

Then he left immediately to return to the south.

Related to this is Wang Mien's prediction of the downfall of Yuan. Again the two versions are somewhat different. In Hsü's story, Wang, in his return to the south in 1348, passed through Suchou where he told the author of his biography:

> "The Yellow River will flow to the north, and the whole world will
> be in great turmoil. I am retiring to live in the south, in order to fulfill
> my own wishes. I hope that you will take care of yourself."

> 黃河將此流，天下且大亂。吾亦南棲以遂志。子其勉之。

But in Sung Lien's account, Wang Mien, after returning to Yueh 越 (the K'uai-chi area), predicted that the whole world would be in great turmoil. At that time, since the country was still peaceful, people thought he was mad. Wang replied, "If I am not crazy, who should be crazy?" Thus he retired to Mt. Chiu-li 九里山, near K'uai-chi, where he planted vegetables and flowers, especially plum trees. There he lived the life of a hermit.

In these several accounts, both authors attempted to portray him as a person of noble character and great learning, worthy of holding high appointments in the government, but declining to take them. Both emphasized his foresight in predicting the collapse of Yuan. All these aspects were the highly revered qualities of a Confucian gentleman which were embodied in Wang Mien.

THE MOST INTERESTING accounts are those concerning Wang's death. There are several different versions, all worth comparing. Hsü Hsien's story, probably written not long after his death, goes as follows:

> "In the year *chi-hai* (1359), when he was taking a nap, a group of rebels came into his home. He called out aloud, 'I am Wang Yuan-chang!' Greatly surprised, the rebels, respectful of his name, took him to the T'ien-chang Temple, where their Grand Marshal received him as the guest of honor, paid him respect, and asked for his advice. Mien said, 'Now as the whole country within the four seas is boiling up, you people do not seem to be able to bring peace and livelihood to the people, but are engaged in plundering and destroying. Thus there is nothing but destruction ahead! If you are righteous, who would not follow you? If you are not righteous, who would not become your enemies? Since the people of Yueh uphold righteousness, they should not be attacked. How could I let you fight against my father, my brothers, and my sons? If you choose to listen to me, you should reform and take the right path. If you do not want to listen to me, kill me now. I do not want to say anything more to you.' The Grand Marshal, paying him more respect, expressed his willingness to follow his instruction. The next day, Wang fell sick and could not get up again. In a few days he died. The soldiers prepared a coffin, dressed him, and buried him by the Orchid Pavilion in Shan-yin, with an inscription saying, 'Mr. Wang's Tomb.' "

> 歲己亥，君方晝臥，適外寇入。君大呼曰，「我王元章也。」寇大驚，重其名，與君至天章寺。其大帥置君上坐。再拜請事。君曰，「今四海鼎沸，爾不能進安生民，乃肆虜掠，滅亡無日矣。汝能為義，誰敢不服。汝為不義，誰則非敵。越人秉義，不可以犯。吾寧教汝與君父兄子弟相殺乎。汝能聽吾，即改過以從善。不能聽，即速殺我。我不與若更言也。」大帥復再拜，終願受教。明日，君疾遂不起。數日以卒。眾為之具棺，服斂之，葬山陰蘭亭之側，署曰王先生墓云。

There are several interesting points about this story. First, Hsü Hsien seems to have written this from very intimate knowledge, since his description is very specific, with dates and locations given. Thus, the whole account seems to be quite reliable.

Second, the rebel leader is mentioned here as Grand Marshal, without any name given. Third, most interesting of all, the whole point of view here is neither pro-Yuan nor pro-Ming, but one of the author's own, based totally on Confucian principles, which are reflected in his comments at the end of the biography.

In Sung Lien's biography, Wang's death is described in the following way:

> "Having captured Wu-chou 婺州 (the present-day Chin-hua 金華, in Chekiang), the Emperor was preparing to invade Yueh-chou. Looking for someone to advise him, he found Mien and appointed him a military advisor in the general staff. But one night, he died of illness."

> 皇帝取婺州，將攻越。物色得冕。寘幕府，授以諮議參軍。一夕以病死。

Here, the whole story is like a summary report, not a first hand account as the previous one. But the author identified the leader as the Emperor. Because of this, his point of view was definitely that of Ming. In fact, Sung Lien was recruited into the service of the first Ming Emperor, Chu Yuan-chang 朱元璋, in 1358 just after the latter had captured Wu-chou, and when the Mongol government was losing hold of the southern part of the empire. Like Wang Mien, he was a Confucian scholar in the Chin-hua area. As a result, in his biography, he was showing respect for both the Emperor and Wang Mien.

A third source, also a contemporary account, is found in Hsü Mien 徐勉's *Pao Yueh lu* 保越錄, which shows the author to have been someone in the service of the Yuan government, for the title itself means the defense of Yueh-chou (K'uai-chi area) against the invading rebels under Chu Yuan-chang. It is a long narrative of the fighting. The section dealing with Wang Mien is as follows:

> "A man of this prefecture, Wang Mien, *tzu* Yuan-chang, who was proud and arrogant, lived on Mt. Chiu-li. When the big army (rebels) arrived, all the people fled to the city, but Mien alone did not do so. Having captured him, the big army wanted to kill him. When Wang told them that he was familiar with military strategy and books on martial art, his life was spared. Some of the generals of the big army, such as Hsieh Chien 謝僉, set him free, accompanied him to Wu-chou, and took him to see T'ai-tsu. His Royal Highness the Emperor summoned him at the gate of the military camp. Mien memorialized the Emperor on his proposal to establish the number of officers and men for the campaign and the strategy and plan for the invasion. Greatly pleased, His Royal Highness immediately gave him an important appointment and ordered him to be at the head of the army to lead the men to attack Shao-hsing . . . ."

> 郡人王冕，字元章，負氣倨塞，居九里山中。大軍至，民皆避兵入城。冕獨不入。大軍執而欲殺之。自言能韜略兵書，得不死。大軍將謝僉等資之，偕行至婺州，領見太祖。高皇帝召對于軍門。冕即奏請定官額，陳設攻取方略。上大悅，即命授以重任，命軍前督衆攻取紹興。

But in the following narrative, Wang Mien's plan did not succeed. The offensive was

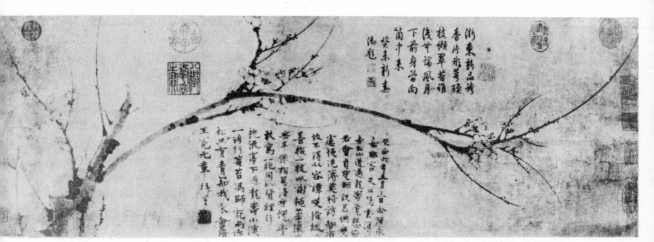

Plate 79   PLUM BLOSSOMS, by Wang Mien.

broken by the defenders. The last part of the story says:

> "The big army, frightened, did not know what to do, retreating while fighting. Some soldiers climbed over the wall, only to die in the river. Our army followed them with attacks, capturing two generals, three heralds, and two horses. Wan-hu (Division Commander) Ho Ch'ing 何清's eyes were hit by flying arrows.
>
> The big army, since its defeat on the right embankment which resulted in the loss of a great number of their men and horses, blamed Mien. From then on they did not seek his company any more."

> 大軍惶怖不知所爲，且進且却，士卒有踰垣而赴水死者。我軍從而擊之，
> 獲大將二人，先鋒三人，馬二匹。而萬戶何清中流矢傷目。大軍自右堰
> 之敗，人馬散亡甚衆，頗咎王冕，由此疏之。

This account, apparently written by someone who was on the side of the defenders of Shao-hsing against the invading "big army" of Chu Yuan-chang, who later founded the Ming dynasty, shows another side of the story. In complete contrast to the other two biographies, this writer was neither sympathetic with Wang Mien, who betrayed his prefecture, nor with the Ming Emperor. However, probably because the book was copied in the Ming period, all the references to Chu Yuan-chang in the text have been changed to "the Emperor" or "His Royal Highness" by some editors. In general, the writer shows extremely low esteem for Wang Mien. That this account is far more detailed and specific than the other two seems to be a definite mark of authenticity.

Among these three accounts, two flattering to Wang Mien and one not, perhaps some conclusions can be drawn. All three, though very different, do share something in common. They all mention Wang's capture or invitation by the rebels, led by either the Grand Marshal or the Emperor. They all relate something about his admonitions or plans to the leader. Thus they seem to agree that Wang Mien must have had some contact with Chu Yuan-chang or some of his generals. Since the biography by Hsü Hsien states that Wang died in 1359, his contact with the rebels must have taken place just before that. This seems to correspond with contemporary historical events. Late in 1358, Chu Yuan-chang's army did capture Wu-chou, and in the first month of 1359 they also took Chu-chi, which was Wang Mien's home district. Late that year, he also captured Ch'ü-chou 衢州 and Chu-chou 處州, both further south. In all these, Chu was fighting against other rebel groups, especially that of Chang Shih-ch'eng 張士誠 who, after a period of independence, made peace with the Yuan government during the late 1350's to become a nominal official of Yuan, though he still acted independently. In this context, the three accounts seem to represent three different points of view. The *Pao Yueh lu* took the position of the Yuan government; Hsü Hsien's biography was written from Wang Mien's point of view, without any sympathy for either Yuan or Ming; Sung Lien saw Wang Mien entirely from the Ming point of view.

DURING THE EARLY Ch'ing period, Wang Mien seemed to have enjoyed a new kind of popularity. At that time, with a new dynasty, Wang Mien could be seen in a more objective way. The earliest scholar to try to straighten out this problem was Ch'ien Ch'ien-i 錢謙益 (1582-1664). In his monumental work, the *Lieh-ch'ao shih-chi* 列朝詩集, he made use of all three sources mentioned above and concluded his biography of Wang Mien with this remark:

> "The biographies and the narrative (the three sources cited above) differ from each other in their reports of what happened to Mien in the rebel army. What Hsü's biography refered to as the 'Grand Marshal' was Hu (Ta-hai) 胡大海, the Duke of Yueh. When the whole world's situation was still unsettled, accusations from opposing powers have come down in letters and records. Those who read them should do some investigation of the circumstances."

> 傳錄載晃軍前事多互異。徐傳所云:「大帥」者，即胡越公也。天下未定，敵國指斥之詞，流傳簡牘，習其讀者，或有考焉。

Next, a friend of Ch'ien Ch'ien-i, the great scholar Huang Tsung-hsi 黃宗羲 (1610-1695), who was a native of Yü-yao 餘姚, not far east of K'uai-chi, cited Wang Mien as a man with a great political philosophy whose work unfortunately did not survive in his own famous treatise, *Ming-i tai-fang lu* 明夷待訪錄. Written in 1662, this treatise was the embodiment of his own idea of kingship and the relationship between the ruler and the ruled. A philosopher in the tradition of Chu Hsi 朱熹, Huang did a great deal of research in Ming history and the history of philosophy. Thus it is not accidental that he took an interest in Wang Mien.

It was Chu I-tsun 朱彝尊 (1629-1709) who took the greatest interest in Wang Mien in the Ch'ing period. Appointed to the Han-lin Academy as an editor of the official history of the Ming dynasty, he wrote another biography of Wang Mien. Living more than three hundred years after Wang Mien's time, again he could be much more objective in his approach. He described the episode of Wang's contact with Chu Yuan-chang as follows:

> "After (Ming) T'ai-tsu had captured Wu-chou, he sent Hu Ta-hai to

attack Shao-hsing. Hu stationed his army in Mt. Chiu-li. While all the
inhabitants in that area fled, Mien was not shaken. Having captured
him, the soldiers took him to see Hu Ta-hai. Asked by Ta-hai for advice,
Mien said, 'The people of Yueh uphold righteousness and should not be
attacked. If you are righteous, who would not follow you? If you are
not righteous, who would not become your enemy?' When T'ai-tsu
heard about his name, he wanted to appoint Mien a military advisor,
but Mien died."

太祖既取婺州，遣胡大海攻紹興，屯兵九里山。居人奔竄，冕不爲動。
兵執之，與俱見大海。大海延問策。冕曰，「越人秉義，不可以犯。若爲
義，誰敢不服。若爲非義，誰則非敵。」太祖聞其名，授以諸議參軍，
而冕死矣。

In his final comment to the biography, Chu expressed the idea behind his rewriting
of Wang's biography:

"During the late Yuan period, there were many cultivated people living
in retirement, among whom was Wang Mien. But since the appearance
of his biography by Sung Wen-hsien (Lien), all people have regarded him
as a military advisor. But did he ever serve as military advisor for even
one day? Reading Hsü Hsien's *Pei-shih chi chuan*, one came to realize
that Mien died because he would not yield his will. Therefore, I have
written another biography for the Archive of History in the hope that
their editors could have a choice (for the official history)."

當元之季多逸民，冕其一也。自宋文憲傳出，世皆以參軍目之。冕亦何
嘗一日參軍事哉! 讀徐顯稗史集傳，冕蓋不降其志以死者也。因別爲傳，
上之史館，冀編纂者擇焉。

This comment actually contradicts the conclusions drawn from the three major
sources of late Yuan and early Ming and also differs radically from Ch'ien Ch'ien-i's
idea. Perhaps now in the Ch'ing period, Chu I-tsun, free from the obligation to
flatter the Ming Emperor, was trying to depict him as a model literatus. Again it was
the Confucian tradition that was behind this emphasis.

   It is interesting to see that, perhaps because of the influence of Chu's biography,
Wang Mien was fictionalized as the perfect model of the literati in the introductory
chapter of the famous *Ju-lin wai-shih* 儒林外史 (Unofficial History of the Literati),
a biting satire by Wu Ching-tzu 吳敬梓 (1701-1754). While using the biographical
sources as his basis, Wu made many changes in his novel to depict Wang Mien as the
great literatus. Again it is the last part dealing with Wang's relationship with the
Ming Emperor that is most interesting. However, since it is too long to translate
here, a summary of Wu's treatment is sufficient.

   In the novel, Chu Yuan-chang is depicted as a great leader who, after defeating
Fang Kuo-chen 方國珍 to gain control of Chekiang, made a special trip to visit Wang
Mien in the latter's humble hut. During this visit, Chu became so respectful of Wang
that they carried on their conversation until dusk, with Wang emphasizing the
importance of righteousness as the ruling philosophy for the visitor (as mentioned

first in Hsü Hsien's biography). The story ends with Wang Mien, aware that the new emperor after establishing his own empire would invite him to serve in the government, quietly moving away to live in Mt. K'uai-chi for the rest of his life. This he did to preserve his integrity.

This final change in the attitude toward Wang Mien in the Ch'ing period seems to be very much in line with the outlook of both Chu I-tsun and Wu Ching-tzu. While they may have been somewhat affected by the loyalty toward Ming which persisted long into the Ch'ing period, their own unfortunate careers with the Ch'ing government and the official examination system probably made them look at Wang Mien differently, not so much as a man who was anxious to present his ideas of righteousness for action, but as one who found withdrawal from society as the best means to preserve his own integrity. It was still part of the Confucian tradition, though with some mixture of Taoism.

THIS MATTER OF the various points of view concerning Wang Mien's relationship with the first Ming emperor can be left to rest here except for the fact that it should be seen in another context, namely the strong Confucian tradition, especially of the Chu Hsi School. For the Chinese, the roots or native traditions are always very important in the consciousness of the leading men, especially the literati. K'uai-chi, or Yueh-chou, of which Wang Mien's native Chu-chi was a part, was an area filled with many glorious traditions from the ancient past. The great flood-controlling emperor of the legendary Hsia dynasty, Yü 禹, was supposed to have been buried here. During the early fifth century B.C., Kou-chien 勾踐, the Prince of the State of Yueh, spent years after a defeat by the Prince of Wu planning and training his men for his revenge. He finally succeeded and became the great cultural hero of perseverence and loyalty to an ideal. During the period of the Six Dynasties, the famous Lan-t'ing 蘭亭 (Orchid Pavilion) Gathering held by the great calligrapher Wang Hsi-chih 王羲之 (321-379) here became the great model for all literary gatherings of later periods, symbolic of the cultural brilliance and artistic achievement of this area.

In the case of Wang Mien, what is most interesting is the fact that, except in the case of *Pao Yueh lu*, which was a field narrative of the defence of the area from the Yuan point of view, all the other biographies from Yuan to Ch'ing were trying to glorify him as a Confucian sage. Although this is nothing very unusual in Chinese historical writing, there were some very special circumstances of that time that made this quite logical. The meeting between Wang Mien and Chu Yuan-chang or some of his generals took place at the most important juncture in Chu's long struggle for power. For up to 1358, although he was already building up a great power base, he remained somewhat of a "bandit hero" because of his own humble origin, lacking culture. But in that year, he captured Wu-chou (Chin-hua), which had been for two hundred years the Neo-Confucian center and undoubtedly the most important area of Confucian studies in the Yuan period. A whole stream of leading scholars, including the so-called "Four Gentlemen of Chin-hua," namely Ho Chi 何基 (1188-1268), Wang P'o 王柏 (1197-1274), Chin Li-hsiang 金履祥 (1232-1303), and Hsü Ch'ien 許謙 (1269-1337), carried on the philosophy of Chu Hsi into a flourishing development. In addition, during Wang Mien's time, there were the "Three Masters of ku-wen of Late Yuan," namely Liu Kuan 柳貫 (1270-1342), Huang Chin 黃溍 (1277-

1357), and Wu Lai 吳萊 (1297-1340). It was after the capture of Wu-chou that Chu Yuan-chang began to recruit a group of Confucian scholars to serve on his staff. Here he invited a group of thirteen scholars to take turns in giving lectures to him and his staff on the classics and history, to re-establish centers of studies in the prefectures, and to discuss government and political philosophy. Of this group the most famous was Sung Lien (1310-1381), a pupil of both Liu Kuan and Huang Chin, who became one of the most important advisors of Chu Yuan-chang during those years of struggle against the Yuan armies and other rebels. From then on, Chu, undoubtedly under the influence of Sung Lien and the other Confucian scholars, was transformed from a "bandit hero" to a Confucian leader, eventually gaining control of the empire. It was about the same time that another rebel leader, Chang Shih-ch'eng, who made his headquarters in Suchou, attempted to recruit the scholars and literary talents of that cultural city to his staff.

As mentioned above, Wang Mien at that time was living in the K'uai-chi area, which lay north of Wu-chou and was the next target in Chu Yuan-chang's campaign. When Wang was captured by Chu's army, his life was spared because he was a well-known scholar and poet. Eventually, there was also an attempt to try to recruit him into the service of the leader Chu Yuan-chang. Whether he tried to claim to be a military expert and to offer some strategy for the Chu army as a way to save himself, as the *Pao Yueh lu* indicates, or was asked for advice by either Chu Yuan-chang or Hu Ta-hai, as the other biographers mention, can never be ascertained. But there is reason to believe that both Hsü Hsien and Sung Lien, as Confucian scholars, might have colored Wang Mien's biography to make him appear as a noble upholder of righteousness. Clearly, this was Hsü Hsien's attempt. In the case of Sung Lien, who on the one hand had to show his loyalty to Chu Yuan-chang and on the other needed to extol some of the literati from his own area, he thus depicted Wang Mien coming into the service of the future emperor, just as he himself had done.

Wang Mien was also eulogized by another Confucian scholar of the Chin-hua School, Liu Chi 劉基 (1311-1375), who was also recruited by Chu Yuan-chang in Wu-chou at about the same time. Together with Sung Lien, Liu was one of the closest advisors on Chu's staff. Both of them helped the leader to develop the political and institutional foundations of the future Ming Empire. In his preface to the volume of collected poems of Wang Mien, Liu Chi told about how he first came to read his poems at K'uai-chi in 1354 and wrote that his poetry expressed "the feeling of loyalty to the ruler and of love of the people and the determination to eliminate the evil and to remove the corrupt", which were basically Confucian. Unlike these two scholars, Wang Mien seemed to have no luck and failed to impress the Emperor. However, to the eyes of some of the later writers his untimely death made him a more perfect example of a literatus in a world of turmoil, one who was not involved in the politics of the chaotic world but preserved his own personal integrity through withdrawal.

IT IS IN THE same context that we can see Wang Mien as a painter of plum blossoms in the Confucian tradition from the K'uai-chi area. Though he was born and raised in Chu-chi, he later, after his trip to Peking, retired to K'uai-chi and planted a thousand plum trees on Mt. Chiu-li. In the history of Chinese painting, K'uai-chi was for a long time closely associated with paintings of plum blossoms, at least from the time of Monk Hua-kuang Chung-jen 華光仲仁 (late 11th century), who was the originator of the ink plum blossom tradition in connection with the literati painting development of Northern Sung. From this time this type of painting must have taken roots in K'uai-chi. Although the two most important followers of ink plum blossom painting in Southern Sung, Yang P'u-chih 楊補之 (1079-1169) and his nephew, T'ang Cheng-chung 湯正仲, were from Kiangsi, they may still have some links with K'uai-chi. T'ang was known to have spent some of his later years in Huang-yen 黄岩, in the southern part of Chekiang, not far from K'uai-chi.

It was during the Yuan period that plum blossom painting became a most exciting tradition in this area. The two most important plum painters in this period, Wu T'ai-su 吳太素 and Wang Mien, were both natives of this area. Wu, who was best known for his treatise on plum painting, the *Sung-chai mei p'u* 松齋梅譜, and whose surviving works are all in Japan, was from K'uai-chi, while Wang, though a native of Chu-chi, spent his last years in this area. Between the two, while Wu was more influential in theory, Wang was the more innovative as a painter, calligrapher, poet, and seal-carver, thus a standard literati artist, in addition to a Confucian scholar.

Wang Mien became the most influential painter of plum blossoms during the first half of the Ming period, when all of the famous plum painters were from the same area. Ch'en Lu 陳錄 (fl. ca. 1440), a native of K'uai-chi, was probably the closest follower. Liu Hsueh-hu 劉雪湖 (fl. first half of the sixteenth century), also a native of the same area, was another close follower. A third painter of this genre was Wang Ch'ien 王謙 (fl. ca. 1500), who came from Ch'ien-t'ang, slightly to the west. However, none of them seemed to have the same mastery of painting, calligraphy and poetry as Wang Mien, or could match his brillance and innovation. It was only during the sixteenth century, that another native of K'uai-chi, Hsü Wei 徐渭 (1521-1593), introduced a different and freer type of ink painting of flowers and plants, thus putting an end to the persistent influence of Wang Mien.

Wang Mien was the master of plum blossom painting *par excellence*. By his command of the art of painting, calligraphy, and poetry, and by his combination of Confucian learning and personality, he elevated this type of painting to a high form of expression of the literati. Plum blossoms, as one of the three friends of winter with the pine and the bamboo, thus became symbolic of the perfect literati in China. This can best be seen in a painting, *A Branch of Plum Blossoms over Water*, executed in 1355, on which he wrote a long essay entitled "Biography of Mr. Mei", an allegorical account of the genealogy of the plum, which concludes in the following passage:

> "Mr. Mei 梅 (Plum) was an elegant and noble man in the dusty world. Showing pure taste and refined manners, he had the style of the gentlemen of the past. How could worldly comforts corrupt him! It is no wonder that he is so much admired and loved by the people of the world!"

> 梅先生翩翩濁世之高士也。觀其清標雅韻，有古君子之風焉，彼華映綺麗，烏能辱之哉。以故天下人士，景愛慕仰，豈虛也耶。

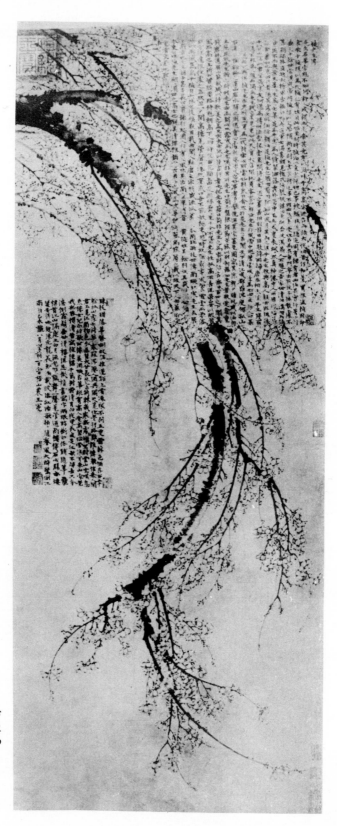

Plate 80 A BRANCH OF PLUM BLOSSOMS OVER WATER, by Wang Mien. Top right: Biography of Mr. Mei.

Plate 81 ORCHID SCROLL, by Cheng Hsieh. The inscription: *"How prosperous are the youths of Black Costume (Lane)...."*

Plant Paintings of Two Yang-chou Masters

By **Laurence C.S. Tam**

THIS ARTICLE is a study of some paintings and poems by two painters of the Ch'ing dynasty, Cheng Hsieh 鄭燮 (1693-1753) and Wang Shih-shen 汪士慎 (1686-1759), two representatives of the Eight Eccentrics of Yang-chou 揚州八怪 who were active during the reigns of Yung-cheng and Ch'ien-lung. The majority of these artists were not natives of Yang-chou, but their painting activities were centred there.

Cheng Hsieh, a native of Chiangsu, is now better known by his pseudonym, Pan-ch'iao 板橋. He obtained his *chin-shih* degree in the reign of Ch'ien-lung and was consequently appointed to the magistracies of Fan Hsien 范縣 and then of Wei Hsien 濰縣. After retirement, he led the life of a scholar-painter in Yang-chou. His favourite painting subjects are bamboo and orchid.

Wang Shih-shen, a native of Anhui, spent his life largely in Yang-chou as a recluse. He was a good friend of Chin Nung 金農, the most renown of the Yang-chou circle. In his old age he lost the sight of one eye, hence he sometimes used a seal bearing the characters "*Tso-mang-sheng*" 左盲生, meaning "scholar whose left eye is blind". His most famous painting subjects is the blossoming plum.

ALTHOUGH PAINTERS before them had employed inscriptions as constructive elements in painting, it was in the hands of Yang-chou masters such as Cheng Hsieh and Wang Shih-shen that inscriptions were used with the greatest inventiveness. Cheng Hsieh would use inscriptions to enhance or stabilize pictorial movement or to replace certain realistic pictorial details. Wang Shih-shen would use inscriptions to guide the movement of his pictorial forms, and to imbue his paintings with poetic atmosphere. By analyzing the paintings and poems presented below, we hope to throw light on the artistic insights of these two men, and by so doing bring out their contribution to eighteenth century painting in their bold breakthrough from orthodox compositional format.

Among the earliest dated paintings of Cheng Hsieh is an orchid hanging scroll which he executed in 1752. In it he painted nothing but orchids arranged in four separate groups at different levels (Pl. 81).[1] As Chinese hanging scrolls are usually painted from the bottom upwards, and are meant to be viewed that way, we shall start our visual journey into the painting from its lower margin.

There we are welcomed into the scene by a small clump of orchids in the lower left corner of the painting. The orchid leaves grow mostly upwards, inclining slightly to the right. This first group, announcing the opening of the scene, has its two longest leaves arranged in a V shape, diagonally facing the other side of the painting. Such an arrangement of leaf forms naturally leads us to the second group which grows more profusely, in a graceful and vigorous manner. Immediately above it, along the right margin of the painting, is a third clump shown only by the upper parts of some leaves and two flowering stalks, one pointing towards the centre of the painting, another shooting upwards along the right margin. Following this upward movement, we come to the orchids growing on the highest level, with flowers and leaves which seem to be dancing triumphantly in the air.

The pictorial movement, which accumulates strength as it ascends the picture plane, has thus reached a climax and begins to make its descent, and the orchids' dangling leaves usher us on to the inscription. This vertical column, reading downwards, leads our eyes back to the first orchid clump, the starting point of our journey. Thus the inscription is not only useful in completing this

---

[1] This painting was published in *Shina Nanga Taikan* 支那南畫大觀 (Tokyo, 1926), vol. 10, pl. 6. Another orchid scroll dated 1761, of similar composition and with the same inscription, is reproduced in *Shina Nanga Taisei* 支那南畫大成 (Tokyo, 1935-37), vol. 1, pl. 184.

circular configuration, but also essential in achieving compositional balance.

In fact, all four groups of orchids have prominent leaves pointing towards this inscription, which consists of a poem followed by the date of execution and Cheng's signature. The poem reads:

> How prosperous are the youths of Black
>   Costume (Lane),
> And so similar are they to the Southern
>   Dynasty's Wang and Hsieh clans.
> Abundant were the virtues planted by
>   their ancestors for a hundred years;
> So, naturally, the nine fields all come to
>   bloom.

烏衣子弟何其盛，
酷似南朝王謝家。
百歲老人多種德，
自然九畹盡開花。

In this poem, Cheng demonstrates his skill in the play of words as subtly as he exhibits his mastery of brushwork in the painting. The use of the term "youths of Black Costume (Lane)" in the first line has a historical connotation. The lane was actually a place situated in what is now southeastern Nanking where many nobles of the Chin dynasty (265-420) used to live, while the so-called "Black Costumes", made from a coarse black cloth, were a kind of fashionable dress worn by those gentlemen. The term "youths of Black Costume" denotes youths of noble breed, and makes us think of the orchids on the painting, which are executed in black ink. This term receives further clarification in the second line through the mention of Wang Tao 王導 (267-330) and Hsieh An 謝安 (320-385), once renowned inhabitants of that area, both prominent officials of the Chin dynasty. They were noted for their scholarship, talents and integrity of character, qualities which, according to Chinese tradition, are symbolized by the orchid.[2] Then, in the third and fourth lines, a

causal relationship between successive generations is exemplified by the pronouncement that Wang Tao and Hsieh An's merits brought forth their descendants prosperity. In a moralistic manner, the poet conveyed to us his belief in the Taoist idea of ch'eng fu 乘負, which asserts that the meritorious services or evil acts of a person will affect the future lives of his descendants.[3]

It is interesting to note that Cheng Hsieh used such words as "plant" and "nine fields" to link up the theme of his poem and the representation of orchids in his painting. The word "plant" 種, which can also mean "seeds", carries the metaphor between good deeds done by past generations and seeds that grow unnoticed in the ground: both are sure to lead to later prosperity. The term "Nine Fields" 九畹, a poetic substitute for blooming orchids,[4] continues this idea of prosperity and echoes the painting's cheerful growth of orchids. Thus our thoughts complete a circuit of ideas as we peruse the poem and view the painting.

Skilled in brush work, Cheng Hsieh can execute gradations in ink tones with the effect that his heavier strokes stand out like accents in Chinese poems. Large areas of empty space sometimes occur in his plant paintings, giving us the feeling of a natural open space where the plants are supposed to grow. Sometimes these spaces function like long pauses in a poem, preparing our thoughts for new realms of ideas as our eyes leave one group of plant forms to meet another with

---

[2] For the biography of Wang Tao, cf. the *Chin Shu* 晉書, *chuan* 65, Biographical Section 35, pp. 1-10. In the same *chuan*, pp. 10-17, are biographies of his sons and grandsons. The biography of Hsieh An is given in the same text, *chuan* 79, Biographical Section 49, pp. 4-8, and biographies of his sons and grandson, his brothers and nephews are on pp. 8-23.

[3] This idea of Cheng was also expressed in a letter to his brother, Mo 墨; cf. *Cheng Pan-ch'iao chi* 鄭板橋集, (Shanghai, 1965), p. 4.

[4] "Nine fields" is a literal translation of the Chinese term "*chiu wan* 九畹". It was originally used to indicate an area of land. In the *Li Sao* 離騷, a long poem of the *fu* style by Ch'u Yuan 屈原 (343 B.C.-?), a line goes like this:

> I have cultivated orchids of uni-floral stalk
>   in chiu wan.

余既滋蘭之九畹兮

According to Pan Ku 班固, author of the *Han Shu* 漢書, "*wan*" is equivalent to twenty "*mou*" 畝 (1 *mou* ≏ 6,000 sq. metres), while Hsu Shen 許慎 in his *Shuo wen* 說文 took "*wan*" to be equal to 30 "*mou*". Later scholars used the term "*chiu wan*", here translated as "nine fields", to mean "a place of land for growing orchids", or, simply, "orchids".

different structural details.[5]

AMONG THE EXTANT works of Cheng Hsieh are some large bamboo paintings in the form of scrolls or screens. The way in which these were painted is told by him as follows:

> People think that it is difficult to execute a large bamboo painting, but I think it easy. Everyday I paint only one stalk, completing it to my full satisfaction. In five or seven days, five or seven stalks are painted. Each stands by itself and is complete in all its excellence. Then bamboos in light ink tone, bamboos of smaller sizes and bamboos in broken form are woven into the pattern. The forms can be arranged widely separated or close together. The ink tone may vary from dark to light. Their forms can be long or short, and fat or slender. The tempo (of painting) may be fast or slow according to the state of my mind. A large composition is completed in this way.[6]

畫大幅竹，人以爲難，吾以爲易。每日只畫一
竿，至完至足。須五七日畫五七竿，皆離立完
好。然後以淡竹小竹碎竹經緯其間，或疏或
密，或濃或淡，或長或短，或肥或瘦，隨意緩
急，便構成大局矣。

Now let us study a large bamboo scroll which he painted in 1757 (Pl. 82) and try to interpret the course of its execution in the light of the passage cited above. This is a big painting, measuring 223.5 cm. x 91.3 cm.. To start with, we can number the ends of the twelve stalks from left to

right as *1* to *12*. According to the method he himself described, it would not be too far-fetched to suppose that he painted stalks *1, 2, 3, 5, 11* and *12* first. These are the major structural stalks in the painting, the main pillars in a building. They are so arranged that stalks *1* and *2* form one pair, *3* and *5* a second pair, and *11* and *12* a third. In each of these pairs, the lower ends of the stalks are drawn apart from each other but are joined together at the top. After this, stalk *4* was drawn to join the second and third pairs of stalks together. Stalk *6* was further added to support stalk *4* in its slanting position.

Of all these, stalk *2*, supported by stalk *1*, has been given the greatest height, its side stalks loaded with leaves drawn mainly in the traditional form like the Chinese characters *che* 介 or *ke* 个. Each layer of leaves is a repetition of these forms or their component parts. Decreasing in density and weight as they ascend in height, the leaves extend over the top portion of stalk *3*, bringing the first two pairs of main stalks together, and pointing diagonally downwards, counterpoising the upward movement of the slender pyramid formed by stalks *4, 11* and *12*.

Working from this orderly arrangement of pictorial elements, Cheng Hsieh wove in additional bamboo patterns according to the tempo of his own thoughts, paying attention to the relative density of ink tones and the arrangement of forms. He first broke the regularity of the feet of the bamboo stalks by adding stalks *7, 8, 9* and *10*. Stalk *10* was probably added last to accentuate the density of the stalks on the right side. Stalk *7* was put in for another function. It shoots right up to the top of the pyramid and sends out five sprays of leaves in lighter ink tones. These eliminate the monotony of the scaffolding appearance at the top of the pyramid, and act like a transmitting station, receiving the message of downward movement sent from the leaves above, and passing this message down along the stalks which form the pyramid.

To find a point of concentration for the upward force of the stalks and the downward movement of the leaves above, Cheng Hsieh stressed the more profuse growth of leaves on top of the shorter, and younger, stalks *8, 9* and *10*, and arranged them in a concave shape as if in a gesture to receive the downward thrust from above. The densest growth of leaves here seems to take place at a point about

[5]The system of four tones in the Chinese language, and the application of unaccented tones (*p'ing* 平) and accented tones (*che* 仄) in poetry, were fully discussed as early as the Six Dynasties by Shen Yueh 沈約 (441-513) in his *Ssu-sheng-p'u* 四聲譜, and by Chou Yung 周顒 (?-485) in his *Ssu-sheng ch'ieh-yün* 四聲切韻. For a fuller discussion of the development of the tones and sounds of Chinese characters, cf. Chang Shih-lu 張世祿, *Chung-kuo sheng-yün-hsueh kai-yao* 中國聲韻學概要 (Taipei, 1969). A comprehensive study of the part played by tonal patterns in Chinese poetry is found in Huang Hsu-wu 黃勗吾's *Shih-tz'u-chü te yen chiu* 詩詞曲的研究 (Taipei, 1966).

[6]*Cheng Pan-ch'iao chi*, p. 224.

Plate 82   BAMBOO SCROLL, by Cheng Hsieh. The inscription: *"Wen Yü-k'e, in a poem which he inscribed on an ink bamboo painting, said: 'I will use a section of the finest silk. . . .'"*

1   2 3   4 5 6 7 8 9 10 11 12

one-third up the length of stalk *11*. From this point, leaves spread out in spray forms in various directions. Some shoot out towards the right, filling up the empty space beyond stalk *12*, while several heavy clusters reach up towards top left, and join the upward movement of the tallest stalk, thus completing a circuit of pictorial movement in the upper half of the painting. Some sprays of leaves go downwards and, pointing towards the left, lead our eyes back to the area of the main stalks which started off the composition. The major leaves were executed in undiluted ink, and some clusters of leaves were drawn to overlap one another. The use of varying, light ink tones gives thickness to the bamboo grove as well as a three-dimensional effect to the leaves themselves. Sometimes these leaves in lighter ink tones act as bridges linking two heavy forms.

IT IS RATHER unusual for an inscription to be placed the way it is in this painting. The bamboos on the left look as if they are growing out from the inscription. In a way, the whole inscription may be looked upon as a solid mass. Cheng's use of inscriptions to simulate the effect of rocky masses, or their surface textures, can be seen elsewhere in his other works: a bamboo painting dated 1753 (in the Tokyo National Museum collection), a painting of auspicious plants growing out from a rock, dated 1761 (exhibited in the Hamburg Exhibition of 1949), and a painting of fragrant orchids and bamboos dated 1762 (reproduced in *Yang-chou pa-chia hua-chi* 揚州八家畫集, Peking, 1961). In a painting of orchids and bamboos done by Cheng at the age of seventy (Pl. 83), he replaced the textural strokes of the upper rock mass with an inscription. If the inscription is removed from the painting, the rock jutting out from the right margin will look uninterestingly bare, and the strokes representing the orchid plant and the bamboo leaves will appear as unduly heavy and somewhat out of balance. The presence of the inscription adds weight to the rock mass, giving the rock sufficient latent force to hold the orchid and bamboo firmly in place.

Returning to Plate 82, we can interpret the inscription as a rocky mass coming into the picture plane from behind the bamboo stalks at the lower left corner. The downward movement of the calligraphy not only balances the strong upward

Plate 83   BAMBOO SCROLL, by Cheng Hsieh. Dated 1762.

movement of the major stem, which sends its leaves right to the top of the picture plane, but also gives added interest to the spaces between the tall bare bamboo stalks in that corner of the picture. Also, it counterpoises the bend of stalk *11* and the leaves on stalks *2* and *7* towards the right. The first line of the inscription is put alongside a stalk leaning towards the left, which makes quite obvious the painter's intention: he wanted to accentuate the left-bending force of that stalk to keep the painting in visual balance.

The following is a literal translation of the words in the inscription:

Wen Yü-k'e (Wen T'ung 文同, 1018-1079), in a poem which he inscribed on an ink bamboo painting, said:

"I will use a section of the finest silk,
To sweep on wintry stalks a myriad
feet in length."

Mei Tao-jen (Wu Chen 吳鎮, 1280-1354) said:

"I, too, have a pavilion deep in the
bamboo grove,
And also the thought of returning
home to hear the autumn sounds."

Their poetic thoughts are most exquisitely pure. They are remembered not for their paintings alone. Because they are remembered not only for their paintings, their paintings are therefore even better remembered. I am proficient in neither poetry nor painting. Yet I exert myself to inscribe a few lines:

"They said that the frosty stalks had
withered.
Who knew that green leaves would
again abound?
Gusts and thunder over the clear river
last night
Released the dragon's descendants (i.e.
young bamboo shoots) ten thousand
in number."

These are words from a vulgar person not worthy to be compared with those of the early masters. I wish that my dear old friend and classmate Shih-lan[7] will correct this.—

Painted and inscribed by Cheng Hsieh, in the year *ting-ch'ou* in the reign of Ch'ien-lung (i.e. 1757).

文與可題墨竹詩云，擬將一段鵝溪絹。掃取空
梢萬尺長。梅道人有云，我亦有亭深竹裏。也
思歸去聽秋聲。皆詩意清絕，不獨以畫傳也。
不獨以畫傳而畫益傳。余不能詩又不能畫，然
亦勉題數句曰，只道霜筠幹已枯，誰知碧葉又
扶疏。風雷昨夜清江上，拔出龍孫一萬株。鄙
夫之言，有愧前哲也，唯石蘭同學老世長兄政
之。乾隆丁丑板橋鄭燮畫並題。

The Sung dynasty painter Wen T'ung has often been hailed as the founder of the most influential school of bamboo painting known as the Hu-chou School 湖州派.[8] Executing bamboo leaves and sections of the stalks each with one single stroke of the brush, he presented his plants according to a natural system of growth, so that we can clearly discern how each small stem grows out from a larger stalk, and how a leaf in turn grows out from a small stem. In the Yuan dynasty Wu Chen continued the Hu-chou School but went one step further. He freed himself from the bondage of weaving the brush-strokes according to realistic patterns of growth, and took bamboo painting as a kind of ink play through which he tried to capture the momentary impression of the plant in his mind.[9] Thus his brushstrokes demonstrate greater freedom and spontaneity than those of Wen T'ung.

In the inscription cited above, Cheng Hsieh acknowledged Wen T'ung's achievement as a painter of bamboo, and emphasized the magnitude and heroic feeling of his brushwork. The sheer length of the tallest bamboo stalk in Cheng's painting, measuring well over seventy inches, with emphasis laid on its bare, leafless upper part, distinctly reminds us of the "wintry stalks a myriad feet in length" in Wen T'ung's poem. But

[7] Shih-lan 石蘭 was the pseudonym of Chiang Tao 江燾, a calligrapher from Hsi Hsien 歙縣 of Anhui Province; cf. *Chung-kuo li-tai shu-hua-chuan-k'e-chia tzu-hao so-yin* 中國歷代書畫篆刻家字號索引 (Peking, 1960), vol. 1, p. 385.

[8] Yü Feng 于風 states this view in his *Wen T'ung, Su Shih* 文同, 蘇軾 (Shanghai, 1960), pp. 13-17.

[9] This analysis is carried in Ku Lin-wen 顧麟文's *Yang-chou pa-chia shih-liao* 揚州八家史料 (Shanghai, 1962), p. 6.

we are also reminded by Wu Chen's lines that Cheng's style, though inherited from the Hu-chou School, is in fact less close to Wen T'ung's style than to Wu Chen's in that it is not a mere reconstruction of bamboo forms but a reflection of the untrammelled spirit and integrity often attributed to a virtuous scholar. Cheng's own poem tells us of his joy in finding new growth emerge from old plantings, his interest and concern for bamboos which echo Wu Chen's desire to return to the bamboo grove, and his expectation of a new generation of bamboo shoots "ten thousand in number" to burst soon into luxuriant growth. Thus, with the insertion of a short poem of four lines, Cheng successfully high-lighted the subject matter of his painting, and rounded up the multiple background thoughts associated with its composition.

A THEME WELL-LOVED by literati painters of the 18th century was the "Four Gentlemen" represented by the blossoming plum, orchid, chrysanthemum and bamboo. Painters would choose among these plants those that suited their own tastes and make personal interpretations of them. Cheng Hsieh was fond of the bamboo and orchid, while his contemporary Wang Shih-shen specialized in the blossoming plum, and both gave us paintings that form testimony to their idiosyncrasies.

A painting of the blossoming plum by Cheng Hsieh well illustrates the difference between his and Wang Shih-shen's treatment of the plant. This is an undated work, now in the collection of the Palace Museum, Peking (Pl. 84). In it, plum branches are presented together with two stalks of bamboo which, in a rather unusual arrangement, cross one another almost at right angles just inside the small rectangle formed by the plum branches. The bamboos are executed in fewer strokes than the plum branches but, because of the radiating placement of their leaves, the density of ink tone and their clearcut shapes, they emerge more distinctly than the plum branches and blossoms. The plum in this painting lacks the control, precision and musical rhythm of Cheng's bamboos and orchids. The reason underlying this is explained in the inscription, a seven-word *chüeh-chü* poem which reads:

Plate 84 BLOSSOMING PLUM SCROLL, by Cheng Hsieh. The inscription: "*I have never painted plum blossoms so far in my life. . . .*"

*I have never painted plum blossoms so far
  in my life;
Nor have I known a reclusive home in
  lonely hills.
Today, I painted plum blossoms as well as
  bamboo,
In this cold season my mind fills with
  smoky mists.*

一生從未畫梅花，
不識孤山處士家。
今日畫梅兼畫竹，
歲寒心事滿烟霞。

In the very first line of this poem, Cheng openly announced that plum blossom painting is not his specialty. The second line explains why he chose not to paint that subject—because he had never had any intention of leading a reclusive life. The third line turns to the subject of the painting and specifies the plants in it. The last line reveals the condition of the painter's mind at the moment of creating the work. This painting was probably done not long before Cheng Hsieh retired from his official career in the year 1753. Not satisfied with being a government official, he had thought of leading a life of retirement in his own native place which, however, was not to his taste either. Thus at that time his mind was not peaceful, but veiled by "smoky mists". In fact, this painting can be taken as an attempt by Cheng Hsieh to record, through the use of different plant symbols, a critical moment in his life when he had to choose between officialdom, as represented by the bamboo, and retirement, as represented by the blossoming plum. The tall bamboo, with leaves high above the plum blossoms, may be taken as a symbol of an upright official, while the bamboo, lying behind some of the lower plum branches, may symbolize an official who has to bend down to the will of others. In the poem Cheng did not indicate what decision he made, but he did suggest, by arranging the three plant forms at three different levels, that his highest ideal was to be an upright official, failing which he would descend one level and choose to be a recluse rather than an official who has to yield to the will of others.

WANG SHIH-SHEN, Cheng Hsieh's contemporary, who led a life very much like that of a recluse,

holds quite a different attitude towards the blossoming plum. He liked to paint flowering plum branches because he wanted to be identified with them, particularly in his old age. Among such paintings by him, two of the earliest are dated *ping-ch'en, ch'ing-he* 丙辰清和, i.e. the third lunar month in the year 1736 (Pl. 85), and *ping-ch'en, li-ch'iu hou ssu-jih* 丙辰立秋後四日, i.e. four days after the beginning of autumn in the year 1736 (Pl. 86). In both of these works, plum twigs enter the picture plane near the top right corner with the main branch projecting towards the left, diagonally in one, and almost horizontally in the other. Before reaching the left margin, the branch makes a turn and sends forth smaller blossoming twigs towards the right and bottom of the painting. Such a compositional format can be found in quite a few blossoming plum paintings by Yuan and Ming masters, such as those by Wang Mien 王冕 (1335-1407), the most celebrated blossoming plum painter in Chinese art history. But whereas Wang Mien tried to recreate, by a shower of blossoming branches, the gaiety and vigour of plant life in spring,[10] Wang Shih-shen was used to painting only a few branches, being more interested in the arrangement of pictorial shapes than in the beauty of natural and exuberant growth. Rather than try to paint real plum branches, he borrowed their forms to weave a pattern, or to construct a setting for a theme expressed in his inscription.

Wang Shih-shen, a zealous lover of plum blossoms, wrote many poems which contain messages essential for a fuller understanding of his paintings. The scroll painted in the third month of 1736 (Pl. 85) has two inscriptions on it. The shorter one, on the upper right, tells when and where the painting was executed, and carries the signature of the painter. Placed just under where the branches enter the picture, it functions like another plum branch entering the picture and pointing downwards. The long inscription on the lower left, added after the shorter one, reads:

[10][For a discussion of plum-blossom painting by this artist, see the latter part of Chu-tsing Li's article "Problems Concerning the Life of Wang Mien, Painter of Plum Blossoms" in this issue.]

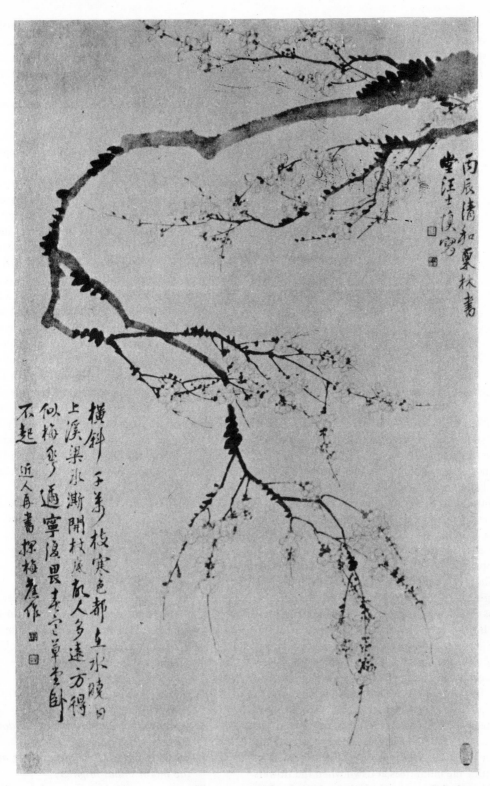

Plate 85 BLOSSOMING PLUM SCROLL, by Wang Shih-shen.
The inscription: *"A myriad branches crisscross. . . ."*

A myriad branches crisscross,
Their wintry hue deep in the water.
Walking on a stream's bridge at dawn,
Ice cracks under my staff.
My old friends are mostly far away,
But seem as close as these plum blossoms.
Why should one still fear the spring cold,
And lie abed in the thatched chamber?

Chin-jen inscribes again a poem composed earlier on visiting plum blossoms.

橫斜千萬枝，
寒色都在水。
曉日上溪梁，
冰漸開杖底。
故人多遠方，
得似梅花邇。
寧復畏春寒，
草堂臥不起。

近人再書探梅舊作

"Chin-jen" is the pseudonym of Wang Shih-shen. From this inscription, we learn that the poem existed before the painting. This longer inscription was probably added to the lower left corner to balance the weight of the branches and the shorter inscription. The two inscriptions thus placed look as if they were defining a passage for the inturning flowering branch. The affinity in form and relation in content of the two inscriptions create a force of attraction between them. This force exerts an invisible pressure on the branches in between, increasing the tension and agility of the lines with which the plant is delineated.

An air of serenity pervades the whole poem. It begins with a picturesque description of blossoming branches by the side of a frozen stream. In this scene an old man walks, staff in hand, across a bridge over the stream, and approaches the flowering plum tree. The poet expresses slight agitation when he thinks of his friends faraway, but he soon calms down in the presence of his beloved plum blossoms and feels glad that he has not stayed late in bed and missed such a beautiful sight. At the end of the poem, he encourages others to join him in visiting the plum trees at dawn when the flowers should look their best, which shows how fond he was of the plum tree. Thus we are led to associate the branches in the painting with that particular plum tree described in the poem, a tree which grew near the stream, bathed in the pale light of the morning sun on a freezing day in early spring. The poem certainly made the picture much more meaningful than a mere sketch of a few flowering branches.

THE PLUM BLOSSOM paintings of Wang Shih-shen lack the obvious musical rhythm which we find in most of Cheng Hsieh's paintings. Yet in them we can sense quite clearly the line of movement indicated by the branches, and the accentuation of such movement indicated by the varying density of plum blossom clusters, moss dots and other elements. In the course of painting the branches, his picture surface was divided into compartments of varying shapes and sizes. This is particularly obvious in the scroll which Wang painted in the autumn of 1736 (Pl. 86). The branches here are painted in such a way that the spaces enclosed by them look very much like rocks with moss and flowering plants growing out from their cracks and hollows. They are so arranged that they have partitioned the picture surface into two, a triangular space on the upper left and a nearly semi-circular shape on the lower right. Inside the triangular space, the painter put the title of the painting in a calligraphic style of the past, reading:

STREAKS OF FRAGRANCE IN THE AIR
written also by Chin-jen in seal script

空裏疎香
近人又篆

The size of the space left in the lower right portion of the painting and the way the flowering twigs point towards it make us expect something significant here. True enough, within this setting, the painter inserted his major inscription:

In the small court are planted plum trees,
*   one or two rows;*
Marking the space, their meagre shadows
*   cover my clothes.*
When frosty crystals melt into water, and
*   the moon shines brighter,*
The east wind brings gusts of fragrance
*   the whole day through.*

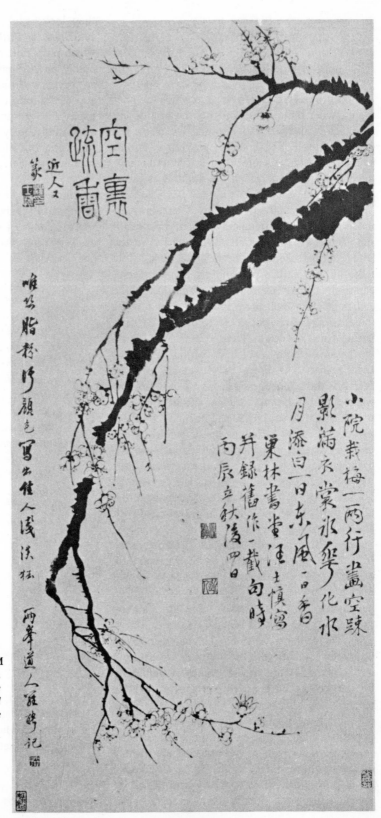

Plate 86 BLOSSOMING PLUM SCROLL, by Wang Shih-shen. Title: *"Streaks of fragrance in the air."* The inscription: *"In the small court are planted plum trees, one or two rows...."*

小院栽梅一兩行，
畫空疏影滿衣裳。
冰花化水月添白，
一日東風一日香。

The poem reveals a garden scene in which the poet stands under plum trees, enjoying the beauty and fragrance of their moonlit flowers. The poem is a picture in itself. The branches of plum blossoms painted here are, therefore, an introduction into the poetic world of which the painting is just a part.

These two paintings done by Wang in 1736 show remarkable differences in their brushwork and methods of execution. The branches in the later painting are done in saturated ink, while those in the earlier painting are done in comparatively lighter ink tones. The branches in the earlier painting look more solid and round, while those in the later one look comparatively flat, irregular and shadowy. Such differences in brushwork can be easily explained by the content of their poems. The poem in the earlier painting describes the plum trees as seen in a cold morning when the branches are still icy and lit by a clear morning sun. According to the poem on the later painting, the poet is looking up at the blossoming branches against the moonlight above, thus the branches appear to him as flickering black lines. To emphasize this shadowy effect and to keep the black ink strokes from being overly dominant, the upper part of the main branch was painted with abrupt narrowing.

Wang's plum blossom paintings are distinguished from those of other painters by their casual look of brush strokes for the branches. Often he formed each branch with one single stroke of the brush, moving the tip of the brush along the painting surface and varying its applied pressure. Unless when adding moss dots, he seldom tried to retouch the branches with the brush, or at least tried not to show his retouching strokes. Although no texture strokes were added, we do not feel the painting is lacking in them. The lines which Wang drew for these branches look very casual but, at the same time, they are full of interest and variation. Some parts of the branches are painted thicker or thinner than they should be. Occasionally, they are made to bend at awkward angles. At certain unexpected points, they are so thin that they look as if about to break. This feeling of casualness is further accentuated by the way in which moss dots are added. They are often placed boldly on the branches, in rows of three or more, at irregular intervals. Unduly large dots may appear abruptly on thin branches. In his effort to make his paintings look effortless, Wang has successfully played with features of apparent casualness to add extra life and vividness to a common subject.

IN THE YEAR 1746, Wang Shih-shen reached the age of sixty (or sixty-one, according to the Chinese way of counting years of age). He wrote a poem on New Year's Day for his own amusement.[11] The poem reads:

Sixty years having passed, the year ping-yin *comes again.*
For long, my tastes in life have merited the description of being humble.
An occasional desire for a cup of tea has become my single weakness.
In age, I cherish the plum blossoms as old friends.
Vegetarian food is naturally superior to rich banquet fare.
A mat-covered window can match a newly ornamented hall.
I tidy the place, sweep the floor, light incense, then sit.
Snow drifts and icicled eaves have already announced the spring.

六十翻頭又丙寅，
多年況味得稱貧。
間貪茗椀成清癖，
老覺梅花是故人。
蔬食原勝粱肉美，
蓬窗能敵錦堂新。
安排掃地焚香坐，
積雪檐冰早占春。

In this poem, Wang tells us of his living conditions and his state of mind at the age of sixty. He admits that he has been poor all his life but, showing no regret for it, expresses quiet joy over

---

[11]Recorded in Wang Huan 王幻's *Yang-chou pa-chia hua-chuan* 揚州八家畫傳 (Taipei, 1960). p. 121.

the peace and simplicity of a poor scholar-painter's life. He takes delight in such plain pleasures as sipping tea, admiring plum blossoms, eating vegetarian dishes and living in a small thatched house. On New Year's Day, when most people are busily engaged in festival activities, he welcomes the coming of spring by sitting quietly in a clean, tidy room admist the fragrance of burning incense, to enjoy the morning scene outside the window. When he said jokingly that he failed to greet the coming of spring as early as the snow and icicle, he is in fact trying to identify himself with nature.

SIX YEARS after this, in the year 1752, Cheng Hsieh wrote an extraordinarily long couplet to celebrate his own sixtieth birthday. The right column reads:

> *Since I am always like a guest (in this world), why ask about my health and safety? As long as there is savings in my purse, wine in the jar and food in the cooking pot, I shall take out a few sheets of my favourite old drafts and release myself in chanting verse. One should have wide interests and a strong body. To have all five senses alert and well is better than to have a thousand offices. Thus, having lived sixty years, one remains a youth.*

常如作客。何問康寧。但佼囊有餘錢。甕有餘釀。釜有餘糧。取數百賞心舊紙。放浪吟哦。興要闊。皮要頑。五官靈動勝千官。過則六旬猶少。

The left column reads:

> *To fix one's desire on becoming an immortal is to create trouble for oneself. I only command my ears to listen to no vulgar sounds, my eyes to watch no vulgar things and my mind to bear no vulgar thoughts. I take any few branches of fresh bloom and arrange them casually. I retire late and rise early. A day of leisure is like two days. Counting time in this way, I am already over one hundred years of age.*

定欲成仙。空生煩惱。祇令耳無俗聲。眼無俗事。胸無俗念。將幾枝隨意新花。縱橫穿插。睡得遲。起得早。一日清閒似兩日。算來百歲已多。

Here, a personality entirely different from that of Wang Shih-shen's is presented to us. Cheng Hsieh starts each of the columns by pronouncing that life and death are not matters for his concern. Yet, from his confession that he does not care for much except some daily necessities and the freedom to do what he wants, we nevertheless sense that, both physically and morally, he was a man of strict discipline. He stresses the importance of good living habits. He also advises against vulgar sounds, vulgar things and vulgar thoughts, and advocates the full use of one's senses and inherent capacity. When reading his couplet, we are confronted with an energetic man who still cherishes the pleasures of life. He favoured the painting of bamboos, rocks and orchids because they symbolize the virtuous qualities of the superior man whom he admired and looked upon as his model. In the course of executing his paintings, he consciously demonstrated his skillful depiction of plant forms, his masterly manipulation of ink tones and his power to control rhythmic movement on the picture plane. In Wang Shih-shen's poem, however, we seem to see an old monk in meditation, with little interest in the material world's excitement and joy. He favoured the painting of plum blossoms because they symbolize the qualities of endurance and purity to be found in eremetic scholars of whom he was one, and in painting plum blossoms he has given them an apparently effortless feeling, a free and easy look, as if the plant forms flowed naturally from his brush.

饒宗頤：明季文人與繪畫
Painting and the Literati in the Late Ming

By Jao Tsung-i

Translated by James C. Y. Watt

This article is a partially abridged translation of Professor Jao Tsung-i's paper delivered at the Symposium on Painting and Calligraphy by Ming I-min 明遺民, i.e. those who remained loyal to the Ming cause after the fall of the dynasty in 1644. The symposium and its accompanying exhibition were held at the Chinese University of Hong Kong in August-September 1975. In analyzing the art of this critical period of Chinese culture, Professor Jao, Professor of Chinese Literature at the Chinese University of Hong Kong, pointed out that the works of Ming I-min are characterized by their scholarly spirit 士氣, their free imagination and their "uncommon" artistic expression. Among the painters of the late Ming there was hardly a professional; they were scholars skilled in various arts, poetry and other literary studies and their versatility was in a way the basis of their skill as painters.

Introduction

The literati of the Ming period were almost all skilled in painting and calligraphy. It has for some time been assumed that the practice of painting and calligraphy among the literati first became prevalent in late Ming times. Teng Shih 鄧實, for example, attributes the beginning of the fashion to the example of Tung Ch'i-ch'ang 董其昌. However, many literary figures at the beginning of the dynasty, such as Liu Chi 劉基, were well versed in the art of painting.

The Categories of "hua-shih" (畫士) and "shih-hua" (士畫)

From late Ming times, various artists and critics have attempted to group painters into categories. Ku Ying-yuan 顧凝遠 in his *Hua-yin* 畫引 singled out Tung Ch'i-ch'ang as the grand innovator. The rest were categorised as: (1) Scholarly master painters, such as Shen Chou 沈周, Wen Cheng-ming 文徵明 and T'ang Yin 唐寅; (2) Literati painters, such as Ch'én Ch'un 陳淳, Lu Chih 陸治 and Hsü Wei 徐渭; (3) Painterly painters, (Chou Ch'en 周臣 is one of four in this category); (4) "Contemporary" literati painters (Li Liu-fang 李流芳 and Chung Hsing 鍾惺 are among the five in this category). The term "Painterly Painters" (*hua ming-chia* 畫名家) probably referred to professional painters as opposed to the literati.

In the album of works by contemporary painters dedicated to Chou Liang-kung 周亮工 (recorded in the *Shih-ch'ü San-pian* 石渠三編) is a long colophon by Kung Hsien 龔賢 on the painters of the early Ch'ing. In it he divided the painters of his time into two streams and three classes. The three classes were: the "masterly" (能), the "inspired" (神) and the "sublime" (逸), in ascending order of merit. The masterly and the inspired were grouped in the "main stream" and the sublime was regarded as the "other stream". (Then he went on to qualify his statements by saying that the sublime class of painters, because they were really beyond classification, should really be called true masters of painting (畫土). He also warned against a too strict division of painters into the literati and painterly schools, and criticised the habit of connoisseurs of calling any painting of high artistic merit a "literary painting" and also the practice among the less discerning of using the term "scholarly painting" as a form of damning praise. Of the painters of Nanking, Kung Hsien regarded K'un-ts'an 髡殘 and Ch'eng Cheng-kuei 程正揆 as the two leaders among the few who belonged to the sublime class. Again, only a few belonged to the inspired class, and the rest were seen as masterly.

In the inscription in an album of landscapes recorded in the *Hsü-chai Ming-hua Hsü-lu* 虛齋名畫續錄, Kung Hsien discussed the rules (法) of painting: "According to Hsieh Ho 謝赫 of Nan-ch'i 南齊 there are six rules in painting. In my opinion, there are only four essentials (*iao* 要). The first is the brush (*pi* 筆), the second is ink (*mo* 墨), the third 'mountains and valleys' (*ch'iu-huo* 丘壑) and the fourth is 'life' (*ch'i-yün* 氣韻). The brush should be handled with authority, the ink should be rich, the mountains and valleys should be stable. If these qualities are all present, there is life in the painting. The authoritative brush should be tempered with delicacy. If it is wielded with strength and no delicacy, the painting is withered. Richness of ink does not imply a wet brush. Mountains and valleys are just another way of saying "composition"; the composition should be balanced, but then it must have elements of the unexpected without which the balance achieves nothing. Mere balance is the characteristic of the non-gifted painter, while the unbalanced painting is produced by the hand of an amateur. Now there are two streams of painting, the professional and the scholarly. The professional painting is balanced and the scholarly painting lacks balance. It is surely better to be amateurish than to be uninspired. If one combines strength and delicacy, delicacy with richness, richness with the unbalanced, and the unbalanced with the balanced, then one would reach the highest peak of achievement in painting. And who can accomplish this but the supremely gifted person who is skilled through dedicated study? In a painting by such an artist exists poetry and order, and the vibrancy of life. Truly, painting is no mean art."

From the passages quoted, it can be seen that Kung Hsien rated the sublime as the highest category in painting and named only two artists worthy of a place in this class. He also regarded the element of the unexpected in a painting as the mark of creativity and rated innovation above technical competence.

In the opinion of the author, Kung Hsien's theory of the four rules of painting represents an advance on the six rules theory of Hsieh Ho. It points out the inter-relationship of the different aspects of artistic creation.

Chou Liang-kung records Fang Heng-hsien 方亨咸's comments on Kung Hsien's theory: "Pan-ch'ien (Kung Hsien)'s discussion on scholarly paintings and professional painters is both true and well argued. It makes one feel that Hsieh Ho's theory is incomplete. My only comment is that it is perhaps not right to rate the sublime above the inspired. For the inspired painter the hand perfectly reflects the movements of the mind, brush and ink becomes one, and the whole work defies analysis. The painting is individual and completely unified in its every aspect. The sublime on the other hand transcends and is removed from the world of common convention.

It is unfettered like the heavenly horse galloping in the sky. It also has its place in the order of things. The *Ch'an* (禪) masters would call it the divine tradition outside orthodoxy or "the meeting on the other peak". The inspired is in the state of a Tathāgata and the masterly is but a pratyeka Buddha. In the military world, Sun-tzu 孫子 and Wu Ch'i 吳起 were the inspired and Ch'eng Pu-shih 程不識, who commanded with absolute discipline, was the masterly, while the relaxed General Li Kuang 李廣 was the sublime. The inspired is the ultimate of the masterly and there is no single way to achieve it. Therefore, the inspired is in a class above the masterly and the sublime. It should not be discussed on the same level as the others, far less being considered as inferior to any. Perhaps for Kung Hsien the inspired represents only the complete mastery of rules. In any case, painting is a (rarefied) and cultured activity. If one is not well read and is unrefined, one will always remain an artisan however much time and effort one puts into the practice of painting. This is why the discerning person differentiates between the refined and the vulgar. There is surely no cause for us to consider all paintings by scholars sublime."

Thus Fang Heng-hsien's point of view is markedly different from that of Kung Hsien and the difference depends on the interpretation of the term "inspired".

According to Fang I-chih 方以智, the division is between the "artisan's brush" and the "scholar's brush", neither of which is the middle way. He says: "According to the world's opinion, the artisan's brush is impeded by rules, and the scholar's brush is impeded by the lack of impediment. This dilemma must be resolved before the natural process of creation can run its course."

There is thus considerable difference among the views of late Ming painters on the relative merits of the three classes of painting, but there is general agreement on the superiority of the "literary" over the "artisan".

Tao-chi 道濟 wrote in an album of old trees painted for Ming-liu 鳴六 and dated 1694 (reproduced in *The Paintings of Tao-chi*, p. 108): "These men painted from the fundamentals, without inheriting it from the family—noble painters such as Pai-t'u 白禿 (K'un-ts'an), Ch'ing-ch'i 青溪 (Ch'eng Cheng-kuei) and Tao-shan 道山 (Ch'en Shu 陳舒), elegant painters like Mei-huo 梅壑 (Cha Shih-piao 查士標) and Chien-chiang 漸江 (Hung-jen 弘仁), dry and lean painters like Kou Tao-jen 垢道人 (Ch'eng Sui 程邃), eloquent painters like Pa-ta Shan-jen 八大山人 (Chu Ta 朱耷) of Nan-ch'ang 南昌, expressive painters like Mei Ch'ü-shan 梅瞿山 (Mei Ch'ing 梅清) and Hsüeh-ping-tzu 雪坪子 (Mei Keng 梅庚), these are all painters of our generation who have understood. I alone have failed, and so my paintings are clumsy and devoid of meaning. Those who know would simply laugh."

This passage was written in the thirty-third year of K'ang-hsi, twenty years after Kung Hsien's colophon quoted above. It is certain that by this time, the question of the literary painter and the artisan was no longer considered crucial.

Painters and Writers

The literati of the late Ming were mostly versed in all the literary arts as well as in painting and calligraphy, but their achievements in these diverse activities were not equal. The following are examples of literary figures who also painted and painters who also wrote:

(*a*)   Essayists who painted: Hou Fang-yü 侯方域, Wang Ssu-jen 王思任.

(b) Poets who painted: Chung Hsing 鍾惺, Ch'eng Chia-sui 程嘉燧.

(c) Dramatists who painted: Ch'i Chih-chia 祁豸佳.

(d) Painters who wrote poetry: Ch'eng Sui, Hu Tsung-jen 胡宗仁, Yün Ke 惲格, Wu Li 吳歷, Chiang Shih-chieh 姜實節.

(e) Calligraphers who painted: Hsing T'ung 邢侗, Ni Yuan-lu 倪元璐, Huang Tao-chou 黃道周.*

The Relation between Style in Poetry and in Painting

Nearly all painters of the late Ming wrote poetry, and many true poets were accomplished painters. Poetry is the expression of one's nature and temperament, and differences in temperament and experiences give rise to differences in style. Temperament is determined at birth, but learning is a consequence of application. Talent is innate and knowledge is acquired. The power of expression varies with the individual but the artistic form is learned through exercise. In short, poetic style is formed as a result of the interaction between nature and practice, and the same can be said of style in painting. Thus one often finds parallels in the styles of poetry and painting, and the cause is none other than similarities in temperament, taste and inclinations.

It is not possible to discuss all the painters of this period, but those who are represented in the Chih-lo Lou 至樂樓 Collection may be categorised as follows:

(1) Gifted Painters: These are not specialists in painting but their talents are much in evidence and there is a refreshing quality to their painting. Their compositions are often unexpected and different from common productions. Such painters are: Yang Lung-yu 楊龍友 (Wen-ts'ung 文從), Chang Ta-feng 張大風, Huang Hsiang-chien 黃向堅, Fu Shan 傅山, Cha Chi-tso 查繼佐.

(2) Masterly Painters: These are true painters who are well trained in the technique of painting. In spite of differences in style they can all be grouped in the same category. Such painters are: Ch'en Hung-shou 陳洪綬, Lan Ying 藍瑛, Hsiao Yün-ts'ung 蕭雲從, Ku Fu-chen 顧符稹, Wen Tien 文點.

(3) Monkish Painters: Their paintings are prompted by moments of inspiration and not by any desire to represent reality. The works originate from the spirit and assume forms which are entirely individual. Such painters are: Wu-k'o 無可 (Fang I-chih), Tan-tang 擔當, K'un-ts'an, Chien-chiang (Hung-jen), Shih-t'ao 石濤 (Tao-chi), Pa-ta (Chu Ta).

According to the differences in learning, experiences, personal vision and skill with the brush and ink, the styles of these painters can be grouped into the following eight types:

(i) The closed and complex. Mountains and peaks are juxtaposed and the imagination is given free rein, e.g. Wu Pin 吳彬, Kung Hsien.

(ii) The open and sparse. A few brush-strokes suggest a rarefied landscape, e.g. Ch'eng Chia-sui, Pa-ta (Chu Ta).

*Following this classification, the original article gave biographical notes on the painters mentioned, quoting extensively from critics to show the nature of their art.—TRANS.

(*iii*)   The dry. The texture strokes are rendered with a dry brush but the representation is complete, e.g. Ching Sui, Tai Pen-hsiao 戴本孝.

(*iv*)   The moist. There is no impending storm but the atmosphere is saturated with moisture, e.g. Cha Shih-piao, Tan Ch'ung-kuang 笪重光.

(*v*)   The rich and ornamental. Technically brilliant and all six methods of painting are employed, e.g. Lan Ying, Wang Chien 王鑑.

(*vi*)   The quiet and leisurely. All clichés are done away with and the statement is personal and direct, e.g. Shao Mi 邵彌, Shen Hao 沈顥.

(*vii*)   The full and rounded. The vertical brush is used to achieve a simple charm, e.g. Tsou Chih-lin 鄒之麟, Ch'eng Cheng-kuei.

(*viii*)   The finely-balanced. The expression is powerful though it lacks apparent design, e.g. Huang Tao-chou, Ni Yuan-lu.

Lui Hsieh 劉勰 in his *Wen Hsin Tiao Lung* 文心雕龍 discussed literary styles under eight categories. I have used his approach as a model for my discussions, but I do not wish to imply that these are the only eight styles in painting or that the painters mentioned are restricted to one particular style. Of all the painters of the late Ming, Shih-t'ao was the most versatile. Most of the others developed individual styles to an extreme and disregarded the "golden mean". In this way they all found original expressions.

When we study the poetry of these masters, we can often observe the relationship between their artistic and the literary styles. It was said that when Li Liu-fang painted, he "opened up an infinite vista with a few dots and washes" (*Keng-tzu Hsiao-hsia Chi* 庚子消夏記) and that his poetry "seemed casual, but revealed the depths of his being" (*Lieh Ch'ao Shih Chih* 列朝詩集). The poetry of Chung Hsing is profound and finely balanced, so are his paintings. Li Jih-hua 李日華's short poems are most elegant and greatly enhance his paintings. Ch'ien Ch'ien-i 錢謙益 said that Li's poetry was "made known through his paintings and not obscured by them". Hsü Fang 徐枋's brush work is orthodox and regular and so is his poetry, there being no trace of extravagance. Hung-jen's paintings are dry and lean, coldness emanates from his rocks. Similarly his poetry has the penetrating quality of fragrant snow. Fu Shan's poetry and calligraphy are completely unbridled and his paintings are like those of a madman. The poems of Chu Ta are like riddles, and his paintings are often allegories. Thus the poetry of painters is made of the same stuff as their painting and derives characteristic styles from highly individual personalities. Their poetry and painting explain each other. More examples can be given, but the ones mentioned will suffice.

Painting as Poetic Illustration—a few Examples

Paintings illustrating poems were popular among artists of this period. At times, early poetry also provided the themes. The following are a few examples:

(*i*)   Tai Pen-hsiao: an album of landscapes on the poems of Tu Fu 杜甫.
(Lu Hsin-yuan 陸心源, *Hsü Hsiang-li Kuan Kuo-yen Lu* 續穰梨館過眼錄)

(*ii*)   Fu Shan: Painting on a poem by Li Shang-yin 李商隱. (*Hsü Hsiang-li Kuan Kuo-yen Lu*)

(*iii*)   Shao Mi: Album on T'ang poems. (*Hsiang-li Kuan Kuo-yen Lu*) (*iv*)   Kao Chien 高簡: Album on T'ao Ch'ien 陶潛 poems. (Chih-lo Lou Collection)

(*v*)   Yeh Hsin 葉欣: One hundred paintings on poetic lines of T'ao Ch'ien. (*Tu-hua Lu* 讀畫錄)

(*vi*)   Cha Shih-piao: Album of eight leaves illustrating poems by Fang Heng-hsien. (*Ku-kung Shu-hua Lu* 故宮書畫錄)

Among the illustrations of contemporary verse, those by Tao-chi on the poems of Huang Yen-lü 黃研旅詩集 (in the Chih-lo Lou Collection) are well-known.

Literary Writings as Source Material for Art History

In the collected works of late Ming and early Ch'ing literati are often found poems and inscriptions addressed to contemporary artists. These writings provide valuable information for the history of painting.†

Conclusion

Literati of the Ming period eschew the artisan's brush. They wish to be scholars who paint rather than masters of painting. To them, nature is their garden, brush and ink their diversion, literature their outpouring and painting the gift among friends. Artistic activity is the means of expression of friendship. He who inscribes repays the painting with a poem, and he who paints uses (substitutes) the painting for a poem. Painting and poetry assuage longing. Wang Shih-chen recorded a poem by the painter Sung Chueh 宋珏: "When I came, the prunus was still lean and it was not yet time for the blossoms. After we parted the weeping willows were sprouting golden shoots. Should you think of me, look at my painting, you will see that west-wards beyond the plank bridge is where I live." To see the painting is to see the painter, and the use of the painting rises above a common feeling of friendship. Thus the best of paintings are often painted for best friends, and if the best friend is himself a painter then the painting would be better still, and its meaning even more profound, because it is painted for someone who understands. Ch'eng Sui inscribed on a painting dedicated to Cha Shih-piao: "Could I but share the enlighten-ment of my Mei-huo, who has found it in painting." Such words are not lightly spoken even among friends. As it is said in *Wen Hsin Tiao Lung*, "the message in music is hard to understand, and it is hard to meet someone who does. Perhaps it may be a thousand years before one finds such a person." The Ming scholar painted not for gain but for those who understood. This is what Chang I 張怡 in his preface to Chou Liang-kung's *Tu-hua-lu* meant when he talked of "finding meaning in it" and "the communion of spirits".

---

†In the original article, examples are quoted from the writings of Yü An-ch'i 俞安期 on Ting Yün-p'eng; Huang Tsung-hsi 黃宗羲 on Wei Hsueh-lien 魏學濂; Ch'üan Chu-wang 全祖望 on Huang Tao-chou; Ch'ien Ch'ien-i on Yang Wen-ts'ung; P'eng Sun-i 彭孫怡 on Ch'en Hung-shou; Shen Shou-hung 沈受弘 on Yün Ke; Wang Shih-chen 王士禎 on Ku Fu-chen; Fang Shou 方授 on Hsiao Yün-ts'ung; Yün Ke, Huang Shih-chai 黃石齋 and Li Yin-tu 李因篤 on Ch'eng Sui; T'ang Yen-sheng 湯燕生 on Hung-jen; Ch'ien Ch'ien-i on Shen Hao, Wang Shih-chen and Ch'eng Chou-liang 程周量 on Tai Pen-hsiao; and the inscriptions of Ta Shan 大汕 on his own paintings.—TRANS.

(For Chinese text see page 209)

Notes on Keng Chao-chung

By **Thomas Lawton**

ALTHOUGH RECOGNIZED as one of the most discerning of Ch'ing dynasty connoisseur-collectors, Keng Chao-chung 耿昭忠 (1640-1686) remains a strikingly enigmatic figure. His well-known collector's seals, which appear on many of the finest ancient Chinese paintings, are eloquent proof of his virtually infallible judgment in matters of quality and authenticity. That unusual degree of discernment is all the more remarkable in light of the fact that Keng died when only 47 *sui*.

Unlike many of his contemporaries, Keng Chao-chung apparently never compiled a catalogue of his extensive holdings. Examples of his colophons on scrolls that had been in his collection are extremely rare, lending a special importance to the few that have survived. Among those are four short colophons written by Keng Chao-chung on album leaves in the Freer Gallery. The first colophon appears opposite a round album leaf depicting plants and insects. The painting, a work attributed to the tenth-century court painter Huang Chü-ts'ai 黃居采 ,[1] was acquired by Charles Lang Freer in 1911.[2] (see cover of this issue). Keng Chao-chung's colophon (Pl. 87), written only two years before his death, can be rendered:

> "[In painting] grasses and insects, such artists as
> Ku Yeh-wang[3] and T'ang Kai[4] are the most able,

---

[1] The third son of Huang Ch'üan 黃筌 (active ca. 900-965), who was a native of Szechwan and a noted court painter in Shu specializing in precise, brightly colored representations of birds and flowers. Huang Chü-ts'ai continued the academic painting style developed by his father. In 965, Huang Chü-ts'ai accompanied the last ruler of Shu to the Sung capital of K'ai-feng. His work was greatly admired by Sung T'ai-tsung (r. 976-994) and he was appointed painter-in-attendance in the Imperial Painting Academy.

[2] Height: 9¼ inches (23.4 cm.); width: 9⅜ inches (23.8 cm.). Ink and color on silk. Another version of this composition appears in *Sung-jen hua-ts'e* 宋人畫册, pl. 77. That painting is attributed to an anonymous Sung artist. Imperial seals of the Ch'ien-lung (r. 1736-1795) and Chia-ch'ing (1796-1820) emperors are affixed to the album leaf.

[3] A native of Soochow, Ku Yeh-wang lived during the period of the Kingdom of Ch'en 陳 (557-588). He was a precocious scholar. His paintings seem always to have been rare. *Hsüan-ho hua-p'u* 宣和畫譜 (preface dated 1120) records only a single work by Ku, a scroll depicting insects and grasses.

[4] Little information is available concerning T'ang Kai other than that he worked during the Five Dynasties and that he excelled in painting animals, fruit and aquatic life.

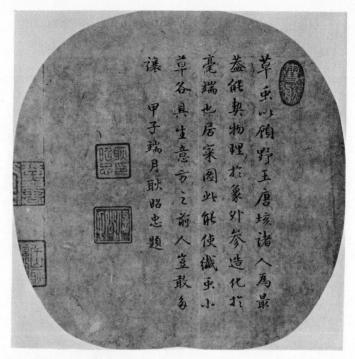

Plate 87 ALBUM LEAF carrying a painting attributed to Huang Chü-ts'ai (see cover of this issue). On this side, Keng Chao-chung's colophon: *"[In painting] grasses and insects, such artists as Ku Yeh-wang and T'ang Kai are the most able. . . ."*

because they can portray the inner nature of things through their outer form, and reveal the macrocosm in microcosmic images. In handling this type of subject matter, [Huang] Chü-ts'ai succeeds in imbuing minute insects and tiny blades of grass with vitality. When [Huang Chü-ts'ai] is compared to the earlier artists, how do they dare not yield? Keng Chao-chung inscribed in the *tuan* month of the *chia-tzu* year [i.e. February 15 – March 15, 1684]."

草蟲以顧野王唐垓諸人爲最。蓋能契物理於象外。
參造化於毫端也。居采圖此。能伎纖蟲小草各具生意。
方之前人。豈敢多讓。

甲子端月耿昭忠題

The three other colophons are written opposite well-known album leaves in the Freer collection.[5] The paintings and colophons were originally part of an album of eighteen leaves entitled, *Li-tai ming-pi chi-sheng* 歷代名筆集勝, all of which are recorded in P'ang Yüan-chi's 龐元濟 (ca. 1865-1949) catalogue, *Hsü-chai ming-hua lu* 虛齋名畫錄 (preface dated 1909), *chüan* 11:9a-15b. Fourteen more leaves from that album, now in the Hui-hua-kuan 繪畫館, Peking, are reproduced

[5]Reproduced: *Chinese Figure Painting* (Washington, D.C., 1973), entries 52 and 53. Osvald Sirén, *Chinese Painting: Leading Masters and Principles*, vol. III, pl. 265.

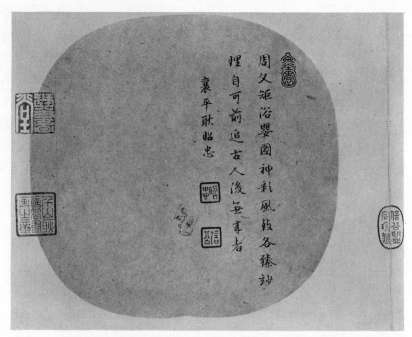

Plate 88   ALBUM LEAF carrying a painting by Chou Wen-chü. On this
side, Keng Chao-chung's colophon: *"In Chou Wen-chü's painting of [palace
ladies] bathing children...."*

and discussed in *Sung-jen hua-ts'e* 宋人畫册.[6] Unfortunately, none of
Keng Chao-chung's colophons on those paintings has been reproduced.
The whereabouts of the eighteenth painting from the album, a square
leaf attributed to Liang K'ai 梁楷 (active early 13th century), remains
unknown.

Two of the colophons (Plates 88, 89) are written on paper bearing
the seal *Chin-su-shan ts'ang-ching chih* 金粟山藏經紙. That seal is said
to have been found on Sung dynasty *sūtra* paper belonging to the
Chin-su Temple, located at the foot of Chin-su Mountain in Chekiang
province.

The colophon facing the first of the two leaves traditionally
attributed to the tenth-century court painter Chou Wen-chü 周文矩,[7]
(Pl. 88) can be rendered:

> "In Chou Wen-chü's painting of [palace ladies]
> bathing children, the countenance and manner of
> each attains the utmost in marvelousness and correct-

[6]Plates 1, 3, 5, 14, 16, 17, 27, 39, 53, 57, 79, 80, 86.

[7]Active from 916-975, Chou Wen-chü served as painter-in-attendance at the
court of Li Yü 李煜 (r. 961-976), the last ruler of Southern T'ang. The Sung
critic Mi Fei 米芾 (1036-1101) states that the only feature which distinguished
the work of Chou Wen-chü from that of the T'ang court painter Chou Fang 周昉
(active 780-810) was his use of *chan-pi* 顫筆, or "tremulous brushstroke". That
characteristic type of brushstroke is traditionally said to have been developed by
Li Yü for his calligraphy.

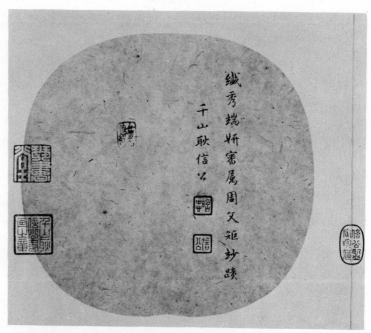

Plate 89 ALBUM LEAF carrying another painting by Chou Wen-chü. On this side, Keng Chao-chung's colophon: *"The delicacy, elegance, dignity and beauty. . . ."*

ness. [Chou Wen-chü] himself can emulate the ancient [masters] who preceded him, and [among] later [artists] none can approach him." Signed, "Keng Chao-chung of Hsiang-p'ing."[8]

周文矩浴嬰圖。神彩風致。各臻妙理。自可前追古
人。後無來者。

襄平耿昭忠

The inscription facing the second leaf (Pl. 89) reads:

"The delicacy, elegance, dignity and beauty [of the figures in this painting] are such as to prove [that the painting] belongs among the marvelous works of Chou Wen-chü". Signed, "Keng Chao-chung of Ch'ien-shan".[9]

纖秀端妍。審屬周文矩妙蹟。

千山耿信公

In the original album, the third colophon, written opposite a

[8]Hsiang-p'ing Hsien, located in present-day Liao-ning province.

[9]A spur of Ch'ang-pai Mountain 長白山, the Ch'ien-shan forms the mountainous spine of the Liao-tung Peninsula.

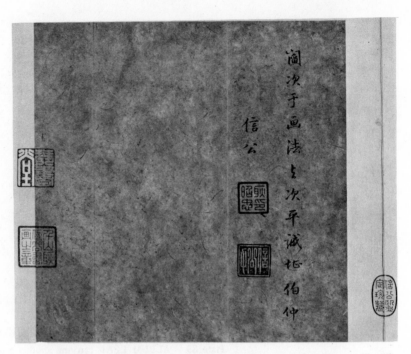

Plate 90   ALBUM LEAF carrying a landscape by Yen Tzu-yu. On this
side, Keng Chao-chung's colophon: *"Yen Tzu-yu's painting style. ..."*

landscape by Yen Tzu-yu,[10] appeared immediately after a leaf attributed
to his brother, Yen Tzu-p'ing 閻次平. Keng's colophon (Pl. 90) reads:

> "Yen Tzu-yu's painting style and [that of Yen]
> Tzu-p'ing [show the two album leaves are] surely
> worthy of the brothers." Signed, "Hsin-kung."

閻次于畫法與次平誠堪伯仲。

信公

Keng Chao-chung's calligraphy is neat, but undistinguished. His
comments about the individual paintings are frustratingly vague, pro-
viding no insight into his knowledge of Chinese aesthetics or any
indication of how he acquired the paintings. It is exactly this paucity
of information that explains, in part, why no study has ever been made
of the full extent of Keng Chao-chung's collection, how he assembled
it, or what happened to all of the paintings after his death. However,
some general information about the Keng family is known.[11]

[10] Younger son of Yen Chung 閻仲, who served as court painter under Sung
Hui-tsung (r. 1101-1126) and Sung Kao-tsung (r. 1127-1162). Both Yen Tzu-yu
and his elder brother, Yen Tzu-p'ing 閻次平, continued the style of their father
in painting landscapes and figures, but their work is said to have been more
refined. Both sons served as court painters under Hsiao-tsung 孝宗 (r. 1163-1189)
of Southern Sung.

[11] The best source available concerning the various members of the Keng
family in English is *Eminent Chinese of the Ch'ing Period*, pp. 415-417.

The Keng family were originally natives of Shantung province, but one of Keng Chao-chung's ancestors emigrated to Kai-chou 蓋州 in Liao-tung 遼東. No doubt the geographical proximity of their new home to the Manchu heartland was a compelling reason for the support which several generations of the Keng family gave to the Manchus during their conquest of China. His grandfather, Keng Chung-ming 耿仲明, was awarded the title of Huai-shun Wang 懷順王 in 1633, in recognition of his military victories in the Manchu cause. In 1642, when the Banner system was extended to the entire Chinese army on the Manchu side, Keng Chung-ming became a Chinese bannerman attached to the Plain Yellow Banner. As a reward for his victorious campaigns against the followers of Chu Yu-lang 朱由榔 (1623-1662), the Ming prince Kuei Wang 桂王, Keng Chung-ming received the title of Ching-nan Wang 靖南王 in 1648. In spite of Keng Chung-ming's many military accomplishments and his official honors, he chose to commit suicide on December 30, 1649, rather than face charges resulting from an inquiry into the actions of his subordinates in receiving and concealing runaway slaves.

Keng Chung-ming's eldest son, Keng Chi-mao 耿繼茂, was with him at the time he died and was placed in command of his father's troops. During his long career, Keng Chi-mao's brutal but successful actions against Ming loyalists won him many honors from the Manchu rulers. Keng Chi-mao strove to bind the fortunes of his family even more closely with those of the Manchu nobility; before his death in June, 1671, he witnessed influential marriages for his three sons. In their youth, all three sons had accompanied Keng Chi-mao on his military expeditions. But in 1654, Chi-mao petitioned the throne requesting that his eldest son, Keng Ching-chung 耿精忠, together with Keng Chao-chung, his second son, be sent to wait upon the Emperor. Keng Chao-chung was only 15 *sui* at the time. The early Manchu rulers understood the importance of strengthening their ties with Chinese sympathetic to their administration and Chi-mao's request was granted; the Emperor awarded both sons the title of *Tzu* 子 ("viscount") of the first rank. The Emperor also arranged marriages for the two sons. Keng Ching-chung was married to a daughter of Haoge 豪格 (1609-1648); Keng Chao-chung was married to the daughter of an Imperial Princess of the Second Degree, *To-lo hsien-chu* 多羅縣主, who was the grand-daughter of Prince A-pa-t'ai 阿巴泰 (1589-1646). As the husband of an Imperial Princess, Keng Chao-chung received the title *To-lo-o-fu* 多羅額駙, a title equivalent to that of *Fu-ma* 駙馬 under earlier dynasties.

According to the funerary epitaph composed by Hsü Ch'ien-hsüeh 徐乾學 (1631-1694) and recorded in *Kuo-ch'ao pei-ch'uan chi* 國朝碑傳集,[12] Keng Chao-chung was born during the second month of the *keng-chen* 庚辰 year of the Ch'ung-te 崇德 period (March 22/April 20, 1640) and died during the first month of the *ping-yin* 丙寅 year of the K'ang-hsi 康熙 period (January 24/February 21, 1686). Hsü also

___

[12]Chüan 6:10b-12b.

records that following his marriage, Keng Chao-chung was given the honorary position of *T'ai-tzu shao-pao* 太子少保 ("Junior Guardian of the Heir Apparent") and the title *Ho-she-o-fu* 和碩額駙. Subsequently, his honorary title was raised to that of *T'ai-tzu shao-shih* 太子少師 ("Junior Preceptor of the Heir Apparent"), and another honorary title, *Kuang-lu tai-fu* 光祿大夫 ("Minister of Banqueting"), was conferred upon him. Keng Chao-chung's first wife died when he was 23 *sui* and he then married a woman *née* Yü 喻, who received the title *I-p'in fu-jen* 一品夫人, a title normally given to the wife of a *Kuang-lu tai-fu*.

In 1656 Keng Chi-mao received imperial permission to send his third son, Keng Chü-chung 耿聚忠, to the court, where he was married to a daughter of Yolo 岳樂 (1625-1689). Like his brother, Keng Chü-cheng then received the title *Ho-she-o-fu* and the honorary position of *T'ai-tzu t'ai-pao*.

The fate of all members of the Keng family was seriously compromised by the precipitous actions of Keng Ching-chung. In 1671, on the death of his father, Keng Ching-chung was placed in charge of his father's posts and inherited the title *Ching-nan Wang*. In 1674, when as part of the San-fan Rebellion 三藩之亂 (1673-1681), Keng Ching-chung supported rebel forces in Fukien, the K'ang-hsi Emperor decreed that Keng Chao-chung and his younger brother, Chü-chung, be seized. But the following year an Imperial edict absolved the two brothers of any role in Keng Ching-chung's revolt and their former titles were restored.

In 1676 the rebel forces commanded by Keng Ching-chung took Ch'ao-chou 潮州 on the eastern border of Kwangtung province. Keng Chao-chung was awarded high military rank and ordered by the Emperor to go to Fukien to take over his brother's post. Finally, after considerable delay and negotiation, Keng Ching-chung surrendered his forces in November 1676.

In spite of the well-founded suspicion the Manchus must have felt toward Keng Ching-chung, the other members of the Keng family apparently remained in favor. In 1678 the Emperor permitted Keng Chao-chung to have the remains of his grandfather, Keng Ming-chung, reinterred in the family cemetery at Kai-chou, Liaotung. However, Manchu resentment against Keng Ching-chung for his part in the San-fan Rebellion finally resulted in his execution by quartering in Peking in 1682. His son, Keng Hsien-tso 耿顯祚, was decapitated, and the family's property was confiscated. Once again, both Keng Chao-chung and Keng Chü-chung were spared, probably because the Emperor honestly felt they had played no part in the uprising and because of the loyalty and military accomplishments of their father and grandfather.

During Keng Chao-chung's final illness, the K'ang-hsi Emperor sent medicines prepared by his own physicians, and when Keng died in 1686, he was buried with all the honors befitting his noble rank. He received the posthumous title *Chin-hsi* 勤僖. According to Hsü Ch'ien-hsüeh, it was Keng Chao-chung's son, Keng Chia-tso 耿嘉祚, who had him buried together with his first wife in T'ang Hsien 唐縣, Honan province.

Keng Chia-tso's seals occasionally appear on paintings together

with those of his father, suggesting that the collection remained intact
after Keng Chao-chung's death.[13] Further support for the assumption
that Keng's paintings were not immediately diapersed comes from the
report that Tao-chi 道濟 (1641-ca. 1720) was able to see the collection
during his visit to Peking from 1689-92, because of the influence of the
Manchu connoisseur Po-erh-tu 博爾都 (died 1701).[14] In addition, An
Ch'i 安岐 (ca. 1683-ca. 1744), who was an infant when Keng Chao-
chung died, mentions having seen a copy of *Hsia-ching shan-k'ou tai-tu
t'u* 夏景山口待渡圖 in his collection.[15] During the 18th century the
bulk of Keng's collection was acquired by the Ch'ien-lung Emperor.

These random facts reveal something of the unsettled social and
political world in which Keng Chao-chung lived. But they tell us virtually nothing about his keen interest in art collecting or about how he
managed to acquire such an impressive collection. Although Keng Chao-
chung's name is not recorded in any of the standard biographical
dictionaries of Chinese artists, there is at least one painting extant
attributed to him.[16] Keng Ching-chung's precipitous action in siding
with the southern rebels during the San-fan Rebellion appears to have
overshadowed every other event in the lives of that generation of the
Keng family. However, it is one of the ironies of history that if Keng
Ching-chung's infamy dominates in official records, the seals and
colophons of his younger brother, Keng Chao-chung, are considerably
more famous today. They have, in fact, come to be regarded by
scholars as reliable indications of quality.

[13]There is some confusion between the seals of Keng Chao-chung and those
of Keng Chia-tso illustrated in Victoria Contag and Wang Chi-ch'ien 王季遷, *Seals
of Chinese Painters and Collectors*, p. 564. Chia-tso and Hui-hou 會侯 are
erroneously listed as two of Keng Chao-chung's *hao*. Seals 1, 3, 8, 9, 12 and 15
are those of Keng Chia-tso. In the supplement, p. 674, seals 18, 19, 24 and 25
belong to Keng Chia-tso.

[14]Cheng Cho-lu 鄭拙廬, *Shih-t'ao yen-chiu* 石濤研究, Peking, 1961, p. 28.

[15]*Mo-yüan hui-kuan* 墨緣彙觀, *chüan* 3, entry on Tung Yüan 董源's *Hsiao-
hsiang t'u* 瀟湘圖.

[16]The large hanging scroll, executed in ink and color on silk, is an extremely
competent copy of a scroll entitled *Wen-hui t'u* 文會圖, now in the National
Palace Museum, Taiwan (reproduced: *Ku-kung ming-hua san-pai-chung*, pl. 92).
The Palace Museum scroll, which is attributed to Sung Hui-tsung, bears a number
of Keng Chao-chung's seals. indicating that it was once part of his collection
(*Ku-kung shu-hua lu, chüan* 5, p. 58). In his long inscription written on the upper
left section of his copy, Keng Chao-chung curiously describes his work as having
been based on a composition by Chou Wen-chü.

向　達：明清之際中國美術所受西洋之影響

European Influences on Chinese Art in the Later Ming and Early Ch'ing Period[†]

By Hsiang Ta

Translated by Wang Teh-chao

Plate 91　MAP OF CHINA, 1626. Colored Engraving by John Speede. Reproduced from *THE CHATER COLLECTION, Pictures Relating to China, Hongkong, Macao, 1655-1860,* by James Orange. Published by Thornton Butterworth Ltd., London, 1924.

[†]This article first appeared in *Tung-fang Tsa-chih* (東方雜誌), Vol. 27, No. 1 (Issue on Chinese Art I), January 10, 1930, and was later collected into *T'ang-tai Ch'ang-an yü Hsi-yü Wen-ming* (唐代長安與西域文明, Ch'ang-an and West Areas Culture in the Period of T'ang), Harvard-Yenching Press, Peiping, 1933, and San-lien Bookstore, Peking, 1957. In addition to the original footnotes, the English translation printed in these pages carries the translator's annotations, indicated by the sign *, which can be taken as supplementary notes.

I Introduction

AFTER THE ARRIVAL of Matteo Ricci (利馬竇 1552-1610), there was a period when Western learning was continuously introduced into China. The study of astronomy and mathematics, physical sciences and philosophy then flourished, reaching a climax at the time of Emperor K'ang-hsi and declining only in the reign of Emperor Ch'ien-lung. Early in the seventeenth century, the Jesuit mission had brought to Peking a collection of Western books of more than 7000 volumes[1] which can be compared unequivocally both in quality and quantity with Hsuan-tsang's celebrated collection of Buddhist works from India in the early T'ang dynasty. Though most of these books are no longer known today,[*] the magnitude of the contribution was obviously considerable. Many modern scholars, in fact, have devoted their energies to an exposition of the transmission of Western scholarship to China in the later Ming and early Ch'ing period, but few have done this with respect to fine arts. Based on the results of earlier studies by Chinese and overseas scholars, this article aims to elucidate the possible relationship between Chinese and Western art and its vicissitudes during the 200 years from the beginning of the reign of the Ming Emperor Wan-li to the end of the reign of the Ch'ing Emperor Ch'ien-lung.

---

[1] It was mentioned in Wang Cheng's *Ch'i-ch'i T'u-shu Lu-tsui* (王徵, 奇器圖說錄最) and Li Chih-tsao's "K'e Chih-fang Wai-chi Hsü" (李之藻, 刻職方外記序), "Shih Huan-yu-ch'uan Hsü" (釋寰有詮序) and "K'e Tien-hsueh Chu-han T'i-t'zu" (刻天學, 初函題辭). Both Wang and Li flourished in the late Ming period. Li also indicated that it was the French Jesuit Nicolas Trigault (金尼閣) who brought to China this collection of books.

[*] According to a study by Fang Hao (方豪), there were 757 titles in 629 volumes of the original collection still in existence in the library of the Pei T'ang (北堂 North Church) in Peking in 1940's. See Fang Hao "Pei T'ang T'u-shu kuan Ts'ang-shu Chih" (北堂圖書館藏書志), in *Fang Hao Liu-shih Tsu-ting Kao* (方豪六十自定稿), Vol. II, pp. 1840-46. Taipei, 1969.

II Traffic between East and West in the Late Ming and Early Ch'ing Period

IN THE FIFTEENTH and sixteenth centuries, both the East and the West made great efforts to try to communicate with each other. On China's side there were Cheng Ho's Seven Expeditions into the "Western Seas", reaching as far as Somaliland on the east coast of Africa and bringing the Chinese hegemony to a height which had never been reached in former times. On the part of Europe, Christopher Columbus reached America in 1492; Bartholomew Diaz discovered the Cape of Good Hope in 1486; Pedro de Caviiham discovered the Indian Ocean in 1487; Vasco da Gama arrived at Calicut on the southwestern coast of India in 1496. From that time on more and more Europeans came in succession and colonized the islands in the Indian Ocean and the territories along the coast of the subcontinent of India.

In 1514, a Portuguese named Jorge Alvares arrived at Shang-ch'uan Island in Kwangtung; in 1517, another Portuguese Rafaël Perestrello also arrived in Kwangtung; and in 1520, yet another Portuguese reached Canton and brought in his ship an envoy from the Portuguese Governor of Malacca to be sent to the Imperial Court in Peking. The coming of the Europeans to China, interrupted after the fall of the Yuan dynasty, was now resumed.[2] In the wake of the Portuguese came the Dutch, the Spanish, the English and the French, one after another. They chiefly assembled in Macao in the Hsiang-shan District of Kwangtung, but also appeared at coastal places such as Chang-chou, Ch'uan-chou, Ning-po, etc. In Kwangtung where most foreigners landed, a profitable foreign trade existed, and even the monthly emoluments of the provincial civil and military officials were partly

---

[2] Henri Cordier, Histoire Generale de la Chine, tom. III, Chaps. X-XIX.

Plate 92   VIEW OF CANTON c. 1780. Engraving. From *THE CHATER COLLECTION.*

paid with exotic goods. Under the reign of the Ming Emperor Chia-ching (1522-66) the trade was prohibited and, as a result, hardly any foreign ships arrived, which caused financial difficulties in both local government and private life. In 1535, the Portuguese were officially permitted to live in Macao (Ao-Ching in *Ming Shih*) where, in time, rows of high and spacious buildings were erected in exotic styles. Fukien as well as Kwangtung merchants crowded into Macao to do business with the Portuguese. Later on, more and more merchants from overseas came to Canton to trade and, henceforth, there was the rise of the "Thirteen *Kung-hang*" (Co-hongs) in Canton to carry out transactions with foreign traders. As the Hong merchants had a monopoly of foreign trade, they became very rich. A description was given by Ch'ü Ta-chün, a Cantonese scholar of the seventeenth century, in one of his well-known folk songs (*Kuang-chou Chu-Chi Tz'u*)[3] as follows:

> *In a rush the seafaring ships of government-enrolled merchants*
> *Sail through the Cross Gate straight to the two Oceans East and West.*
> *Out-going are the fine Kwang satins of five and eight threads;*
> *The Thirteen Hongs are heaped to the full*

with silver coins.

P'eng Yü-ling also said:[4]

> *Before the reign of Hsien-feng (1851-61), no other port was open to overseas trade, and foreign merchants crowded into Canton. There, many businessmen became very rich through skillful purchases and investments. For example, the Thirteen* Kung Hong, *which had a monopoly of the trade, accumulated an enormous wealth and were admired throughout the country. When there was a need to ask for subscriptions, millions would be raised in a moment.*

What Peng described concerns the period immediately preceding the reign of Hsien-feng, but there was probably no great difference in the early Ch'ing period as can be seen in Ch'ü Ta-chun's folk song quoted above. At that time, the Thirteen Hongs were not only known for their unrivalled wealth, but also widely admired for the architecture of their buildings which resembled those seen in Western paintings.[5] Western countries such as Denmark, Spain, France, the United States,

---

[3]Ch'ü Ta-chün, *Kwang-tung Hsin-yü* (廣東新語), Vol. XV, Article "Sha Tuan" (紗緞).

[4]P'eng Yü-ling, *P'eng Kang-chih Kung Tsou-kao* (彭剛直公奏稿), Vol. IV, "Hui-tsou Kwang-tung T'uan-lien Chüen-shu Shih-i Che" (會奏廣東團練捐輸事宜摺).

[5]Shen Fu (沈復), *Fu-sheng Liu-chi* (浮生六記, *Six Chapters of a Floating Life*), Vol. IV, "Lang-yu Chi-k'uai" (浪遊記快).

Sweden, Holland and Great Britain also built their factories in Canton.[6]

In the seventeenth century, Western missionaries also enthusiastically reported their discoveries in China when they returned to Europe. Chinese Classics, such as *The Great Learning* (*Ta Hsueh*) and *The Doctrine of the Mean* (*Chung Yung*), were translated into Western languages.[7]* It was not uncommon for Chinese converts to accompany Western missionaries to Europe. It has been said that Turgot's economic thought was deeply influenced by these Chinese whom he had met in Europe,[8] and that the doctrine of the European Physiocrats was also enriched with Chinese ideas.[9]

[6]H. F. MacNair, *Modern Chinese History: Selected Readings,* Chap. II, Section 5, "The Co-Hong and the Factories."

[7]A. Reichwein, *China and Europe*, p. 20. In Jules Aleni's (艾儒略) "Ta-hsi Li Hsien-sheng Hsin-chi" (大西利先生行蹟), it is said that "Matteo Ricci had translated the *Four Books* (四書) of the Chinese classics into Latin and sent back the manuscripts to his native land. It is owing to his effort that his countrymen, after reading his translations, know that the ancient Chinese classics could recognize the real source of life and never mistake superficials for essentials." Moverover, in *Mo-ching Chi* (墨井集), A. Pfister's (費賴之) *Notices biographiques et bibliographiques* is quoted as saying that, when Philippe Couplet (柏應理) was going back to Europe, "he arrived in Holland early in October, 1682, and thence went to Roma to present the four hundred books, which the Jesuits in China had translated from Chinese, to the Pope. The Pope was pleased and, by his order, the books were to be kept in the Papal Library as of great value."

*Of more recent studies related to the relevant subject, see Sueo Goto, *Chūgoku Shisō no Furansu Seizen* (後藤末雄, 中國思想のフランス西漸), new edition, 1969; Chu Ch'ien-chih, Chung-kuo Shih-hsian tui-yü Ou-chou Wen-hua Chih Ying-hsiang (朱謙之, 中國思想對於歐洲文化之影響), 1940; Wang Teh-chao, "Fu-erh-teh Chu-tso chung so-chieh chih chung-kuo," (王德昭, 伏爾德著作中所見之中國) *New Asia Journal* (新亞學報), Vol. IX, No. 2, 1970.

[8]Li Yung-lin, "Ching-chi Hsueh-che Tu-erh-k'e yü Chung-kuo Ch'ing-nien Hsueh-che chih Kuan-hsi," (李永霖, 經濟學者杜爾克與中國青年學者之關係), *Pei-ching Ta-hsueh She-hui Ko-hsueh Chi-kan* (北京大學社會科學季刊), Vol. I, No. 1. In it are also mentioned other Chinese christians who visited Europe in the seventeenth and eighteenth centuries.

[9]A. Reichwein, *China and Europe*, pp. 101-109, "The Phsiocrats."

III   The Appearance of Western Missionaries and Western Art in China

ST. FRANCIS XAVIER, the Bishop of Goa, arrived at Shang-ch'uan Island and died there without fulfilling his wish to preach the Gospel in China. Three years after his death, Dominicans, Augustinians and Franciscans came to Canton or Fukien occasionally to preach, but, as a rule, were soon expelled. In 1579, the Jesuit Michael Ruggieri arrived in Canton;[10] and two years later, Matteo Ricci came to China. It is from that time on that Catholicism began to take root in China and, as a result, the introduction of Western learning ensued. In fact, it was Matteo Ricci who first introduced Western arts into China. In his memorial to Emperor Wan-li in 1600, Matteo Ricci wrote:

> Your Majesty, I herewith humbly present before your Royal Presence one portrait of our Heavenly Lord, two portraits of our Holy Mother, one copy of the Bible, one cross inlaid with pearls, two clocks, one copy of the World Atlas, and one clavichord. These are all things of little value. We present them only because they have been brought to China from the Far West, which makes them a little different from other things.

The portraits which Matteo Ricci presented are, therefore, the first Western artistic works ever known to have been introduced into China. The French sinologist P. Pilliot, judging from a description in Chiang Shao-wen [shu]'s *Wu-sheng Shih Shih* (姜紹聞[書], 無聲詩史,* History of Speechless Poetry), considered that this was the only provable occasion of Matteo Ricci's present-

[10]Hsiao Jo-se, *Tien-chu Chiao Ch'uan-hsin Chung-kuo Kao* (蕭若瑟, 天主教傳行中國號), Vol. I, pp. 103-112.

*The author made a mistake in the designation of the author of *Wu-sheng Shih Shih* (無聲詩史). It is Chiang Shao-shu (姜紹書), not Chiang Shao-wen (姜紹聞).

ation of portraits. Chiang's description is as follows:[11]

> The Portrait of the Heavenly Lord of the Western countries, which Matteo Ricci brought to China with him, depicts a woman carrying a child in her arms. The facial features and the lines of clothing look like images of real things in a mirror, vividly alive. The dignity and elegance of the figures are beyond the technical capability of Chinese painters to produce.

What Chiang designated as the portrait of the Heavenly Lord is in fact a portrait of the Holy Mother. The confusion was due to his lack of knowledge of the Christian tradition. Also in the reign of Wan-li, Ku Ch'i-yuan (顧起元) had a chance to see the portraits brought by Matteo Ricci. Ku said:[12]

> Matteo Ricci, a European, with fair skin and curly beard and deep eyes coloured yellow like a cat's, came to Nanking and is now living in a barrack west of the Cheng-yang Gate. Ricci knows Chinese. He said that his countrymen worship a Heavenly Lord who is the Creator of the universe and all things in it. The Heavenly Lord is presented in pictures as a little child carried in the arms of a woman called the Heavenly Mother. The pictures are painted in five colors on copper plates. The features are lifelike; the bodies, arms and hands seem to protrude tangibly from the picture. The concavities and convexities of the face are visually no different from a living person's. When people asked how this was achieved, he replied: "Chinese painting depicts the lights (Yang) but not the shades (Yin). Therefore, when you look at it, people's faces and bodies seem to be flat, without concavities and convexities. Painting in our country is executed with a combination of shades and lights, so faces are presented with high and low lights, and hands and arms all look round. A person's face, when it faces the light straight on, will be all bright and white. When it turns sideways, then the side which faces the light will be white, and on the other side which does not face the light, the recessed parts of the eyes, ears, nose and mouth will all have dark shadows. Because the portrait painters of our country know this method and use it, they can make their portraits indistinguishable from the living person." Ricci brought with him a great number of books in which every leaf of white paper is printed on both sides, with words all running horizontally. The paper is thick and strong like our Yunnan rag paper and the printing as well as the ink used is very fine. There are incidentally illustrations [engravings] in which figures and buildings are exquisitely executed in lines as fine as thread or human hair....

Ku's description was not only more detailed than that in Wu-sheng Shih Shih, but also gave an illustration of the Western principle of using chiaroscuro to represent light and shade in painting. (Kuo-ch'ao Hua-cheng Lu 國朝畫徵錄, Eminent Painters of the Imperial [Ch'ing] Dynasty, also referred to the same incident but not in accounts as detailed as Ku's. See a reference in the concluding part of this article.) Western paintings and the Western principles of painting were, therefore, all first introduced into China by Matteo Ricci. Also, from Ku's description, we know that upon Ricci's arrival in China, he had brought with him works of art which included not only portraits of Jesus and the Virgin Mary, but also Western engravings, which also became known to the Chinese literati. The engravings represented a variety of topics including human beings and buildings. In addition, Ku said:[13]

> Later the priest Joao da Rocha [羅儒望], a junior of Matteo Ricci's, came to Nanking. In intelligence Rocha could not compare with Ricci, but the objects he brought with him were similar to Ricci's.

[11]P. Pelliot, "La Peinture et le Gravure Européenne en Chine au temps de Mathieu Ricci" (T'oung Pao, 1922, pp. 1-18).

[12]Ku Ch'i-yuan, K'o-tso Chui-yü (顧起元, 客座贅語), Vol. VI, "Li-ma-tou" (利瑪竇傳).

[13]Ibid.

Therefore we know that, in general, the missionaries who arrived in China after Ricci and made Nanking their working base often brought with them Western paintings. As the fashion spread, it is reasonable to suppose that Chinese painters would be impressed and would respond to its influence.

Little is known now about the engravings brought in by Matteo Ricci. However, in Ch'eng Ta-yueh's work, *Mo Yuan* (程大約, 墨苑, Elect Specimens of Ink), four Western religious pictures were included, which may be the earliest existing Western artistic works brought in by the missionaries in the Ming period, and still known to us. The four engravings are: (1) Christ and St. Peter, (2) Christ and the Disciples on the Road to Emmaus, (3) the Destruction of Sodom, and (4) Christ in the Arms of the Holy Mother. Interpretations in Chinese and Romanized script are attached to the first three pictures. All four engravings were given to Ch'eng Ta-yueh by Matteo Ricci and then incorporated by Ch'eng into his *Mo Yuan*. Very

probably, these were the kind of engravings carved in the illustrated books which Ku Ch'i-yuan described. *Mo Yuan*'s four engravings were lately reprinted in collotype and published by Ch'en Yuan (陳垣) in 1927, with the title *Ming-chi chih Ou-hua Mei-shu chi Lo-ma-tzǔ Chu-yin* 明季之歐化美術及羅馬字注音 (Westernized Arts and the Romanization of Chinese in the Later Ming Period). Ch'en wrote a colophon at the end of the collotype copy, of which the following is a summary:

The above four Western religious pictures and three texts appear in Ch'eng-shih Mo Yuan (程氏墨苑), *following page 35, Vol. VIb, but without page numbers, because they were added after the book had already been printed. There is also a goodwill address from Matteo Ricci in Vol. III, separately paginated for the same reason. Among the existing copies of* Mo Yuan *known to us,*

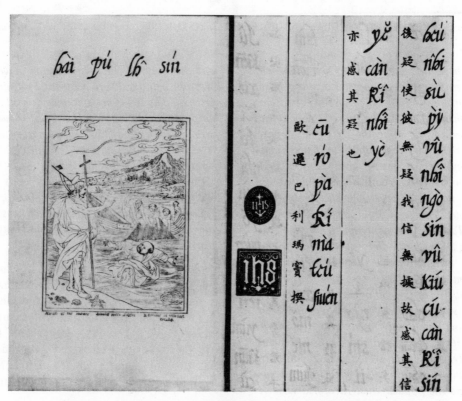

Plate 93   CHRIST AND ST. PETER, with interpretations in Chinese and Romanized script. From the *Ch'eng-shih Mo Yuan*, by Ch'eng Ta-yueh.

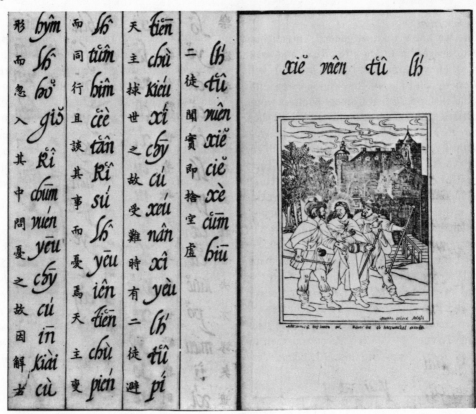

Plate 94   CHRIST AND THE DISCIPLES ON THE ROAD TO EMMAUS. From the *Ch'eng-shih Mo Yuan.*

some have the pictures but no text and some have neither. The expurgation must have been made at times when an anti-Christian movement was rife. The present copy is the treasure of the Ming-hui Lu (鳴晦廬) collection of the Wang family in T'ung-hsien, rare indeed for having both pictures and texts intact. Mo Yuan is composed of six parts, namely: Heaven, Earth, Personages, Precious Things, Confucianism, Buddhism and Taoism. The denominative term Tzu-huang (緇黃, black and yellow robes) on the book margin means that Buddhism and Taoism are combined into one part, with Catholicism at the end of this part. When Mo Yuan was compiled, Matteo Ricci had been in China for only five or six years, yet in the eyes of the Chinese literati, Catholicism had already won a status comparable with both Buddhism and Taoism. From this one can imagine the popular trust Ricci had won. It is not surprising that Western paintings appeared in China in the later Ming period,

but this must be the only occasion in which Western paintings were accepted by Chinese artists, adapted on stationery, and incorporated into a book. The use of romanization to respell the Chinese explanatory notes is also new. When Nicolas Trigault (金尼閣) wrote his Hsi-ju Erh-mu Tzu (西儒耳目資, Phonological and Morphological Aids for Western Scholars to Learn Chinese), he followed the same method, which was believed at that time to be the easiest way to learn Chinese characters . . . .

As Ch'en's colophon was mainly a piece of scholarly writing on source criticism with few comments on the four pictures themselves, Hsu Ching-hsien (徐景賢) followed up at a later time with an article entitled "明季之歐化美術及羅馬字注音考釋" (Exegesis to Ch'en Yuan's Westernized Arts and the Romanization of Chinese in the Later Ming Period),[14] in which he gave a compendious trans-

[14] Hsu's article was published in the monthly *Hsin Yueh* (新月), Vol. I, No. 7.

lation of the Latin words on the four religious pictures in *Mo Yuan* and suggested that the Madonna which Matteo Ricci had presented to the Ming Emperor and the one on which Hsu Kuang-ch'i (徐光啟) had contributed an encomium[15] were the same picture as that incorporated into *Mo Yuan*. According to Ku Ch'i-yuan's account, this suggestion is groundless. The Madonna Hsu Kuang-ch'i had seen in Nanking must be the one Ku had seen in the same city, but the picture presented to the royal court could not be such a very modest engraving. Moreover, as Ricci said clearly in his memorial, that picture was brought to China all the way from the West, while the engraving in *Mo Yuan* was in fact produced in the East (see below). One can see, therefore, that the two could not be the same.

Both Ch'en's colophon and Hsu's exegesis made no effort to trace the origin of the four pictures. As we know, B. Laufer has discussed the Western religious pictures in *Mo Yuan* in his article "Christian Arts in China", and in 1922 P. Pelliot wrote an article on the introduction of Western paintings and engravings into China in the time of Matteo Ricci.[16] The latter ascribes the original of the picture which Ricci gave to Ch'eng Ta-yueh to the authorship of Jean Nicolao, a Jesuit missionary in Japan. Nicolao, an Italian Jesuit, arrived in Japan in 1592. He taught painting to Japanese youths and later worked in the Seminaire des Peintures established by the Jesuits in Nagasaki. At the bottom of the Madonna in *Mo Yuan*, there is a line of Latin which reads *in Sem Japo 1597*. Here, *Sem* is an abbreviation of *Seminaire*, and *Japo*, *Japon*. In 1597 Nicolao was still working in Japan. The picture, therefore, must be an engraving made in 1597 by another Jesuit, based on the original work of Nicolao. It fell by chance into Ricci's hands and the latter gave it to Ch'eng. This hypothesis made by P. Pelliot is a very likely one,

and a useful supplement to both Ch'en's and Hsu's expositions.

Besides the portraits of Christ and the Holy Mother presented to the imperial court by Matteo Ricci and the four religious pictures given by Ricci and printed in *Mo Yuan*, pictures and statues were also presented to the imperial court by Joannes Adam Schall von Bell (湯若望). In Huang Po-lu's (黃伯祿) *Cheng-chiao Feng-pao* (正教奉褒, The Holy Religion Praise) there is an account of that occasion, which reads as follows:

In the 13th year of Ch'ung-chen 崇禎 *[1640], in November, Adam Schall presented to the royal court a fine sheepskin album of colored pictures illustrating the life of Christ and a set of colored statues cast in plaster, depicting Christ and the Adoration of the Kings. These were gifts from the Prince of Bavaria [Germany], who sent them to China and asked Adam Schall to present them to the Ming Emperor. Adam Schall, after adding in neat Chinese characters an annotation to each of the holy stories in the pictures, took them to the court himself and presented them to the Emperor respectfully.*

These pictures presented by Adam Schall were later engraved and published, but it is not known whether there are still copies in existence. In Yang Kuang-hsien's collected anti-Christian work, *Pu-te-i Shu* (不得已書, I Cannot Do Otherwise), there is an article entitled "Lin T'ang Jo-wang Chin-ch'eng Tu-hsiang Shu" (臨湯若望進呈圖像說, An Explanatory Note to the Copies of the Pictures Presented by Adam Schall). In the introduction to this article, Yang wrote:

After my letter to Mr. Hsü [Chih-chien, 許之漸] had been sent out, I regretted that, when my P'i-hsieh Lun *(闢邪論, Writings to Expose the Evils) was written, I failed to put the pictures printed by Adam Schall at the head of the treatise. The pictures depict how the Hebrews applauded Jesus and how Jesus was nailed to death by law. These pictures would make all people in the world know that Jesus was put to death as a convicted criminal, so that not only would scholar-officials not write prefaces for their [Chris-*

---

[15] In "Hsu Wen-t'ing Kung Hsin-shih" (徐文定公行實) it is said that, "in the autumn of 1603, the Honourable [Hsu Kuang-chi, 徐光啟] was again in Nanking. As he had friendship with Matteo Ricci, he went over to the latter's place to pay a visit. Ricci was not in, but [Hsu], when he entered Ricci's house, saw a portrait of the Madonna. His spirit seemed suddenly to soar to the supernatural and was unconsciously converted."

[16] See Note 11.

tian] writings, but people of the lower classes would also be ashamed to believe in that kind of faith. The album Adam Schall presented to the imperial court is composed of 64 leaves of writings and 48 pictures; an annotation was put on the left side of every picture. Being unable to reproduce all the pictures, I copy only three pictures and their respective annotations for the present moment. They are the people applauding Jesus, Jesus being nailed on the cross, and Jesus on the cross. This will show all the world that Jesus was not an orderly and law-abiding person, but a subversive rebel leader, who was convicted and executed. The annotations are put to the left of the pictures.

The three pictures are copied from the original Nos. XXVIII "The Triumphal Entry", XLII "The Crucifixion" and XLIII "Jesus on the Cross." Since Adam Schall's original pictures have now disappeared, it is only in these copies in *Pu-te-i* that one can still gain some idea of their appearance. But on close examination, it can be seen that the presentation of facial features, and especially also the lance and halberd in picture XLII and the sword in picture XLIII, have all been sinicized and lost their original European characteristics, unlike the four pictures in *Mo Yuan*, which still keep intact the main features of the original. However, it is also understandable that, as *Mo Yuan*'s illustrations were the work of the painter Ting Yun-p'eng (丁雲鵬) and the sculptor Huang Lin (黃鏻), both great masters of the time, and as the work itself purported to be an artistic object designed for the adornment of a scholar's studio, the pictures therefore must be refined and enjoyable. On the other hand, *Pu-te-i*, being compiled in a hurry for the purpose of propaganda, was bound to be far inferior to *Mo Yuan* in quality. But as the main features of some of Adam Schall's pictures are known to us only through these copies in *Pu-te-i*, the fragments thus preserved are therefore still invaluable.

Western paintings brought into China in the later Ming period are mostly religious paintings, because the missionaries knew that the Chinese people in general were fond of paintings and thus made use of paintings to propagate their religion. In both Matteo Ricci's Latin work *The Christian*

Plate 95   The Triumphal Entry

FROM THE PU-TE-I SHU,
by Yang Kuang-hsien:

Expedition into China (De Christiana expeditione apud Sinas) published by Trigault in 1615, and Franciscus Sambias (畢方濟)'s Chinese work *M'eng-ta Hua-ta** (夢答畫答, Discourses on Dream and Painting) written in 1629, it is related that the use of Western paintings and engravings was very helpful in propagating Christianity in China. The same indication is also seen in a letter sent to Europe by Nicolaus Longobardi (龍華民) in 1598, in which Longobardi made a request for more pictorial books, explaining that the Chinese people were very fond of Western paintings because the very

---

*The two discourses are mutually complemental and were co-published in a book. See Hsu Tsung-tse, *Ming-ch'ing Chien Yeh-su-hui Shih I-chu T'i-yao* (徐宗澤，明清間耶穌會士譯著提要), pp. 340-341, reprint, 1958.

Plate 96   Jesus on the Cross

Plate 97   The Crucifixion

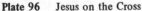

Copies of three engravings originally presented to the court by Johannes
Adam Schall von Bell.

life-like presentation of lights and shades in Western paintings was lacking in Chinese painting.[17]

In the later Ming period the number of Western paintings brought into China must have been considerable but no missionary who was also skilled in painting was known to have taught painting to Chinese artists.[18] Not until the early Ch'ing period

did the Imperial Studio begin to have Western missionaries serving in it, among whom the most famous were Joseph Castiglione (郎世寧) and Ignatius Sickelparth (艾啟蒙). Castiglione, whose family had made painting a profession for generations, was an Italian. He came to Peking in the 54th year of the reign of Emperor K'ang-hsi (1715) and was immediately called to the service of the palace; he died in the 31st year of the reign of Emperor Ch'ien-lung [1766].[19] One of his

[17]Ibid.

[18]Seigai Omura (大村西崖) wrote in his *Shina Bijutsu Shi* (支那美術史) that, "in the year of 1582, Matteo Ricci, an Italian Jesuit, arrived in China. He was also versed in painting and capable of portraying Madonnas." (Ch'en Pin-ho tr. *Chung-kuo Mei-shu Shih* 陳彬龢譯, 中國美術史, p. 196). It is not known on what evidence did Omura make this statement, as no sources known to the author [Hsiang Ta] have ever mentioned that Ricci was also able in painting.

[19]In Huang Po-lu's *Cheng-chiao Feng-pao* (黃伯祿, 正教奉襃), it is recorded that J. Castiglione died in 1764. But, according to P. Pelliot's "Les Conquêtes de l'Empereur de la Chine" (*T'oung Pao*, 1920-1922, pp. 183-274), as late as in July, 1765, Castiglione had still a letter sent to Europe, instructing how the "Triumph over the Dzungars and the Hui-pu" should be engraved. The date given in *Cheng-chiao Feng-pao*, therefore, must be wrong.

Plate 98 THE IMPERIAL ARMY SURPRISES TA QUA TSI, 1755. Engraving from "Triumph over the Dzungars and the Hui-pu". Hong Kong Museum of Art.

commentators said that he "is skilled in painting flowers, birds and animals, executed in Western methods." Again, "Castiglione's painting is rooted in Western techniques, complemented with Chinese methods. He can give his flowers a very life-like air, which makes him so much greater than other mediocre Western painters who can only adhere to traditional standards." In the Ch'ing palace catalogue *Shih-ch'ü Pao-chi* (石渠寶笈), 56 of Castiglione's works were recorded, of which most were paintings of flowers, birds and animals, with horses as the most favored subject. Among the 56 works, two hand scrolls depicting scenes on the battlefield represented a part of the great composition "Triumph over the Dzungars and the Hui-pu (回部, Moslem tribes)".[20] The hand scrolls were produced in the 20th (1755) and the 24th (1795) year of the reign of Emperor Ch'ien-lung respectively. It was in the 30th year of Ch'ien-lung (1765), after the conquest of the Dzungars and the Hui-pu, that the Emperor selected a number of Western missionaries from those serving in the Imperial Academy to record the important battles in painting, with the

purpose of making his military achievements remembered forever. The paintings were sent to France to be engraved. The French scholar Henri Cordier describes the matter as follows:[21]

There are altogether four paintings depicting the conquest of Dzungaria. Three of them were first commissioned from Joseph Castiglione, Ignatius Sickelparth and Jean Denis Attiret (王致誠), *all Jesuit missionaries serving in the Imperial Academy. Later, as they proceeded too slowly with their work, another Italian, Giuseppe Panzi* (潘廷璋), *was added to the team. The fourth was commissioned from an Augustinian missionary, Jean Damascéne* (安德義). *When the paintings were completed, Emperor Ch'ien-lung, demanding perfection, wanted them to be engraved in Europe. He decreed that the Governor-General of Kwangtung handle the matter. At first the Governor-General planned to send the paintings to England, but the Bishop of Kwangtung, J. Louis le Febvre,*

[20]Hu Ching, *Kuo-ch'ao Yuan-hua Lu* (胡敬, 國朝院畫錄), Vol. I.

[21]Henri Cordier, op. cit., Tom. III, pp. 349-350, and P. Pelliot, "Les Conquêtes de l'Empereur de la Chine."

persuaded him to send them to France, maintaining that French art was supreme in Europe and that people there were very competent in this work. On 26th, the Fifth Month of the 30th Year of Ch'ien-lung (July 13, 1765), the paintings were sent to France with the permission of the Emperor. After their arrival, the Director of the Royal Academy of Painting, Marquis de Marigney, commissioned the work from Charles Nicolas Cochin and recruited a group of well-known engravers, such as Le Bas, Saint Aubin, B.L. Prevot, Aliamet, Masqulier, Née and Choffard, to work under him. The whole set of engravings was completed and sent back to China in 1774. When they were presented, the Emperor, on seeing them, spoke highly in their praise.

One of Castiglione's paintings still in existence is the *Scroll of 100 Horses*. In this painting, the horses are presented in all kinds of motions and postures, crouching, stretching, bending, leaning, and the use of a combination of lights and shades is completely in the Western style. In *Shih-ch'ü Pao-chi*, nine paintings by Sickelparth are recorded. It is said in Chinese writings that Sickelparth was at his best in painting birds and animals.[22]

At the time of K'ang-hsi and Ch'ien-lung, there was a considerable number of Western missionaries serving in the Imperial Studio and the Imperial Observatory. Under their influence there emerged artists such as Chiao Ping-chen (焦秉貞) who successfully combined the Eastern and Western traditions in pictorial art, initiated a new school of Ch'ing court painting and became its first master.

When a British embassy was sent to the Ch'ing court at the time of Ch'ien-lung, among the presents it brought were fourteen French tapestries of cut silk, of which four are still in existence. The designs on these tapestries illustrate European figures in color. This is another example of Western works of art introduced into China in the early Ch'ing period whose history can be traced.

[22] See *Kuo-ch'ao Yuan-hua Lu*, Vol. II. There are eight scrolls of horses painted by Sickelparth still kept in the Ku-wu Ch'en-lieh So (古物陳列所, Gallery of Antiquities) in Peking. He also painted in 1771 a picture entitled "Hsiang-shan Chiu-lao Tu" (香山九老圖, Nine Elders in the Mount Fragrant). There were in it Nine Military Elders, Nine Civil Elders, and Nine Retired Elders. The celebrated painter Tsou I-kuei (鄒一桂) was one of the Nine Retired Elders. See Wu Chang-yuan, *Ch'en-yuan Chih-lüeh* (吳長元, 宸垣識略), Vol. XI.

Plate 99 THE IMPERIAL ARMY FOUGHT TA QUA TSI ON THE BANK OF THE RIVER D'ELY, 1755. Engraving from "Triumph over the Dzungars and the Hui-pu". Hong Kong Museum of Art.

IV   Western Portraiture
in Later Ming and Early Ch'ing Painting

AS WE KNOW, in later Ming and early Ch'ing, Western churchmen who came to China as missionaries often made use of religious paintings as a medium of conversion, catering to the known tastes of the Chinese people. Quite a few Western missionaries who came to the East were versed in painting,[23] and, in the early Ch'ing period, a considerable number of them served in the Imperial studio. Moreover, churches everywhere set up holy images for religious worship, and among the Chinese converts there were numerous good painters. All these factors made Western influence in Chinese art certain and inevitable. It is first seen in portrait painting and, according to the opinion of modern scholars, the first painter who adopted Western techniques in painting portraits was Tseng Ching (曾鯨), a Fukienese of the later Ming period. Chiang Shao-wen [shu] wrote of Tseng as follows:[24]

> Tseng Ching, courtesy-named Po-ch'en (波臣), was a native of P'ut'ien (莆田), Fukien, but took up residence in Nanking. He was a man of neat and handsome looks, and of noble appearance. Everywhere he went, he always made his abode a pleasant residence, with graceful verandas and rooms built on an elegant and magnificent plan. The portraits he painted were all like images reflected in a mirror, with the expressions of the models skillfully captured. His use of color was splendid, and he could make the eyes of his figures look very vivid, so that their every look or glance, smile or frown, though only on paper or silk, showed full of true life. His skill was such that not even Chou Fang (周昉)'s portrait of Chao Tsung (趙縱) could surpass it. Whether the subject were a dignitary or a recluse, a beauty or a religious man, every inch of beauty or ugliness in his portraiture resembled the real person. When he was face to face with his subject, he would always concentrate his whole attention on it until the self and the subject would become interpenetrated. Every time a portrait was being painted, he would never tire of adding washes and shades, often tens of times, until he achieved real artistry. It is therefore not without reason that Tseng Ching was unequalled among contemporary artists and was famous far and wide. He died at the age of eighty-three.

In his Kuo-ch'ao Hua-cheng Lu, Chang Keng (張庚) also wrote:[25]

> There are two schools of portraiture: one puts more emphasis on brush strokes; only after the structure has been worked out in lines of ink are colors applied to represent different sensuous qualities in the subject, while the spirit of the portrait has already been manifested in the brush strokes. This is the school of the Fukienese painter Tseng Ching. Another school uses at first a little light ink to make out a rough sketch of the main features of the subject, but finishes wholly with color washes. This is the method

---

[23] According to Yin Kuang-jen and Chang Ju-lin's Ao-meng Chi-lüeh, (印光任, 張汝霖著, 澳門記略), Vol. II, there was a world atlas in the St. Paul's in Macao. (In Section "Ao Fan" 澳番, Foreigners in Macao.) The same atlas was also mentioned in Ch'ü Ta-chün's Kwang-tung Hsin-yü, Vol. II. It has been said above that in the church in Nanking, there were portraits of Christ and the Holy Mother. The following description is found in Chao I's Yen-pao Tsa-chi (趙翼, 簷曝雜記), Vol. II: "The Catholic Church is situated inside the Hsüan-wu Gate (宣武門). The portrait of Christ worshipped in the church looks like a handsome youth. His name is Yeh-su, and he is the holy one of his countrymen. The portrait was painted on the wall, but looks like a round body protruding from the wall. (In the article describing Western telescopes and music instruments.) A similar description can be seen in the same author's rhyme "Inspect Western Music Instruments with Friends" in Ou-pei Shih-ch'ao (甌北詩鈔). In Wu Chang-yuan's Ch'en-yuan Chih-lüeh, Vol. VII, it was also said that "people worship in church the portrait of Christ, which, though it is a painting, looks like a statue, with its ears and nose protruding as if they were parts of a living body."

[24] Chiang Shao-wen [shu], op. cit., Vol. IV, "Tseng Ching".

[25] Chang Keng, Kuo-ch'ao Hua-cheng Lu (張庚, 國朝畫徵錄), Vol. II, biographies of Ku Ming (顧銘) et al.

which painters in Kiangnan (江南) *have taught for generations; and in it Tseng Ching was also well versed. I have seen a portrait of Hsiang Yuan-pien* (項元汴) *painted in ink by Tseng Ching, the spirit of which shows the same qualities of any painting in color. We can understand, therefore, why in painting brush strokes are to be emphasized.*

Hence in Ch'en Heng-k'o (陳衡恪)'s opinion, "With Tseng Ching's work, a new approach was initiated in the tradition of spiritual rendition [in Chinese painting]. Tseng put more emphasis on brush strokes than on color, and applied washes and shades, which shows that he was influenced by Western painting."[26] Seigai Omura (大村西崖), a Japanese historian, also said:

In the 10th year of the reign of Wan-li [1582], Matteo Ricci, an Italian Jesuit missionary, came to China. He was versed in painting, and adept in the portraiture of the Holy Mother of Jesus. Tseng Ching adapted Ricci's method of painting portraits and inaugurated the so-called Kiangnan (江南) *school of portraiture.[27]*

Matteo Ricci arrived in China at the time when Tseng Ching was living in Nanking. The Western-styled portraits of Christ and the Holy Mother, which were set up in the church in Nanking and seen by Ku Ch'i-yuan and Hsu Kuang-ch'i, would also have been seen by Tseng Ching. Tseng's usual practice of applying washes and shades, often tens of times, in painting a portrait, as Chiang Shao-wen [shu] tells us, was a method which Chinese painters had never known before. Tseng had abruptly initiated a new school of portraiture, whose method was more or less close to Western painting. Accordingly, we can believe what Ch'en Heng-k'o and Omura had said, that Tseng had successfully combined the Chinese and Western elements in his art to make it his own. But Omura was obviously mistaken in asserting that Matteo Ricci came to the East in 1582 and that Tseng's art pertained to the Kiangnan school. As regards the question whether Ricci was also versed in painting or not, since no positive written proofs have ever been found and the evidence on which Omura made his assertion is not known, we can only leave the matter unresolved.

Tseng Ching's art had a great number of followers, among whom Hsieh Pin (謝彬), Kuo Kung (郭鞏), Hsu I (徐易), Shen Shao (沈韶), Liu Hsiang-sheng (劉祥生), Chang Ch'i (張琦), Chang Yuan (張遠), Shen Chi (沈紀) are the most well-known. Hsu Yao-p'u (徐瑤圃) was rightly rated as a talented pupil of Shen Chi: not only did his portraits closely resemble the real persons, but also in them the brush strokes, the ink and the washes merged completely into a whole.[28] In the time of K'ang-hsi and Ch'ien-lung, the school of Tseng Ching undoubtedly occupied a leading position in portraiture. When Shang-kuan Chou (上官周)'s "Wan-hsiao T'ang Hua-chuan" (晚笑堂畫傳, Illustrated Biographies from the Wan-hsiao Hall) appeared in the time of Ch'ien-lung, the consummation of Tseng Ching's art had been achieved.

As has been said above, the school of Tseng Ching put more emphasis on brush strokes than on color and applied washes and shades. When a picture was being worked out, tens of layers of washing and shading were often used. Nevertheless, it was still essentially a Chinese approach with engrafted Western methods. When we come into the early Ch'ing period, the importation of Western art grew more and more in scope, and there then began to appear painters who used purely Western methods to do portraits. The primary representatives of this school were Man Ku-li (莽鵠立), Ting Yün-tai (丁允泰) and the latter's daughter Ting Yü (丁瑜). In *Hua-cheng Lu* it was said:

Mang Ku-li, courtesy-named Cho-jan (卓然), *a Manchu, Director of Salt Administration of the Ch'ang-lu* (長蘆) *Area, was skilled in portraiture. His method was essentially Western oriented, which, without giving first a structure by brush strokes, used only washes, shades and surface lines to make a picture. His portrait painting always closely resembled the real person and one who saw the picture*

[26]Ch'en Heng-k'o, *Chung-kuo Hui-hua Shih* (中國繪畫史), p. 39.

[27]Seigai Omura, op. cit. (Ch'en's translation), p. 196.

[28]Chang Keng, op. cit., Vol. II, biographies of Pien Yün (卞允) et al.

could easily tell whom it was depicting. He had a student named Chin Chieh (金玠), *courtesy-named Chieh-yü* (介玉), *a native of Chuki* (諸暨) *of Chekiang province.*[29]

It was again said in *Hua-cheng Lu:*[30]

Ting Yü, courtesy-named Huai-chin (懷瑾), *was a native of Ch'ient'ang (*錢塘*, Hang-chow). Her father Yün-tai was skilled in portraiture, following entirely the Western*

[29]Chang Keng, *Kuo-ch'ao Hua-cheng Hsü-lu* (畫徵續錄), Vol. I, biography of Man Ku-li.

[30]Ibid., Vol. II, biography of Ting Yü.

method in using washes and shades. Yü inherited his art and specialized in figure painting, being very adept in representing figures in their every possible attitude of looking up, bending down, leaning sideways.

These painters adopted a new approach which was known to follow the Western principles entirely. It was different from that of Tseng Ching, which was characterized by a combination of both Chinese and Western elements. But, besides Mang, Chin and the two Ting, no other painters of the school were wellknown. It can be inferred, therefore, that the school was not much welcomed by the artistic circles of the time.

V The Imperial Studio in Early Ch'ing and Westernization in Chinese Painting

ACCORDING TO Ch'ing custom, no official rank was given to painters who served at the Inner Court. The Emperor set up a studio called Ju-i Kuan (如意館) in the south of the courtyard known as Ch'i-hsiang Kung (啟祥宮), and there painting, copying, jade-carving, scroll-mounting, book-binding, etc. were being carried on. At first only artisans were recruited, but gradually literati, either recommended by high officials or recommended by their own talents, were also assigned work there. But the status of the latter was still different from that of literary courtiers.[31] In K'ang-hsi's time, Western missionaries served at the Inner Court as painters, and in the Imperial Observatory they filled most of the leading posts. Their Chinese colleagues grew familiar with their ideas, absorbed their art in painting, and were influenced by them unconsciously. Beginning with Chiao Ping-chen, the western orientation almost became a fashion in the Imperial Studio, and quite a few Chinese painters emerged as distinguished masters in the new fashion. In the later years of Ch'ien-lung, however, when Christianity was prohibited, the number of Western missionaries working in the Imperial Observatory dwindled, and the new tendency in Chinese painting towards an eclectic art was abruptly stopped.

[31]*Ch'ing Shih Kao* (清史稿), "I-shu Chuan" (藝術傳) III, biography of T'ang Tai (唐岱).

In his *Hua-cheng Lu* Chang Keng wrote:[32]

Chiao Ping-chen, a native of Tsining (濟寧) *[of Shantung Province], was a high officer of the Imperial Observatory. He was skilled in figure painting. In his paintings, figures far and near, big and small, were represented with an exactitude devoid of the slightest mistake. This was accomplished by applying the Western method.*

A more detailed description was given in Hu Ching (胡敬)'s *Kuo-ch'ao Yuan-hua Lu* (國朝院畫錄, Court Paintings in the Imperial Ch'ing Dynasty) as follows:[33]

Chiao Ping-chen, skilled in painting figures, landscapes and palatial buildings, complemented his art with the Western method. His Late Majesty K'ang-hsi once copied Tung Ch'i-ch'ang (董其昌)'s *calligraphy Ch'ih-shang P'ien* (池上篇) *by his own imperial hand, and left a remark on the copy which reads: "In the spring of the 28th year of K'ang-hsi [1689], I once copied Tung Ch'i-ch'ang's calligraphy Ch'ih-shang P'ien, and instructed Chiao Ping-chen, an officer in our Ob-*

[32]*Kuo-ch'ao Hua-cheng Lu*, Vol. II.

[33]*Kuo-ch'ao Yuan-hua Lu*, Vol. I.

servatoay, to work out a painting representing what Tung's writing had described. When people of the past commended paintings, they conferred, time and time again, the same praises, such as 'out of a single brush touch a fly,' 'man in an inch and horse in the size of a bean,' 'like the four saints in painting,'* 'like Ku K'ai-chih (顧愷之)'s two excellences,'** etc. Chiao Ping-chen as a painter is unique. As he has long been versed in the measurement of the latitudes of the heavenly bodies and the topographical differences of the earth, he can show, within the space of a single foot in his paintings, layer upon layer of mountains and high peaks which represent distances as far as ten thousands of li. *This is even more than what one [like Chang Tsao (張璪)], who could simultaneously manage two brushes, can do. I, therefore, write these few lines to record the occasion." In my humble opinion, the Western method excels in painting shades. It dissects the picture into minute parts to distinguish* yin *and* yang, *front and back, slanting and upstanding, long and short, and applies colours either heavy or light, bright or dark, according to the distribution of shades. Therefore, viewed at a distance, figures, animals, plants and houses all seem to stand out and look rounded. In addition, the casting of daylight, the spread of mist and cloud, and every depth and extremity [in nature] are represented distinctly on a small piece of paper or silk. Chiao had worked in the Imperial Observatory and was versed in the science of survey and mathematics. This helped him appreciate the Western method and adapt it to his own painting. His Late Majesty K'ang-hsi's commendation of his painting is accordingly also a commendation of his scholarship in mathematics.*

---

*It is not known to whom did the "four saints in painting" actually refer. Most probably it referred to Ku K'ai-chih (顧愷之, c. 344-406), Lu T'an-wei (陸探微, fl. c. 475), Chang Sheng-yu (張僧繇, fl. c. 530), and Wu Tao-yuan (吳道玄, fl. c. 725).

**It has been said that Ku K'ai-chih had three excellences (Hu-t'ou San-chüeh, 虎頭三絕): One in talent, one in painting, and one in naïveté.

In *Shih-chü Pao-chi*, six of Chiao Ping-chen's paintings are entered, of which the most famous is *Keng-chih T'u* (耕織圖, Illustrations of Grain and Seri-Culture). Chiao was already in service at the Inner Court before the 28th year of K'ang-hsi (1689). Castiglione arrived at Peking only in the 54th year of K'ang-hsi (1715), Sickelparth was called to service at Ju-i Kuan in the 10th year of Ch'ien-lung (1745), and both Panzi and Attiret were also taken into the service of the Court in the time of Ch'ien-lung. Therefore, it is likely that Chiao acquired his new method in painting from the missionaries who were working with him concurrently in the Imperial Observatory, and not from Castiglione, Attiret or any other known missionary painters.

After Chiao, men like Leng Mei (冷枚), T'ang Tai (唐岱), Ch'en Mei (陳枚) and Lo Fu-min (羅福旻) were all wellknown for their adoption of Western methods in painting.[34] In Feng Ching-po (馮金伯)'s *Kuo-ch'ao Hua-chih* (國朝畫識, Notes on Paintings of the Imperial Dynasty), an account of Ch'en Mei was quoted from *Lou-hsien Chih* (婁縣志, History of Lou County) as follows:

> *Ch'en Mei's painting first followed the Sung masters, but it was tinged with the style of T'ang Yin (唐寅) and complemented furthermore with the Western method. He could present multiple ranges of mountains and valleys on a small piece of paper or silk, and if one looks with the help of a magnifying glass, one can find on it hills and woods, houses and bridges, people moving to and fro, and all other imaginable things, painted with a finesse comparable to what one*

---

[34]There is a biography of Leng Mei in *Kuo-ch'ao Hua-cheng Lu*, Vol. II and *Kuo-ch'ao Yuan-hua Lu*, Vol. I; A biography of Ch'en Mei in *Kuo-ch'ao Hua Chih* (國朝畫識), Vol. XI and *Kuo-ch'ao Yuan-hua Lu*, Vol. I; another biography of T'ang Tai in *Kuo-ch'ao Yuan-hua Lu*, Vol. II; and a biography of Lo Fu-min in the same work. There is also a biography of Leng Mei in *Tao-Kuang Chiao-chou Chih* (道光膠州志), Vol. XXX. According to the latter, "Leng was formerly a disciple of Chiao Ping-chen and became a painter as well-known as Chiao himself. Leng was skilled especially in figure-painting, which was incomparable in his time. He served at the Inner Court during the reign of K'ang-hsi. When Chiao was committed to paint a *Keng-chih T'u* at the royal order, Leng helped him in producing the work."

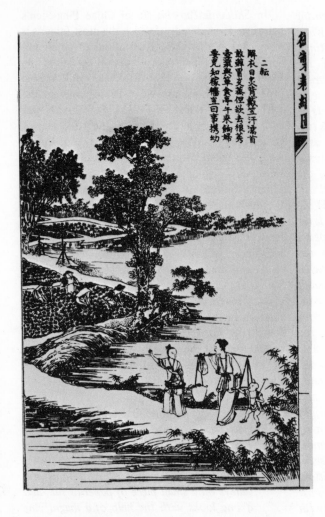

二耘

降衣日炙背戴笠汗濡首
敲辣冒炎蒸但欲去恨莠
妻嬰與單食寺午来餉婦
豐見知家橋豆日事携幼

召耘耘朴圖

Plate 100
SECOND HARROWING
From Chiao Ping-chen's
Keng-chih T'u,
Ch'ing period.

could expect from a big painting. In the 4th
year of Yung-cheng (雍正, 1726), Ch'en was
awarded a Fourth Grade official title in Nei
Wu-fu (內務府, Office of the Imperial House-
hold) for his worthy service at the Inner
Court, and given special leave to return
home to get married. The generous royal
favour bestowed on him was considered in
the arts circle as a rare honor.

As Ch'en painted with a knowledge of perspective,
the precipitous peaks and mountain ranges that
appear in his paintings can show, within the
compass of a foot's length, a distance of thousands
of miles. Compared with the traditional Chinese
method of *p'ing-yuan* (平遠, level distance) or that
of *kao-yuan* (高遠, high distance), Ch'en's method
certainly yielded more distinctive levels and a

more realistic presentation of space.

During the period from K'ang Hsi to Ch'ien-
lung, Chiao Ping-chen's initial adoption of the
Western method gave rise to a new fashion among
the Ch'ing court painters. The most representative
production of this new school is Chiao's *Keng-chih
T'u*. So far as we know, there was an earlier *Keng-
chih T'u* painted by Lou Tao (樓璹)* in the time
of the Southern Sung (南宋), and it was in the
35th year of K'ang-hsi that the Emperor ordered
Chiao to prepare a new work along the lines of the
older work. From *Yuan-hua Lu* we know that, in
the time of Ch'ien-lung, both Leng Mei, and Ch'en
Mei were each ordered again to paint an album of

*The Romanization of 樓璹 was given in Osvald Siren's
Chinese Painting (Vol. V, p. 91) as Lou Ch'ou.

Keng-chi T'u.[35] It is not known whether the works of Leng and Ch'en have ever been engraved, but Chiao's work, in a series of forty-six leaves, was carved on wooden blocks, printed and distributed among officials as a royal favor. It was re-engraved several times later, and altogether more than ten editions, including the original and its reproductions, are now in existence. From this we can see how the Imperial Studio flourished in times past.

The Sung edition of Lou Tao's *Keng-chih T'u* has long been lost, but there exists a Japanese reproduction, copied by Eiinou Kano (狩野永納) in 1676 from a Ming edition of the time of T'ienshun (天順, 1457-1464), in which one can see a miniature of the Sung original. Scholars like B. Laufer in his "Discovery of a Lost Book" and F.

Hirth in his *Ueber Fremde Einflüsse in der Chinesischen Kunst* (Foreign influences in Chinese Art) and "Scraps from a Collector's Note Book",[36] have done comparative studies of the two sets of *Keng-chih T'u* by Lou and Chiao. Based on the findings of Laufer and Hirth, the Japanese scholar Kyushiro Nakamura (中村久四郎) wrote his "Popular Customs in the Time of Sung and the Influence of Western Painting Seen in *Keng-chih T'u*",[37] which made further contributions to the study of the subject. The following is a summary of these three studies.

In comparing Chiao Ping-chen's *Keng-chih T'u* with that of Lou Tao, three differences can be detected.

First, in Lou's work there are 21 pictures illus-

[35] According to the account in *Kuo-ch'ao Yuan-hua Lu*, Vol. I, Leng Mei and Ch'en Mei had each painted an album of *Keng-chih T'u* of 46 pictures. A list of the contents of Ch'en's album can still be seen in *Yuan-hua Lu*, of which the titles and the order of the pictures are different from the works of both Lou Tao and Chiao Ping-chen. But, in *Chiao-chou Chih*, it has only mentioned that Leng helped Chiao produce the work, not that he produced a work of his own. It is not known which of the two accounts is correct.

[36] B. Laufer, "The Discovery of a Lost Book" (*T'oung Pao*, 1912, pp. 97-106). F. Hirth's "Scraps from a Collector's Note Book" was also published in *T'oung Pao*, but the author [Hsiang Ta] has not yet seen his other work indicated herewith.

[37] Kyushiro Nakamura, "Kōshito ni mieru Sōtai no fūzoku to seiyōga no eikiyo" (耕織圖に見える宋代の風俗と西洋畫の影響), *Shigaku Zasshi* (史學雜誌), Vol. XXII, No. 11, pp. 17-39.

Plate 101
SECOND
HARROWING
From Lou Tao's
Keng-chih T'u,
Sung period.

trating grain-culture: soaking seeds, ploughing, second ploughing, third ploughing, rolling, planting seeds, shadowing, thinning young plants, transplanting, first harrowing, second harrowing, third harrowing, irrigation, scything, grounding, beating grains, winnowing, hulling, pounding, sifting, storing; and 24 pictures illustrating seri-culture: bathing of silk-worm egg papers, taking down egg papers for storage, feeding, first moulting, second moulting, third moulting, screening, picking mulberry leaves, final emerging from moulting, catching the mature silk-worms, transferring the silk-worms to the straw cocks on the screens, warming the screens, gathering of cocoons, sorting the cocoons, holding the cocoons in trays, reeling the silk fibers, silk-moths, thanksgiving, spooling silk, warping, spinning silk fibers into weft yarns, weaving, figure weaving, polishing. In Chiao's work, both grain-culture and seri-culture each consists of 23 pictures. The section on grain-culture contains two other pictures which Lou's work does not have: one illustrating first shoots and another illustrating thanksgiving. The section on seri-culture omitted three pictures from Lou's selection, viz., taking down egg papers for storage, feeding and first moulting, but added two others: one on dyeing and another on tailoring. The order of the pictures in the two works is also somewhat different. From this comparison one can see the change of practices in grain- and seri-culture from Sung to Ch'ing times.

Secondly, pictures in Lou's work are generally simple and plain, while those in Chiao's are fine and luxuriant. Taking the illustration of the second weeding as an example: the structure of the two pictures is mainly alike, both showing four farmers who are weeding, and two women on the field path, one of whom is leading a child by the hand. But in Lou's picture, besides the woman who is carrying a load of tea and food on her shoulder and leading a child, the other woman is portrayed as squatting and fanning a fire in a brazier, while in Chiao's picture this second woman is drawn walking in front of the other woman, not squatting, but carrying a basket in one hand and pointing to a remote place with her other hand. In Lou's picture, the four farmers, each with a bamboo hat on his head and clothes wrapped up, appear to be very busy pulling up weeds. In Chiao's picture,

however, palm-leaf fans are added to the scene: an old man, chest bare, is cooling himself with a fan, and another farmer has a fan stuck in the waist of his trousers behind his back; both men appear to be easy and relaxed. In Lou's picture, the four farmers occupied in weeding are put in the front of the picture, but in Chiao's picture they are placed in the left corner, against a background of fields, trees and bamboo groves. In Lou's picture, the women are short and round-faced, and the child, naked above the waist, holds a palm-leaf fan in his hand. In Chiao's picture, however, the women have slender bodies and slim waists and are depicted in charming and graceful postures, and the child, naked below the waits, holds a whirligig in his hand. (The whirligig was also a popular toy in Italy. It is possible that Chiao chose to put it in his picture because he was influenced by the Italian missionaries of the time.) In other words, Lou's picture presents mainly a view of toil and is true to life, while Chiao's picture, exquisitely and decoratively executed, presents a view of peacefulness and leisure, as if the artist, idling in the calmness of nature and envisioning the life of the countryside, took Lou's work as a blueprint, and used his painter's imagination to limn his own picture, without realizing that he has rendered the scene much more delicately and, in doing so, made it fall short of reality.

Chiao's work was in the main worked out on the plan of Lou's, but after being modified and embellished, the atmosphere of the picture was greatly changed and savored of peace and relaxation. But the greatest difference was that Chiao applied the Western method of perspective in his work. Chang Keng's description that in his paintings "figures far and near, big and small, were represented with an exactitude devoid of the slightest mistake" can be discerned in each of these 46 pictures. Though the woods, houses, figures and landscape were still executed in the traditional style, the presentation of spatial feeling followed the Western method. This way of complementing Chinese painting with Western perspective brought into being a new school of painting that mingled Chinese and Western characteristics. Unfortunately the literati of the time did not welcome it, therefore, when the patronage of the royal court was lost, this style soon disappeared as well.

In the time of Ch'ien-lung, another court painter named Men Ying-chao (門應兆) also adopted Western methods to a great extent in his painting. In the year 1778, on the instruction of Ch'ien-lung, the *Hsi-ch'ing Yen P'u* (西清硯譜, *Ink Slabs in the Royal Collection*) was compiled. The collators of the work were Yu Min-chung (于敏中) and Liang Kuo-chih (梁國治), and the illustrator was Men. In this work, the entire palace collection of ink-slabs was recorded, and a picture was made of each item. Using a purely Western method in presenting light and shade, Men produced real-looking pictures that faithfully depicted the slabs with all their curvatures, indentations and exposed and hidden faces. Early in the time of Wan-li of the Ming dynasty, when Li Chih-tsao (李之藻) wrote his *Pan-kung Li Yo Shu* (泮宮禮樂疏, *On*

State Rites and Music), the ceremonial vessels and music instruments therein recorded were already meticulously illustrated by pictures executed partly in the Western style. Also, at the end of the Ming dynasty, Wang Cheng (王徵)'s translation of *Ch'i-ch'i T'u-shuo* (奇器圖說, *Illustrated Western Mechanical Engineering*) and the Jesuit Ferdinand Verbiest (南懷仁)'s writing of the *Ling-t'ai I-hsiang Chih* (靈臺儀象志, *On the Astronomical Instruments in the Royal Observatory*) both copied their illustrations directly from Western books, and therefore the objects depicted have a three-dimensional appearance, with relevant light and dark, distinct and obscure presentations. It is possible that Men Ying-chao's art was influenced by these earlier works.[38]

[38]Ibid.

VI Western Art and Painters Outside the Court

WESTERN ART enjoyed a certain vogue in the later Ming and early Ch'ing period as the result of royal patronage, but this, naturally, was mainly confined to the court. Outside, among the common people, it had only minimal influence. In Chu K'un-t'ien's *Ti-yü Hsiao-kao* (笛漁小稿, Mélanges) it is mentioned:

> *Chang Seng-yao* (張僧繇)*'s flower paintings appear to have three-dimensional depth when viewed from afar, but, viewed closely, look flat. This way of presentation was well understood by Ts'ao Chung* (曹重)*, courtesy-named Shih-ching* (十經).

This must mean that Ts'ao adopted Western methods in his paintings.

In Li To (李斗)'s *Yang-chou Hua-fang Lu* (揚州畫舫錄, Roaming in Yangchou in a Boat),[39] it is also noted:

> *Chang Shu* (張恕)*, courtesy-named Chin-jen* (近仁)*, was skilled in the Western style of painting. All that he painted fitted the rules*

of perspective down to the last detail, and not even Westerners could surpass him.

Ts'ao and Chang were followers of the Western style among Chinese painters outside the Court. In the *Hua Cheng Lu*'s Biography of Ts'iu Wei (崔鏏),[40] it is said:

> *Ts'iu Wei, courtesy-named Hsiang-chou* (象州)*, a native of Korea* (三韓)*, is a veteran artist skilled in the painting of figures and female portraits. He is a follower of Chiao Ping-chen's painting style. His portraits are cleanly and beautifully colored and are very charming and elegant. Though not great enough to be ranked equally with the ancient masters, he is justifiably one of the foremost painters of his time. His plumblossom paintings, executed in plain ink, are also fine in style. He is now a prefecture magistrate.*

These men all worked outside the Court and can be grouped as painters among the common people. The painter K'ung Yen-shih (孔衍栻) was also one

[39]*Yang-chou Hua-fang Lu*, Vol. II, "Ts'ao-ho Lu" (草河錄).

[40]*Kuo-ch'ao Hua-cheng Lu*, Vol. III, biography of Ts'ui Wei.

of them. He was active in the early years of K'ang-hsi, and was the author of *Shih-ts'un Hua Chueh* (石村畫訣, Shih-ts'un On How to Paint). He invented the method of shadowing with a semi-dry brush, a slight deviation from the methods of the four masters of the Yuan period. It seems that the invention was inspired by the influence of Western painting, but the hypothesis still awaits the judgement of experts.[41]

The painters mentioned so far in this chapter were mainly eclectics who sought to combine and modify the styles of Chinese and Western painting, and in doing so had initiated a new school of painting, but it is not known whether any of them also admired and penetrated into other aspects of Western culture. The first to convert to the Western style was Wu Li (吳歷), courtesy-named Yü-shan (漁山) and style-named Mo-ching (墨井). Wu was a native of Ch'ang-shu (常熟) of Kiangsu province. Known as one of the six masters of early Ch'ing painting, ranking together with Wang Shih-min (王時敏), Wang Chien (王鑑), Wang Hui (王翬), Wang Yuan-ch'ih (王原祁) and Yün Ke (惲格), he was even rated above Wang Hui by Wang Shih-min. Sketches of Wu's life can be found in both *Hua-cheng Lu* and *Mo-ching Chi* (墨井集, Collected Writings of Wu Li).

In his *Ou-pei Yü-hua* (鷗陂漁話, Fisherman's Words on Crane Beach), the scholar Yeh T'ing-kuan (葉廷琯) wrote the following of Wu Li:

> The master had long been converted to the [Western] religion, and had twice visited Europe. Therefore in his later years he loved to apply Western methods in his painting.[42]

Adopting Yeh's information, the Biography of Wu Li in the *Ch'ing Shih Kao* (清史稿, Draft History of the Ch'ing Dynasty) also said:

> In his old age Wu left his family and was converted to Catholicism. He visited Europe twice. He often employed Western methods in painting. The clouds and atmosphere [in his landscapes] extend to a great distance and height, which is very different from the style of his former days.[43]

Both sources say that Wu had travelled to Europe twice, and that in his later years he complemented his painting with Western methods. But the fact is that Wu Li planned to go to Europe in the 19th year of K'ang-hsi (1680), in the company of the Belgian priest, Philippe Couplet (1624-1692), a Jesuit father in China at that time who had received his Society's orders to return to Rome. In the 20th year of K'ang-hsi they were on their way. However, when they arrived in Macau and took up lodgings at St. Paul's Cathedral (now known in Chinese as *San-pa Sze* 三巴寺), Wu Li decided to stay there to become a novice. In the 21st year of K'ang-hsi he entered the Jesuit Order. His *San-pa Chi* (三巴集, The San-pa Collection) was written during his stay in Macau. In it there is this poem, member 29 in his *Au Chung Tsa Yung* (墺中雜詠, Miscellaneous Poems Written in Macau):

> My Westward venture was unaccomplished.
> What should I do?
> I have stayed in Macau for two seasons,
> winter and spring.
> When tomorrow, at Hsiang-shan, I ask people
> again how to cross the ocean.
> They say: it's a long, long voyage, beyond
> the hills lined with plum-trees.
>> —Written on my failure to
>> accompany Father Couplet
>> to Europe[44]

The poem proves that Wu Li never went to Europe. It is only because, after joining the Jesuit Order, he was wholeheartedly devoted to spiritual studies and rarely communicated with the secular world, that it was mistakenly reported that he had left China for Europe. As regards the story of his adoption of Western methods in his later paintings,

---

[41] K'ung's description of his method of shading with a semi-dry brush in *Shih-ts'un Hua Chüeh* can also be seen in a quotation in the Hsien-feng Edition of *Chi-ning Chou Chih* (咸豐濟寧州志).

[42] Quoted in Yao Ta-jung, "Pien Hua-cheng Lu Chi Wang Shih-ku yü Wu Yü-shan Chüeh-chiao Shih chih Wu" (姚大榮，辯畫徵錄記王石谷與吳漁山絕交事之誣), *Tung-fang Tsa-chih* (東方雜誌), Vol. XXIII, No. 21.

[43] *Ch'ing Shih Kao*, "I-shu Chuan" III, biography of Wang Hui.

[44] Li Wen-yü (ed.), *Mo-ching Chi* (李問漁編墨井集), Vol. III, *San-pa Chi* (三巴集).

Plate 102 MACAO c. 1655. Engraving by J. Nieuhoff. From *THE CHATER COLLECTION*.

it could also have been exaggerated. Wu did make some comparisons between Chinese and Western customs, writing and painting. He once said:

> The town of Macau, also called Hao-ching (濠鏡), is not far from the county city of Hsiang-shan. It is a place where fashions of the Greater and Lesser West prevail. Popular rites and customs are the exact opposite of those practised in our own country here. For example, at home when one sees a guest, one always tidies one's own clothes and hat. Here, however, one simply accosts a guest by taking off one's hat. There is also a difference in writing and painting. In our own writing, characters are formed with dots and strokes, then sounds are given to them. In their writing, the sound exists before the written word, and the script is made up of curves and strokes spread out in horizontal lines. In painting, we do not aim at the resemblance to outward forms, nor prize the rigid adherence to formal presentation, and we call

> this spiritual excellence. On the other hand, their painting is entirely devoted to the portraying of yin and yang, front and back, and the capturing of outward forms. With regard to colophons and signatures, our painters always place them on the top of the painting, while their painters always put them at the bottom. The ways of using the brush are different too. There are so many differences that I cannot describe them all.[45]

But in one of Wu's colophons to his own paintings, he said:

> In ancient times, people who could write well did not ask for recommendations, and those who could paint well did not ask for material awards. They said, "We write to impart the thoughts of our hearts; we paint to make ourselves happy." They ate and

[45]*Mo-ching Chi*, Vol. IV, "Mo-ching Hua-pa" (墨井畫跋).

dressed most plainly, and never accomodated themselves to other people. Not even princes and nobles could order them about, because honours and humiliations meant nothing to them. Only such men who have attained spiritual enlightenment can excel in the art of the brush.

Painters without a basic study of the works of Sung and Yuan masters are like chess-players who have only an empty chess-board, but no chess-pieces to play their game with. A painter whose vision is broad and whose thoughts are free will naturally manifest Nature's charm with every brushstroke. In painting, the brush should be given free rein, and the imagination allowed to soar. Tung Yuan (董源) and Chu Jan (巨然) are to painting as T'ao Ch'ien (陶潛) and Hsieh Ling-yun (謝靈運) are to poetry.

This shows that Wu Li attached great importance to the work of imagination in painting, and belittled the mastering of the outward resemblance of forms. Judging from his extant works, we do not see how "the clouds and atmosphere extand to a great distance and heights". Only one painting, entitled *Spring on the Lake*, seems to show some employment of Western perspective, being also somewhat close to the style of Castiglione in the depicting of trees and rocks. All his other paintings, however, are in the old tradition. Thus the saying the Wu Li liked to apply Western methods in his painting in his old age is nothing but a piece of unfounded hearsay.

Plate 103   HORSE: Pi Li Shang, by Giuseppe Castiglione. National Palace Museum, Taipei.

VII Conclusion

IN THE EARLIER sections of this essay, under the titles "The Appearance of Western Missionaries and Western Art in China", "Westernized Portraiture in Later Ming and Early Ch'ing Painting", "The Imperial Studio in Early Ch'ing and Westernization in Chinese Painting", "Western Art and Painters outside the Court", a brief analysis has been made of the influence of the West on Chinese art in the two centuries between the early years of the Ming Emperor Wan-li and the last years of the Ch'ing Emperor Ch'ien-lung. Now we may ask why it is that, after having flourished for two hundred years, Westernized art came to a premature end in China. The reason for this can be traced back to the seventeenth and eighteenth centuries, when France and Portugal competed for the right to preach Christianity in the East. As French missionaries were inflexibly opposed to the practice of ancestor worship and other similar rites by the Chinese christians, Catholic evangelism in China lost much of its success with the arrival of Cardinal de Tournon. In the last years of Emperor Ch'ien-lung, the prohibition of Christianity became more and more severe, dealing a fatal blow to the spread of Western culture, and this has also been the explanation given for the dwindling of Westernized art. However, there were also factors in the so-called Westernized art of the time itself which were responsible for the failure of its further development.

The first factor was the disapproval of Westernized art felt by most Chinese painters of the time. Wu Li, for instance, compared Chinese and Western painting with an emphasis on the difference between what he called "spiritual excellence" and "outward resemblance of form", implying that the former was superior to the latter. (See *Section V*) The same view is even more obvious in the following words of Chang Keng (張庚):

In the Ming dynasty, Matteo Ricci, a European who knew Chinese, arrived in Nanking and took up residence in a barrack west of the Cheng-yang Gate. He painted their religious Master in the form of a little child called the Son of Heaven held in the

arms of a woman. The portraits looked very spirited, and the colouring was fresh and lovely. He once said, "Chinese painting only shows the front side [of an object], and no concavity or convexity is depicted; but the painting of my native country shows both the back and the front [of an object], which makes it look full and rounded on all sides. In treating a human face, which as a rule is light on the front and dark on the back, we blacken the dark side slightly so as to make the front side stand out clear and bright. Chiao Ping-chen adopted this idea and modified it. But it does not meet the standards of real elegance, and is disapproved of by lovers of time-honored ways. [46]

The painter Tsou I-kuei in his treatise on Western painting also said:

Western artists excel in sketching and drawing, thus when they depict light and shade and distance they are exact to the last detail. All human figures, houses and trees in their painting have shadows trailing behind them. The colours and brushes which they use are completely different from those used in China. When they paint a scene, the perspective is presented as from broad to narrow, calculated in the dimensions of a triangle. Their mural pictures depicting palaces look so real that people are almost tempted to walk into them. Students of art may benefit somewhat if they learn a few such knacks. However, being completely lacking in the mastery of the brush, such painting, though elaborate, is afterall nothing but craftsmanship, and is not recognized as

[46] *Kuo-ch'ao Hua-cheng Lu*, Vol. II, biographies of Chiao Ping-chen et al. In a poem by Ch'ien-lung, entitled "Ming Chin T'ing-piao Fu Li Kung-lin Wu-ma-t'u Fa Hua Ai-wu-han Shih-chün (命金廷標撫李公麟五馬圖法畫愛烏罕四駿), a comment was made on Castiglione's painting, which is similar to Wu Li's opinion of painting quoted in the preceding section. For Ch'ien-lung's poem, see *Yü-chih Shih* (御製詩), Vol. III:

painting of quality. [47]

Himself a painter, Tsou examined the differences between Chinese and Western painting, and perceived the merits of the Western ways of perspective and chiaroscuro. While advocating that Chinese painters employ some of this art, he nevertheless rejected it from the ranks of painting for the reason that it is mere craftsmanship. Actually, in the early Ch'ing period, most painters followed the four masters of the later Yuan dynasty, imitating the time-honoured style, and it was rare for any painter to have as great a vision and as much originality as Shih-t'ao (石濤). It was not surprising, therefore, that Westernized painting was mocked at for not meeting the standards of real elegance and rejected from the ranks of painting.

The development of Western painting in China was impeded by another factor—Western people themselves did not like that new kind of nondescript painting produced by Western missionaries in China. In the reign of the Emperor Ch'ien-lung, the Englishman John Barrows went to Peking in the service of the British Ambassador, Lord Macartney, and set up astronomical apparatus in the imperial gardan Yuan-ming Yuan (圓明園). After he returned to England he wrote his *Travels in China* in which he recorded an occasion on which he saw two works by Castiglione:

> *At* Yuen-min-yuen *[Yuan-ming Yuan] I found two very large paintings of landscapes, which, as to the pencilling, were done with tolerable execution, but they were finished with a minuteness of shade, which give force and effect to a picture; none of the rules of perspective were observed, nor any attempt throw to the objects to their proper distances; yet I could not help fancying that I discovered in them the hand of an European.... Having turned over one of the volumes, I observed, on the last page, the name of* Castaglione *[Castiglione], which at once solved the riddle.... On enquiry, I found that Castaglione was a missionary in great repute at court, where he executed a number of paintings, but was expressly directed by the Emperor to paint all his subjects after the Chinese manner, and not like those of Europe, with broad masses of shade and the distant objects scarcely visible, observing to him, as one of the missionaries told me, that the imperfections of the eye afforded no reason why the objects of nature should also be copied as imperfect. This idea of the Emperor accords with a remark made by one of his ministers, who came to see the portrait of His Britannic Majesty, "that it was great pity it should have been spoiled by the dirt upon the face," pointing, at the same time, to the broad shade of the nose.* [48]

It is evident that Westerners of the time did not think highly of this kind of art which combined Chinese and Western styles but was actually neither Chinese nor Western in nature.

A third factor that hindered the development of Western art in China was the fact that even Western painters in the Imperial Studio were unhappy about their own works. In the reign of Ch'ien-lung, men like Attiret and Castiglione serving in the Court gained imperial recognition by their expertise in painting. Wishing to introduce Western methods of drawing, chiaroscuro, etc. to the Chinese, they at first executed portraits and still-lifes in pure Western manner. However, the Emperor disliked their way of presenting flesh tones, matching heavy and light colours and casting shades, and forced them to learn from Chinese painters and study the methods of Chinese painting. Knowing that the royal idea was wrong, they nevertheless had no choice but to obey. In a letter sent to Paris on November 1, 1743, Attiret told of this quandary:

[47] See Tsou I-kuei, *Hsiao-shan Hua-p'u* (小山畫譜), Vol. II. In the First Volume of the same work, Tsou discussed the methods and secrets of painting in a special article. One of the methods taught how to present rocks, in which Tsou advised that "white and black are used to represent light and dark, and blank and solidness to represent convexity and concavity." In the last chapter of J. C. Ferguson's *Chinese Painting* (1927), it is said that, as Tsou had been associated with the Jesuit painters Castiglione and Attiret, he knew quite well how to use Western techniques in painting. It is undoubtedly true as the afore-quoted saying shows.

[48] See John Barrows, *Travels in China.* pp. 324-325. 1806, T. Cadell & W. Davies, London.

*The above account may sound as if I am
casting away all that I have learnt to create a
new style, in order to please His Majesty.
But all that we painted were by order of His
Majesty. At first we observed our own
country's methods and the correct rules of
painting, but when His Majesty saw our
works he was not happy with them, and
many times returned them to us, ordering
changes. We dared not say whether the
changes thus made were appropriate or not;
we could only bend to His Majesty's will.* [49]

There are a number of entries in Hu Ching's *Yuan-
hua Lu* (院畫錄), that bear testimony to Attiret's
words, for example *Ma Chi T'u* (馬枝圖, A Herd
of Horses) by Castiglione and Chang T'ing-yen
(張廷彥); *Pin-feng* T'u (豳風圖, Illustration of the
Poem "Pin-feng"), by Castiglione, T'ang Tai (唐岱)
and Shen Yuan (沈源); and the *Ai-wu-han Ssu
Chin T'u* (愛烏罕四駿圖, The Four Afghan Steeds),
in which Castiglione was ordered by Ch'ien-lung to
paint the horses, and Chin T'ing-piao (金廷標)
painted the reins holders after the style of Li Po-
shih (李伯時). In the last instance, the Emperor
took pride in saying "Castiglione's style seems to
match Li's, and together they have created an art
of excellent quality." He was not aware that this

style of painting was neither fish nor fowl.

From these three factors it can be seen that
what was known as the new painting of later Ming
and early Ch'ing, a mixture of Chinese and Western
styles, was actually facing a very awkward situation.
Not only was it regarded as vulgar by Chinese
connoisseurs, and criticized by Westerners as
ludicrous, but the painters themselves, who were
forced to take to such a style, were also full of
reluctance and regret. Therefore, it was quite
predictable from the start that such a style would
never establish itself in the Chinese art world and
would come to an early end. The saying goes:
"Previous happenings should be remembered as
lessons for the future." The failure of Westernized
art in China in the later Ming and early Ch'ing
period challenges us to think about the future of
Chinese art. Here, the opinions of two art experts,
one Chinese and the other Western, are relevant.

Laurence Binyon, in his comparative study of
Western and Eastern art, attributed the reason for
the different developments in Western and Eastern
painting to the rise of science.

*I have sometimes thought that if our modern
painting had developed continuously from
the art of the Middle Ages, without the
invasion of scientific conceptions which the
Renaissance brought about, its course would
appear to have run on very similar lines to
that of the painting of the East, where the
early religious art, so like in aim to that of
the early Italian frescoes, flowered gradually
into naturalism, always pervaded by a per-
fume of religious idealism.* [50]

According to Binyon, the presence or absence of
the scientific mind was the basic factor which
determined the difference of modern Western
painting from Chinese painting. In his study of
Chinese painting, K'ang Yu-wei (康有爲) showed
deep concern for its many weaknesses, and said:

*To rectify these faults, we should assert the
importance of mastering the form and spirit
[of objects], rather than the expression of*

[49]Tai Yao (戴嶽)'s translation of S. W. Bushell, *Chinese
Art*, Vol. II, p. 196. A similar account can also be seen in
J. C. Ferguson's *Chinese Painting*, pp. 180-182. Both
Bushell and Ferguson based their accounts on Attiret's
own letter published in *Lettres Edifiantes*. Ferguson
wrote again in his book that, when Attiret first arrived at
Peking, he was soon in Emperor Ch'ien-lung's favour
because of his painting. He entered the Court's service a
little later than Castiglione. But the Emperor did not like
his oil painting and, therefore, the Board of Works was
instructed to forward to him the following royal directive:
"Attiret's painting, though well executed, is devoid of
spirit and brilliance. Attiret should be told to make a
change and learn to work on water-colour. A substantial
improvement may thus be expected. When he is employed
to paint portraits, he can be directed to work again on
oils." Herein we can easily see how the Western painters
serving at the Inner Court were inconsiderately restricted
and conducted in their working. The paintings which they
produced were mostly not what they themselves wanted
to paint; and it is conceivable, therefore, that these paintings were not highly valued by both Chinese and Western
connoisseurs.

[50]Laurence Binyon, *Painting in the Far East*, Chap. I,
"The Art of the East and the Art of the West.", New
York, Dover, 1959.

subjective thoughts. We should recognize rule-drawn colour painting as the major school of painting, and regard broad ink painting [only] as a minor school. Valuable as the spirit of the literati may be, the proper way of painting should still follow the style of the Imperial Studio. By this proposal I am seeking to redeem our past five centuries of erroneous art criticism, and to offer a way by which Chinese painting may be doctored and improved. [51]

He also said:

Entering the period of the present dynasty, Chinese painting became utterly lifeless. Worse than that, we do not hear of real painters anymore in the country. The two or three famous masters who still remain with us can only copy the worst of the four Wang's (Wang Shih-min 王時敏*, Wang Chien* 王鑑*, Wang Hui* 王翬 *and Wang Yuan-ch'i* 王原祁*) and the two Shih's (Shih-t'ao* 石濤 *and Shih-ch'i* 石谿*), making dry brushstrokes like blades of grass in an absolutely tasteless manner. How can such art be passed on and hope to vie with the art of today's Europe, America and Japan? The Wang's and the Shih's, though they inherited a little of the Yuan painters' fine brushwork, had already*

departed from the grand tradition of the T'ang and Sung periods, and were unquestionably much inferior to the Sung masters. Apart from Yün Ke and Chiang T'ing-hsi (蔣廷錫)*, whose lovely works have caught the spirit of the ancients, all our present day painters are uniformly uncommendable. Wu Li lacked disciples, as a result of which Castiglione's Western methods prevailed, so in future some great painter may yet rise who will succeed in combining Chinese art and Western art. Japan is already very enthusiastic about this, and Castiglione may well be regarded as an initiator. If Chinese painting continues to stick to old conventions and resists change, it well deserves to perish. Now is the time for our geniuses to rise and fuse the heritages of Chinese and Western art and usher in a new era in painting, an era to which I look forward.*

Disapproving of the romantic painting of the literati, K'ang Yu-wei advocated a return to the classical style of the Imperial Studio, whereby art could be inspired through the discipline of rules, and Chinese and Western qualities combined to open up new paths. While Binyon's words revealed the basic similarities and differences between Chinese and Western painting, K'ang Yu-wei's words indicate a direction which Chinese painting could take in the future. Both, of course, are greatly relevant to students of the history of Chinese painting.

[51] See *Wan-mu-ts'ao-t'ang Ts'ang-hua Mu* (萬目草堂藏畫目).

The Chinese Pictorial Art, Its Format and Program: Some Universalities, Particularities and Modern Experimentations [1]

By Nelson I. Wu

THE ACADEMIC GAME of asking oneself "What is the difference between a Chinese painting and a Western painting?" or "What makes a Chinese painting Chinese?" is a useful one on which a beginner may cut his teeth. He learns to accept the ink-bamboo as a respected tradition and quickly becomes concerned about perspective or the lack of it. It helps him acquire an understanding of what the Chinese painting is trying to do, and an appreciation for the problems it has, as well as the considerable accomplishments it has so proudly achieved. Soon, however, this very exercise will bring on the realization of its own meager importance. The student will quickly recognize that all pictorial expressions have the same building blocks: line, area, color, space, movement, and all the other privileges and limitations that are, part and parcel, the birthright of a two-dimensional art. These components in their analyzed form, simple and pure, are *universalities*, behaving like musical tones, favoring no particular culture or tradition and belonging to all.

With this second and more analytical look at painting comes the revelation one did not seek: Just as there is no pure race, there is rarely such a thing as a thoroughbred painting, be it Zen or Academic, Northern or Southern School, Kano or Tosa, traditional or modern. Everywhere one encounters eclectic art. I often think that each important work of art is a museum of styles, and every artist of consequence a walking incarnation of a host of ghosts of ancient masters plus his own soul. Earth-shaking creative events look important because they crown the pinnacles of long, collective efforts. At the right time, and the right place, an artist becomes great because he has done the right thing. The right thing, considered alone, may seem a small ripple in the historical currents. But the ripple could be the crest of a surging river that breaks the dike and changes the course of a waterway.

Thus, when a painting is examined again, now for the third time, one looks beyond the general properties of the art of painting and discerns the accumulative and collective efforts in each tradition. Here indeed, he sees characteristic differences among traditions, and feels in each its developmental inertia. Each tradition has its

[1] This article is developed from portions of a paper entitled: "Form and Meaning: Universality and Particularity in the Visual and Verbal Language," which I delivered at the Conference on Oriental-Western Literary and Cultural Relations, Part I: China, on October 18, 1974, at Indiana University.

aspirations and finds its own ways to achieve them. The same objective world appears in the eyes of different groups as vastly dissimilar visions, and experimentations based on different ideologies are devised to depict them. And, as traditions develop and seek their next solutions, they zigzag, they deviate, and lo, new directions now fascinate new seekers! In the meantime, enough telltale *particularities* developed by each tradition will reveal to the viewer the goals, the problems and solutions each experimentation had. In the wake of history, there are usually visible differences in meaning and purpose to separate paintings into various families of styles: *even* Chinese and Western.

From differences to similarities and back to a new set of differences, we progress to a deeper and more fundamental appreciation of the efforts of the creative artists, without prejudice for or against. Of course, this is not all there is to be appreciated in painting, nor is it the only way or the best way to approach it. But it does open up possibilities for restudying works we are familiar with as well as gaining control over unfamiliar compositions.

The late Etienne Balazs once asked me how long it usually would take a Western student to become confident in his appreciation of Chinese painting. He wondered whether his students of Chinese history and literature had been taking too long to learn their subjects. My answer to him was: "Five years plus or minus for a student of art, but fifteen years or perhaps more for a student of literature." (A distinguished Japanese professor of Chinese literature once startled a gathering at a Western university by suggesting "two hundred years," and then turned to a colleague and whispered: "I meant never.") This is because the universalities of the visual art—line, color, etc., are elements of a universal language. The student begins his "reading" of painting easily and needs to make special effort only to deal with the particularities, the special cultural imprints. When it comes to these particularities, the visual arts are just as enigmatic and therefore esoteric as literature. And the nationality of the audience has little to do with it: Japanese students are reading modern translations of *The Tale of Genji*, and modern Chinese scholars line their studies with reference works in Western languages and in Japanese to help them better understand Chinese.

In a painting, however, reading only the universalities, there is instant satisfaction. "The Yellow Gourd" by Ch'i Huang 齊璜, more popularly known as Ch'i Pai-shih 齊白石 (1863-1957), delights us all, whatever our cultural background, with its sound and disciplined structure as well as its apparent ease of execution (Pl. 107, p. 192). The picture has comfortable proportions in terms of format, thus affording us an uncomplicated reading of the composition, as the eyes take in the entire picture at one glance. Indeed, having grasped the structure of the pictorial surface, one wanders from the gourd to the leaves to the twisting vine and the vibrantly progressing calligraphy, or the other way around, enjoying the ceaseless movement. Whatever one's cultural background, to his eyes the luminous lemon yellow color would appear to want to push forward, but the moist and heavy black leaves, with a tendency to recess, are holding the yellow gourd in place. In this tension, the surface of the painting is dynamically established. On it the vine and the calligraphy are like athletes or dancers performing. At times they may appear to be below the surface, and suggest depth; and at other times, they almost lift themselves up from it and

Plate 104
ONE DAY IN THE
FUTURE [THE
BROTHERS] WILL
LOOK AFTER EACH
OTHER,
by Ch'i Huang.

soar. But the solid, opaque, and brilliant vermillion rectangle of the seal pinpoints and stabilizes the pictorial surface and reconfirms the birthright of painting as a two-dimensional art.

In another composition with two chicks, Ch'i Huang demands a cultural and a moral endorsement of certain Chinese values of the audience in addition to a biological participation (Pl. 104). The brownish loop, resembling a broken rubber band, between the two little birds, represents an earthworm. The depiction of all images here is deliberately simple so as not to cloud the meaning. For even though we have here in the center of the composition the worm of contention, the fight is not the subject of this painting. The artist gives the title of this work in four bold characters: *"T'a-jih hsiang-hu"* 他日相呼, meaning "one day in the future [the brothers] will look after each other," no doubt alluding to two famous lines in *The Book of Odes:* *"Hsiung-ti ni yü ch'iang, wai yu ch'i wu,"* 兄弟鬩於牆，外禦其務〔侮〕 [2] "brothers may fight within the walls of the courtyard, but they will fight [shoulder to shoulder] against invaders from outside"; a simple biological response to this painting therefore would be inadequate.

A third example involves much more than the subject matter of a narrative. It evokes emotional and physical responses to man's deep-rooted feelings for life and

[2]*Shih-ching* 詩經, IV, *"Hsiao-ya"* 小雅, Decade of *Lu-ming* 鹿鳴, *Ch'ang (T'ang)-ti* 常棣. See J. Legge, Part II, Book I, Ode IV; B. Karlgren, 164.

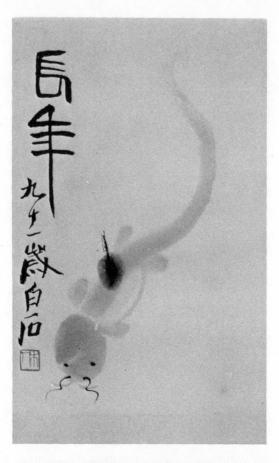

Plate 105
LONGEVITY,
by Ch'i Huang.

death, makes a poetic reference to a fish and plays on the pronunciation of a Chinese word. The painting is that of a catfish, but is entitled "Longevity" (Pl. 105). The word for catfish is *nien* 鮎, and *nien* is also the pronunciation for the word 年 meaning "year," "age," or "life as measured in terms of years." Thus the body of the twisting and swimming catfish is made into a double image: It is not only that of a long and powerful fish, but also that of a long and vigorous life. The almost translucent body of the fish is of the color of the semi-translucent muddy water. The happy fish is in its element. That grandfatherly face sports two wavy whiskers, and there is a twinkle in his eyes. He is healthy, enjoying himself, and not above reminding us of his presence that has been toughened by age. That toughness is in the stiff back fin which demands respect and is the only uncompromising and hard form of the entire organic, pliable body. Its hardness is more menacing and stiffer than seen in the strength of the calligraphy of the title, written in two bold, large characters: "*Ch'ang nien*," or "Long *nien*." Now, is it "Longevity" or "A Long Catfish"?

The rest of the calligraphy must be considered in two parts. The first part echoes the other ink images of the fish, the eyes and whiskers, announcing the age of the artist as ninety-one when the work was done, and flowing more at ease, albeit not without some calculated awkwardness. Beginning with the word "*sui*," 歲 meaning "age," a transformation takes place, and the strokes become more angular as the artist signs his name.

Once the particularities attributable to a culture are discovered, their significance seems to grow more and more. Here, even the simple matter of a date has its share to contribute to it. Although dated, still we cannot be sure whether this painting was indeed done when the artist was ninety-one years old as it says. Ch'i Huang believed what a fortune-teller had predicted: that he was to meet with grave misfortune in 1937 when he would reach the age of seventy-five. At that advanced age, the misfortune could easily spell death. So, in order to escape this fate, he adapted the established procedure known as *man t'ien kuo hai* 瞞天過海, "Fooling the Heaven to cross the sea," to carry him over the dangerous age of seventy-five and to miss his appointment with the heavenly messengers of death who were to come to collect him. The detailed procedure to achieve this I wish I knew. At any rate, Ch'i Huang started in 1937 to refer to his age as seventy-seven, two years older than he really was, and signed his works accordingly.[3] Perhaps he also celebrated his "seventy-seventh" birthday in grand style and did other things to camouflage his true age. As a result he successfully "fooled" Heaven. Since he had no seventy-fifth year, the year in which he was to die, he did not die. He lived twenty more years and died in 1957 at the advanced age of ninety-six. Or was it ninety-four? The same delightful confusion therefore must also surround the date of this painting, "Longevity."

AS BIOLOGICAL BEINGS, people everywhere, now as well as in the past, are very much alike: we perceive colors within the visible spectrum, between the ultraviolet and the infrared; and sound, anywhere between 12 and 20,000 vibrations per second, etc. These biological limits unite us in our common arena of artistic creation.[4] Clearly, it is the cultural particularities that separate us. Thus while red and white have their universally definable properties, white is the color for wedding in the traditional West, but is used for mourning in China, a country whose traditional color for wedding is red, the color that denotes danger in the West. Time further complicates the cultural differences. As modern Chinese have accepted much of the Western ways and marry in white, the so-called "red and white events," meaning the weddings and funerals, have become "white and white events." So, particularities are by no means permanent features in a society. Perhaps ever since the beginning of civilization, man has been adding meaning to simple biological functions. And, revolutions of all categories, political or artistic, are always discernible on the graphs

---

[3] Hu Shih 胡適, *et al, Ch'i Pai-shih nien-p'u* 齊白石年譜, The Commercial Press, Shanghai, 1949, pp. 36-37.

[4] I stated the significance of limitation in greater detail: "The true artist, having learned its potentialities, accepts its limitations and thus excels in that art. Knowing completely what the green color can do, and having all the green colors in the world at his disposal, the bamboo painter created the best picture of the green bamboo with ink alone. The poet accepts the limitations of the meter to set his verse free, and the architect makes invisible the solid of his stone and reveals the majesty of his space. The potentialities of a medium enslave even the greatest master, but a sudden realization of the special limitations transfigures his art. Once the limitation of a medium is identified, more than half of the task is done. Therefore, to our special blindness, we credit the art of painting; and to our special deafness, we credit the art of music. After having fallen from omnipotence, man created art. As silence died, poetry was born. So, let us sing!" Nelson Wu, "Ravana's Struggles," *Art and the Craftsman: The Best of the Yale Literary Magazine, 1836-1961*, J. Harned and N. Goodwin editors, The Yale Literary Magazine and Southern Illinois Press, 1961, p. 272.

of history by a drastic dip to the level of natural or biological existence and values. There the process of developing new particularities no doubt will begin again.

What will happen then, if the process is reversed, and accumulated cultural incrustations are removed? After thousands of years of evolution, the written language of China has become an esoteric communication system. The latest so-called "simplified" style is at times enigmatic even to the learned Chinese scholars. But certain "words," especially the nouns, of the ancient Inscribed Oracle Bones style, which pictorially describe the natural forms of animals, objects, etc., can still be easily identified by us today, whatever our cultural background. This style of writing, in use over three thousand years ago during the Shang dynasty, creates no obstacle, and is virtually forever modern. A similar joy of communication may be experienced with certain petroglyphs in the caves on the Hawaii Islands, in the American Northwest, with Arnhem Land drawings of Australia, or the Ice Age engravings on the fjord cliffs of Norway.[5] Like all art forms, these images are stylized, but not too far removed yet from nature. While over the years Chinese calligraphy has become esoteric by inbreeding and for the sake of efficiency, abstract, Chinese painting has remained this side of total abstraction. Perhaps the energy that has been directed toward developing the many imaginative styles of calligraphy, as well as "ink-play" in painting, has partially satisfied the Chinese appetite for abstract art. This seems very likely the case especially when we consider the fact that almost all Chinese painters practice calligraphy, and calligraphers dabble in painting. Therefore, we should do well by turning our attention back for a moment to the stylized images thus established in the Chinese painting tradition.

The gourd, the chicks, the fish, and even more important, the leaves and the vine, are all characteristically idioms of Chinese painting. Elsewhere, we see the other familiar idioms, the mountains, rocks, trees, waterfalls. But soon we will realize that all nature images are not admissible to artistic representation. There is clearly a selective process that separates what is ju-hua 入畫, "admissible to painting," from what is not (pu ju-hua 不入畫). For example: Old or matured men are admissible, and we see them everywhere in painting, but old women are less so, Young women are, but young men, especially when representing the image of young manhood like those glorified in classical Greek sculpture, are not. Nature always is a favorite object, but not without discrimination. The Chinese painting tradition is perhaps the only one that classifies its artists and production by categories of images. Of natural images, for example, bamboo and orchids are so important that they each merit a special classification. (Apples feature prominently in Western still-life, but one does not think of Cézanne as an "apple-painter.") Stylized and conventionalized mountain-and-water, figures, Taoist and Buddhist priests and deities, horses, flowers and feathers, insects and fishes, and architectual structures are all established idioms. Together they define certain particularities that are characteristic of Chinese painting. The horse in the ink-play manner, even when it is done with oil on canvas, still has something Chinese about it, and today there is no lack of such hybrid art. On the

[5]Nelson Wu, "The Ideogram in the Modern Dilemma," in *Art News*, November, 1957, pp. 34-37, 52-53. And, Johannes Maringer and Hans-Georg Bandi in execution of a plan by Hugo Obermaier, *Art in the Ice Age*, Praeger, New York, 1953.

other hand, a horse by Giuseppe Castiglione, better known by his Chinese name Lang Shih-ning 郎世寧 (1688-1768), even as it dazzled and inspired eighteenth-century China, remains outside of the mainstream of the Chinese tradition.

There is absolutely no narrow-minded chauvinism in these observations. As has been said earlier, there is no thoroughbred art. However, by watching closely the cultural particularities, one finds himself on the trail of the Chinese tradition's historical inertia, and may want to speculate to what goals the modern artist should direct his efforts in order to contribute to the Chinese painting tradition, and what possible contributions that tradition may make to the modern art world.

MILESTONES OF THE HISTORY of Chinese painting mark the specific times when an artistic image, be it a figure style or a landscape convention, established itself as a classic idiom and excelled in a special mode, not unlike the case with calligraphy. Modern artists naturally want to add new idioms to the vocabulary of their painting. Modern images, for instance, automobiles and airplanes, have been introduced to Sung and Ming landscapes of mist and snow scenes, but, as to be expected, no new milestone resulted.[6] Instead, the effort almost caused the Chinese tradition to lose its identity and thus its right to a future.

Obviously, staying with the old idioms and accepting their dated concepts is no solution. Feng Tzu-k'ai 豐子愷 warned his students over thirty years ago that they should not be painting robed old men sitting by the waterfall anymore, because they couldn't have seen such a sight, except in ancient paintings.[7] Today traditional landscapes in all well-known period styles are still being done and taught in schools, just as traditional poetry and calligraphy are being produced and admired. I admire many of these myself, and wish more good ones had been produced. But this has nothing to do with my earnest longing for a new era in Chinese painting. Much can be said about the relationship between direct personal experience and artistic expression, both pro and con. There is nothing intrinsically good or bad in an artistic style; we have to take it for what it is. Besides, much of our aesthetic cultivation is an indirect experience, at least at first. A taste for the various traditional Chinese theatrical styles, *K'un-ch'ü* 崑曲 or *Ching-hsi* 京戲, is usually acquired and induced; and it takes time to cultivate such an appreciation. Poetry is more remote from life than painting because of the medium, language, and calligraphy even more so, to the point of becoming abstract. An appreciation for all these arts thus needs to be induced with different degrees of intensity: from the relatively low requirement for painting to the highest for calligraphy. This does not in any sense rank the arts. In

[6]It is still difficult to assess the achievement of these experiments and to predict any future course except to say that unless new idioms are successfully created, Chinese painting as a tradition may not survive. Many are working along the direction of introducing modern machinery, architecture, clothing, etc. into conventional landscape today. Early pioneers that come to mind include the Cantonese artists Kao Chien-fu 高劍父, Kao Ch'i-feng 高奇峯, and Kuan Shan-yueh 關山月. For some more recent examples of large scale experimentation sponsored by government or otherwise encouraged by it, see Fu Pao-shih 傅抱石 *et al, Shan-ho hsin-mao* 山河新貌 *(New Looks of [Our] Mountains and Waters)*, Kiangsu People's Publications, 1962; and *China Pictorial*, VII, 1964 among many other official publications. Note also the almost uniform "comfortable" proportions of width and height of format.

[7]Personally, I think his own is among the more successful experiments. For a few examples of figures in new landscape by Feng Tzu-k'ai, see Bradley Smith and Wango Weng, *China A History in Art*, Harper and Row, New York, 1972, pp. 282-283.

d   *c*

fact they should not be pitted against each other and compared, but should be regarded as different avenues to revelation in art. However, each has its own imagined ideal form to guide it, and in its concepts of perfection we get a glimpse of the culture's aspiration. In tangible terms, that aspiration is equal to the total sum of all the particularities.

To the Chinese, it is good to see quality poetry, calligraphy and painting, or *shih-shu-hua* 詩書畫, congregate in one artist; and it is auspicious indeed to integrate the artist and the individual, culminating in symbolizing the *wen-jen* 文人, the "cultured human being." (I hope that I may be forgiven for retranslating this much discussed term.) The concept of *wen-jen* has suffered too long from many abuses and its association with the term, *wen-jen-hua* 文人畫, its standardized translation, "literati painting," and the unwanted elitist affiliation as well as class stigma. It should not have anything to do with birth, wealth, and station in life. Nor can low birth, poverty and misfortune rob anyone of his cultured human being status. In its pure and isolated form, the concept of *wen-jen* is perhaps the most important message from the Chinese tradition to our modern world. And today, the modern world seems ready to understand it. It was only yesterday when China was overwhelmed by the West's efficiency, its division of labor, and emphasis on expertism. Now the toiling performer of modern wonders, wherever he may be, longs to be an integrated man.

PRIVATE ART IS DEAD! More and more we hear people say this. "Almost all artists paint with the museum in mind, or at least a large audience [in mind]," Esley Ian Hamilton, a student in my introductory course wrote in a recent examination. "The Chinese painter could pour out his talents for the delectation of one person only, and even that person could not see the whole thing at once."[8] This kind of revelation is widespread among my students. Some marvel at the Chinese formats of the hanging scroll, the handscroll and the album as if they were sheer magic. Others find it maddening to be allowed to see only a portion of a handscroll at a time in museum

[8]Esley Ian Hamilton, examination essay written for the course Art and Archaeology 342, "Introduction to   the Art of China, India, and Japan," Washington University, May 10, 1976.

b   *a*

Plate 106   RIVER CITY AND FISHERMEN VILLAGES.
Handscroll by Wu Yung-hsiang. Sections a, b, c, d.

displays. In either case, the time seems more ripe than ever to consider what the particularities of these formats mean. Having done that, the issue of private art versus public art perhaps may be brought back for more discussion.

The Chinese formats have a wide range of measurements and proportions. Shapes close to the so-called "golden rectangle" indeed exist in large numbers. The height and width of album leaves are usually not drastically proportioned. All three works by Ch'i Huang illustrated here are in comfortable formats that permit the entire composition to be taken in at one glance. Three important points should be kept in mind: First, the biologically comfortable proportions are the universalities in this issue, not important in defining the Chinese ideals. Second, it is remarkable that the format, which exists *before* the painting, should even become an issue. But being *pre*-painting, it is a fundamental issue.[9] Third, the very fact that it *is* an issue is one of the particularities that says something about the aspiration of the culture that has made it so.

The drastic proportions of the height and width of the hanging scrolls and the handscrolls make sure that the entire composition is impossible to be taken in at one glance. It is good form for a viewer to go near a hanging scroll, stoop, stand up, back away and move forward again, taking a long time to go through the painting. It is normal practice to unroll a handscroll a section at a time to read it—pausing, enlarging and narrowing the portion being viewed, going forward and backward when feeling the urge. As the viewers of these formats, albums included, take time to appreciate the art, they add the element of time to it and make painting a temporal art that must exist in time like music, the dance, and poetry. As the viewing progresses, and a special time-space reality is created by virtue of his timing, the viewer, or each viewer if he is in the company of several others, creates his own world in which he is alone with the painting. The impossible happens. The ancients who have seen the same painting are now with him in this reality, and together they leave messages to be deciphered by the future. Colophons testify to these, in spite of

[9]Similar to the situation as related to in *Lun-yu* 論語: "*Hui-shih-hou-su*" 繪事後素 . "The business of laying on the colours follows [the preparation of] the plain ground." See James Legge, tr., *Confucian Analects*, p. 157. The ground could mean the silk on which the painting is done.

h   *g*

the fact that like all good things they often fall victim to self-indulgence.

The simple matter of format also has a vigorous and imaginative presence. It is the format that provides the stage for the performance of *chang-fa* 章法 , structural configuration and program. *Chang-fa* is like the invisible soul, depending upon its incarnation to reveal its existence. A few modern artists experimented with it, but what they did is not as easily noticeable as the automobile in snow, or the airplane in the mist.

"*Chiang-ch'eng yü-ts'un*" 江城漁村 , *River City and Fishermen Villages*, is a long handscroll, 33.25 cm *h* x 694 cm *l*, deceptively conventional in appearance; it does not particularly play up the city or the villages, although it has them among other sceneries (Pl. 106). The title here is not unlike those of the works by the early Cubists that serve to clarify the obvious and conceal the real intent of the artist. This undated work was probably done in the very early 1940's when the artist, Wu Yung-hsiang 吳詠香 (1912-1970), was at her prime.[10] This composition, under the guise of the traditional idioms and brushwork, is a bold experimentation of *chang-fa*, and is ingeniously programed. In the opening section when the first two or three inches are revealed, there is from top to bottom nothing but more or less horizontal lines lightly drawn in moist light color, a serene scene of stability. From this stillness an entire landscape drama of movement and change is to emerge.

A hasty viewer may not notice this by unrolling the scroll too quickly and too

[10]The year in which Wu Yung-hsiang, my late sister, was born is usually given as 1913. Recently this was corrected in a biography published in three installments in *Chuan-chi wen-hsueh* 傳記文學 . (Ch'i Sung 齊崧 , "*Nü-hua-chia Wu Yung-hsiang chuan*" 女畫家吳詠香傳 in *Chuan-chi wen-hsueh*, XXV/3 (148), Sept. 1974, pp. 33-41; XXV/4 (149), Oct. 1974, pp. 54-62; and XXV/5 (150), Nov. 1974, pp. 83-90. Hereafter, this work will be referred to as Ch'i, *Biography*.)

It was considered lucky and good by some northern Chinese that the woman in marriage be three years older than her husband. My sister and her husband,

Ch'en Chun-fu, an established painter in his own right, had a long and obstacle-strewn course of love, and her age, five years his senior, was the last one they had to surmount. To modify the impact the considerable age difference might have on their friends and "to please the parents of both families," for the wedding they changed their ages. She reduced her age by one year, and he increased his also by one year, to make the difference the auspicious three years. See Ch'i, *Biography* (148), p. 34; Michael Sullivan, *Chinese Art in the Twentieth Century*, University of California Press, 1959, p. 97, gives the year of Wu's birth as 1913.

f

e

RIVER CITY AND FISHERMEN VILLAGES.
Sections e, f, g, h.

much at once, thus missing the opening statement of the artist's intent. Few, however, can fail to appreciate her much more elaborate introductory passage that
extends some 90 centimeters to the left, a comfortable stretching of the viewer's
arm. This passage is like an overture of a musical composition, lightly but carefully
introducing the elements and the themes of the work. The life and flow of the water,
which we may liken to the music of the string instruments; the presence of man,
the woodwinds; the mass and the great weight of the mountains, the bass drums;
the jagged progression of the mountains, the punctuation of the percussion instruments, are all here, ready to be introduced, one by one. Having made the image
of the human presence a part of the landscape, she sets things off to a forward
movement (in this case, to the left) by placing two boats and their passengers at a
slight diagonal. Following the rising inertia of this diagonal, she brings the seemingly
docile mountains into view and quickly dismisses them, leaving them rumbling like
muffled thunders in distant clouds. It is not their time to perform yet.

The principal composition that follows is in four movements. They are, if we
may name them while fully aware of the inadequacy of such simple appellations,
The Traveler, The Mountain, The Water, and The Fantasy. These venerated images
are traditional ones, but their thematic treatment, first developed individually and
then put into a sequence, is experimental and exciting.

The first movement begins with an invitation to the viewer to come down to
earth. Hovering over the two boats, he has been a spectator. The people in the boats
do not even look at him. There is no place for him to land, only water below. While
his eyes are still focused on the far horizon, having been led there by the receding
mountains, the scroll unrolls; sneaking up on him, a path appears at the bottom edge
of the handscroll to provide him an entrance into the painting. Wu Yung-hsiang
seems to enjoy using this kind of ploy to splice together major passages of the
composition. She varies her applications, but each time she takes the viewer first in
one direction and then surprises him from another.

It is difficult to decline the invitation to set one's foot down on the path which
has been thrust right under the viewer's nose. Stationed at this point is a fisherman
who, with his boat, comprises the first image, facing right, the direction of the
arriving viewer who begins here to play also the role of a traveler. This is one of the

k   j

RIVER CITY AND FISHERMEN VILLAGES.
Sections i, j, k.

greatest joys offered by the temporal art of a scroll. As the viewer follows himself into the painting, he doubles the pleasure and surprises by maintaining both statuses. What is more, while he identifies himself with other travelers in the painting, or with other images provided by the artist for self-identification purposes, sometimes a horse, other times a tree, etc., he never forgets that he has all the time remained the viewer. Therefore, for him now to see the fisherman and to enter between his boat and the first trees, he is to come into a human settlement, not just arrive at land's edge. As the unrolling on the left side and the rewinding on the right continue, and before the first line of calligraphy comes into view, and as the first few inches of the scroll are rolled up, the composition suddenly seems to complete itself. The newly revealed piece of land forms a triangular area anchoring down the left end and balancing nicely the expanse of space to the right. But the traveler soon realizes that the picture does not end here. The human habitation is not for him to visit; the gate to the yard and the house is shut, the scholar inside is not expecting any guests— his back is turned to the gate and his mind is deeply involved in the book he is reading—even the dog, as if sensing that no guest is expected by its master, barks at the unfamiliar footsteps! So, this is not the end but the beginning of a journey. Following the road, the traveler goes on and around to the backside of the dwelling. Here the beginning of the colophon appears and assures him that much is waiting for him ahead.[11]

When the road re-emerges, an amazing thing happens. It was only a moment ago when the entire height of the scroll was occupied by images: the distant mountains at the top, the river in between, and the trees and houses in the fore-ground. Now the top half is empty. If one rolls up both ends and frames his scenes into small vertical strips, he will see that the images dance up and down along a narrow trail which at times occupies no more than a few centimeters of the format at the bottom ledge. This restricted passageway is where the painter wants the

[11]Here the architecture, the person, and the dog convey the same message—that the traveler should move on—via three different avenues. The gate and the fence, separating the road and the interior of the yard, shut out the traveler spatially. The scholar, reading, rejects him mentally. The dog makes a contact in sound to communicate across the visual and mental separation, but the message is "Move on."

traveler to be. She puts other travelers on the path, at one of the narrowest places, for the visitors to her painting to identify themselves with. The two figures seem to be aware of their passive function, so they, too (like the old scholar), ignore the visitors and only talk to each other. But all the while they serve very well the purpose of just being where they are. As the theme develops, the viewer becomes part of it. He enjoys reading the pictorial space with his feet, and wants to be as sure-footed as he can so that he will not slip off the painting! But how long must he stay with this restricted space?

As his eyes and his feet are concentrating on the few centimeters of ground below, and as he is about to step onto the footbridge, the next movement of the composition already lies in wait for him. Filling up the format to within a few centimeters of the top is the subject of this second movement, the Mountain.

The empty top part of the scroll, which suggests the continuation of the river, is taken up by a poem in the handwriting of the Manchu Prince, P'u Ju 溥儒 (1896-1963), and dated 1944.[12] The positioning of this long poem shows great sensitivity to the composition of the scroll. The calligraphy begins just as the road has reappeared from behind the cottage, thus picking up the narrative. The mental landscape in the poem, and the abstract forms of the calligraphy parallel the journey on foot below, until they come to the land's end, where a footbridge at once separates and connects the first two movements of the composition.

The low level and the narrowness of the land before the bridge serve two purposes: they set us up for the surprise of the height of the mountain, and confine us in a shallow space so that we can better appreciate the expanse and the depth in the second movement. As the great masses lumber forward, carrying along the travelers (some of them have found the going strenuous, and have acquired donkeys), the world in the picture opens up. More mountains come into view, and even more appear through the misty sky to show their peaks on the far horizon. Suddenly we have a vast panoramic scene with all the avatars of the mountain on display! As the landscape expands, we even find that a city nestles in the security of the mountain's lap. But the city is not the theme here; after having given the scene its scale, it is soon dismissed.

Water, the theme of the third movement, re-enters the picture almost as quickly as the mountains established themselves in the previous movement. It is the mist that obscures the mighty mountains, the vapor that lifts their great weight and separates them from their roots, and the sea of moist air that floats them away like so many chunks of drifting ice. Here even color is in danger of being completely bleached away by water. This third movement thus provides a contrast both to what has gone before and to what is to come. At the height of the water's presence, it is the void between solids, the pause between statements, the silence that gives meaning to, and is made meaningful by, the music before and after. We see it in the river, the harbor, the rice field, where the farmers are moving more water into their paddies using their foot-pump. Even more is coming down from the sky.

Now, something different is in the air. It is the wind that is blowing *against*

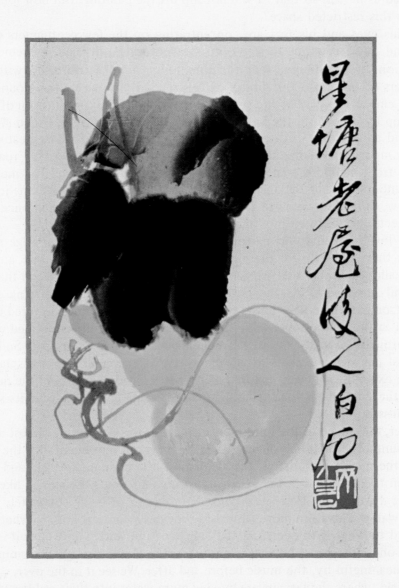

Plate 107   THE YELLOW GOURD, by Ch'i Huang.

our faces, confronting the movement of the scroll. The trees are bending to the right. What ominous message does this bring?

Wedging into the two mountain ranges is a fantastic contortion of jagged rock formations. The unbelievable shapes reaching up from below, coming down from high, defy gravity as they intertwine. Their compositional meaning is not really clear unless one keeps in mind what has gone before. These twisted forms mark the beginning of the fourth movement, which makes its entrance in yet a new stance. The transitions between sequences in this work have been rich in variation. There was a shift from high to low between the overture and the first movement, from low to high between the first and the second, and an overlap between the second and the third. Here, the fourth movement comes in between the distant and the foreground mountains, and halts the forward momentum. Then, as if offering the travelers a chance to reflect, the tortured mountain provides a lookout for them to review the landscape leading to this point, before beginning the journey through the nightmarish world of toppling mountains and sliding forests. Dreams are usually short, and a crescendo must not be held long, and so, peace resumes. The unstable, the diagonal, give way to horizontals again. The lines still have a few gnarled places not yet straightened out, but both the foreground land and the distant mountains are ready to settle down, their horizontality recalling the opening statement.[13] The human images here are all facing the direction we have come from. The last figure, a stooping old man, sums up the composition and serves as a final punctuation. The road, however, goes on, already suggesting a possible new journey on the other side of the hills.

The handscroll is a wonderful format for private art. The viewer in the privacy of his meditation participates in the creation of the landscape—observing, remembering and anticipating. For this reason, a handscroll of this type should not be opened to its full length so that everything is revealed all at once, as we have done here in order to reproduce the entire work. The reader is asked to exercise proper control over his framing of the scenes. After all, who wants to listen to all the movements of a symphony at the same time?

[13]Leaving some of the internal tension unresolved, such as the gnarled lines not all straightened out, to complement the parallel horizontal lines at the beginning of the scroll, is to preserve the *shih* 勢 , the potential. *Shih* can be likened to the potential in a wound-up spring: there is energy poised and emotion unresolved. I have made up a story to illuminate the point with particular regard to the ending of this scroll: Once a scholar became very intrigued by this scroll, and he deciphered one hidden meaning after another as he went along the composition. As tension mounted inside him, his power of observation and ability to penetrate deeper into the meaning of the design increased also. He was sure that something ominous would happen to him or to the scroll, as all the energies that were being liberated by the perfect communication between himself and the masterpiece must have an effect somewhere. When he came toward the end of the scroll, he fully expected that it would end in a peaceful scene represented by a restful grouping of horizontal lines, just as the scroll had begun. Instead, there were the unresolved gnarled lines wanting to be straightened out. Although he felt somewhat less than completely satisfied, he was too thrilled and tired to pursue the matter further. He was relieved, too, that no calamity had befallen him or the ancient treasure because of his deciphering all the artistic secrets. He rolled up the scroll, put it in its box, and left it on his table, still feeling the tension and excitement from looking at it. Exhausted, he put his head down on the table to nap for awhile, and promptly fell asleep. In his sleep, he thought he heard a long slow sigh of relief. There was no one else in the room, and the sound seemed to have come from the box. As if driven by some invisible force, he hurriedly opened the box, took out the scroll, and unrolled it impatiently all the way to the end. There, at the concluding section, the gnarled and kinky lines had just straightened themselves out.

WHAT WE HAVE described is a mid-twentieth century experimentation. Behind it, there was a mid-fifteenth century handscroll of comparable length attributed to the Ming dynasty painter, Tai Chin 戴進 , with a title: "*Chiang-shan ta-kuan*" 江山大觀 , or "A Grand View of Rivers and Mountains," inscribed in seal style by Chou T'ien-ch'iu 周天球 (1514-1595).[14] Wu Yung-hsiang saw the Ming work and was inspired by it. Fascinated by the possibilities it suggested, she re-arranged the composition, changed many of the details, and produced the scroll we have just seen. Previous to this she had spent three years, between 1937 and 1940, at the Chinese Painting Institute in the Palace Museum in Peking studying the former Imperial painting collections housed there. A major part of her time was devoted to making faithful copies of treasured scrolls by ancient masters.[15] She soon earned herself a name for the skill and quality of her reproductions. With the Tai Chin scroll, however, the situation was different. Working for herself and with a special intention in mind, she did not make a copy. Her purpose is best revealed by a quick check against the Tai Chin scroll, and by comparing a number of details in the) two compositions. In the opening section of the Ming painting there are many boats; two of them must be the models for the two in Wu's overture. But there are many other boats of different types going in different directions in the Tai scroll. Moreover, the mountain-water relationship in the earlier work does not exhibit orchestrated characteristics, but progresses rhythmically: water-mountain-water-mountain, many, many, times from the beginning to the end. As correctly observed by Ch'eng Hsi 程曦 , the Tai Chin scroll parades a number of traditional landscape styles. There are the Ma-Hsia 馬夏 School techniques as well as the Mi Family 米家 mountains.[16] This was not an uncommon practice, and it became more popular in the late Ming and early Ch'ing times. By the eighteenth and nineteenth centuries, when eclecticism was in vogue, painters would routinely compose, for instance, an eight-leaf album in eight different historically well known styles. Tai Chin's scroll did not go that far. It exhibits mostly the Chekiang manner Tai Chin had a share in making famous, but the juxtaposition of different styles is nevertheless very noticeable. This feature would have confused Wu's underlying abstract structure had she copied indiscriminately. So, she eliminated two mountain ranges and wide stretches of water to develop her own composition.

The most fundamental difference between the two scrolls lies in the viewpoints the two artists have adopted. The Tai viewpoint is high—the viewer looks down not only at the boats, but also at the flight of birds that are seen against the surface of the water below. Two mountain ranges come rushing toward the viewer, and pass underneath him. Wu Yung-hsiang excluded all these and moved a group of distant mountains from further down the scroll and placed them at the beginning to create the overture. She took out the boats that travel in the opposite direction to insure a

[14]Ch'eng Hsi 程曦 , *Mu-fei-chai ts'ang-hua k'ao-p'ing* 木扉齋藏畫考評 : *A Study of Some Ming and Ch'ing Paintings in the Mu-fei Collection*, Hong Kong, 1965, pp. 7-8. The whereabouts of the Tai Chin scroll was unclear throughout the World War II years. I was most pleasantly surprised to find it in Professor Cheng Te-k'un 鄭德坤 's collection when I visited him in Cambridge, England in 1959 and recognized it as the model my sister had told me about. I am grateful to Professor Cheng for the set of photographs he later sent me.

[15]Ch'i, *Biography* XXV/4 (149), p. 55. At the last count in 1972, six of these long scrolls were still in existence. They all were among the works my sister kept apart never to sell.

[16]Ch'eng, *op. cit.*, p. 8.

good foreward momentum, and added the narrow path to connect the plot of land on which the cottage stands with the footbridge area. She did all this to create the first movement, which describes the human presence and establishes the theme of the journey as soon as the visitor lands.

The landing of the visitor in Wu's work marks the basic difference in attitudes. Tai Chin's high viewpoint keeps the viewer a *viewer*, and his landscape a grand *view* of rivers and mountains. Wu's lower viewpoint, once established, manages to hold the viewer's sympathy with the travelers in the painting, and facilitates his identification with them even when they are far away. Thus, while the last sections of both scrolls contain essentially the same scenes, these different attitudes remain clear in each. The most important change Wu has made occurs at the landing. The Tai Chin scroll has a stable and complete scene outside the cottage gate. An old man holding a staff occupies the space here and he is complemented by the fisherman and his boat. There is no entrance into the painting, and no visitor can come here to crowd the scene. Wu put the entrance here and made the scene dynamic. She vacated the area of the old man, and the space became inviting. The concept of a path she introduced here remains a strong image throughout the entire composition. At the end of the scroll, where the path goes around the hills, the viewer is reminded of the entrance once again.[17]

BOTH IDIOM AND FORMAT challenged the Chinese painter anew after the Second World War. This challenge took place in a much enlarged geographic arena, as the uprooted Chinese roamed all over China or became transplanted far and wide. In this new situation, Chinese painting, which for hundreds of years had been like flowers cultivated in private greenhouses, shed its shyness, forgot its delicate nature, and went public. Sponsored by political or economic forces or both, as a means of communicating with the multitude, the new public art sought its audience among like minds. Whether it took the form of posters, murals, or pictures framed behind glass in homes, it communicated with the masses, and is experiencing an unprecedented, rapid growth. Political persuasions aside, wherever we find it, as public art, it has adopted the format that fits its purpose.[18] Although not necessarily always the golden rectangle, its comfortably proportioned height and width make communication quick, easy and complete. Everything else being equal, a format like this requires less active participation on the part of the viewer as he frames his scenes, and thereby involves his own mind less. Indeed, many can gather in front of a wall painting and receive the same message. (If they do not, then in some way the work must have failed.) But as far as the message is concerned, it doesn't matter whether it extols farm production on a wall in Peking or vows devotion to traditional values in the unchanging landscape hanging in a Hong Kong apartment.

Formats of private art, the long, narrow hanging scrolls, handscrolls, and

[17]Cf. Ch'eng, *ibid.* To my knowledge, the Tai Chin scroll has never been reproduced anywhere else but in this catalogue. Although only two short sections are shown here, they illustrate quite clearly how the entrance was created and the background mountains were moved to the earlier section of the scroll and made part of the overture.

[18]See *Shan-ho hsin-mao*, etc., cited in Note 6. For other examples, see *Chin-pai-nien Chung-kuo ming-chia hua-hsuan-chi* 近百年中國名家畫選集, Vols. *chia* 甲, (1973); and *i* 乙, (1974), Taipei.

planned and programed albums, difficult to mount and impossible to frame under glass, have thus fallen into disuse. The dwindling number of craftsmen who can still mount a good handscroll are faced with the increasing difficulty of finding a dependable supply of good materials, appreciative customers, and interested apprentices to carry on their trade. The modern admirer of traditional Chinese painting is also handicapped by the changing situation. Formats of drastic proportions are not only difficult to mount and maintain, but also expensive and inconvenient to reproduce.[19] We, who have arrived too late to know this private art form in its heyday, must frequently make our acquaintance with its public reincarnations, the reproductions, museum exhibitions, and catalogues. Great scrolls are popularly known only by a few sections, and albums, by a leaf or two. Little wonder that when these monuments of Chinese art are discussed, the emphasis would often be on details or on "*pi-mo*" 筆墨 , brush stroke texture and ink tone, instead of on the movement and meaning of the entire work. But, in the hands of truly creative artists, these old formats still shine brightly in a difficult time for Chinese painting, reward the painter richly with the excitement of experimentation, and promise the tradition a future worth working for.

"*Hui-hsuan*" 廻旋 , an expression which I can only paraphrase as "Hovering and Circling," is the title of just such a work[20] (Pl. 108). Its painter, Ch'en Ch'i-k'uan 陳其寬 , born in 1921 in Peking, earned his B.S. degree from the National Central University in wartime Chungking, and his M.S. from the University of Illinois in architecture, taught at the Massachusetts Institute of Technology, and now, an internationally known architect, living in Taiwan, is just such an artist. He never studied Chinese painting under any famous master, nor has he copied ancient masterpieces. But after having watched a painter friend

Plate 108   HOVERING AND CIRCLING, by *Ch'en Ch'i-k'uan.*

a

g

[19]Although Wu Yung-hsiang's works have been much reproduced, no long scrolls of hers have been published for the same reasons. For her "public" paintings see *Wu Yung-hsiang chiao-shou hua-chi* 吳詠香教授畫集 , *Collection of Professor Wu Yung-hsiang's Paintings*, Ch'en Chun-fu, Taipei, 1973.

[20]Water-color on paper, 22.5 cm. x 184 cm.; a respectable ratio of approximately 1 : 8. Ch'en has done at least one other scroll with the same theme. I often think of this type of landscape as painting without borders. Each is a strip taken out of nature. See Plate 7, "Vertigo," in Catalogue: *Exhibition of Paintings by Chen Chi-kuan* [sic], The Hong Kong Arts Centre, Hong Kong, 1974.

diligently and over a long period of time produce many a bird perching on many a branch, he finally asked: "When will you really begin to paint? If you won't, I shall." Thus, the interesting start of his painting career, in the early 1950's.

"Hovering," painted in 1967, had the benefit of some fifteen years of imaginative experimentation. In it, his art has matured and become an effective form of communication to convey what words cannot express about his new world, his existence, his fascinations and puzzlements. But, what has happened to his format? It is now even impossible to classify this! Is this a hanging scroll or a handscroll? It must be a frustrating question to some, but one really shouldn't worry about such matters when confronted with a delightfully refreshing work like this. Perhaps in this disturbing unorthodoxy lies its loyalty to the venerated tradition. The artist has evoked the spirit of the drastic proportions, and succeeded in creating a work that is full of details to draw the viewer close and surprise him as he rides the movement of the composition. Observing, memorizing, and anticipating, in the best tradition of the scrolls, horizontal or vertical, the viewer participates. Here is an inexhaustible amount of visual fascination that does not depend upon literary narrative to hold the viewer's interest. Like good poetry, this painting, employing only the simple vocabulary of natural forms, creates a mood to permit an

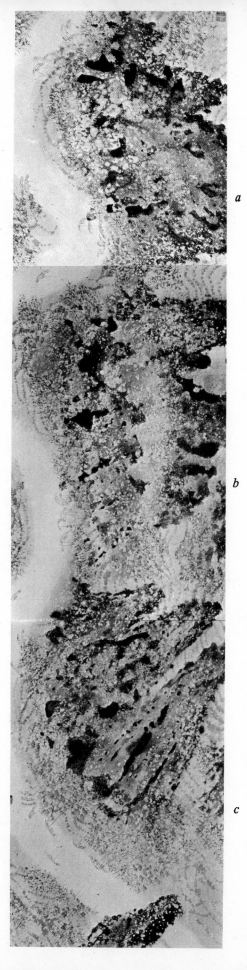

HOVERING
AND
CIRCLING,
Sections
a, b, c:
horizontal
riverscape.

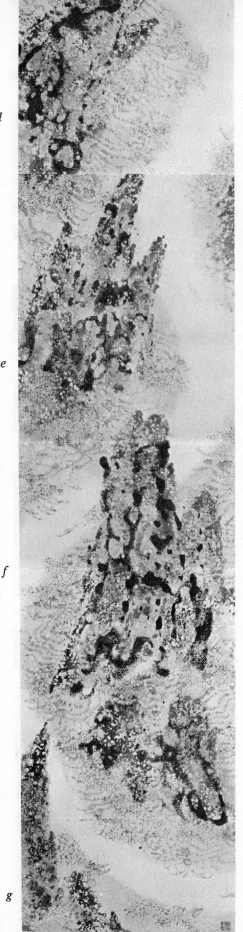

infinite variety of responses from different kinds of audiences.

There are surprises after delightful surprises. Before unrolling, we can see that this is a hanging scroll. But the beginning section clearly shows a horizontal composition of a river landscape, making us wonder if we have been mistaken in our assumption. Several things seem wrong here. Either the painting has been mounted upside down, or it is not going in the expected direction. It seems to be going from left to right! All of these seeming paradoxes, and more to come, must not be dismissed as gimmicks intended to entertain us. They are instead repeated annoyances to nag us out of our complacency, so that we recognize our own new world as revealed to us by the artist. Only when we are forced to discover that nothing is familiar do we realize that indeed, nothing around us is familiar anymore. Therefore, as we accept this, and turn the scroll around, ready to read it from left to right, we wonder what earth-shaking reason the artist had in mind to justify such tactics. Here in the top corner is a seal of the artist, but it lies on its side, at 90° to the horizon! However, as the fascinating river scene and its many dramatic mountain ranges reassure us that the painting is indeed right side up, we decide that the seal may have been an error. But then the earth begins to move and carries the mountains, the houses, the fields, and the river with it. We seem to lose our gravity and stability and find our-

HOVERING
AND
CIRCLING,
Sections
d, e, f, g:
vertical
mountains.

selves on the verge of falling into the painting, or falling from the sky. Somehow I find it very true to the Chinese manner that we should experience in painting the overwhelming sensation of flight without bothering to create an idiom for airplane. But as the land below heaves and falls away, twists and turns, we realize that we are the ones who are hovering and circling. Judging from the stilted houses in the painting, the architecture is more that of southern Asia than China. But, with so many unfamiliar experiences in such a short time, it is now difficult to work up an enthusiasm to resolve the question of whether it is the landscape or the viewer that has been *transplanted*. Still, the land continues to agitate, and we continue to hover, eyes glued to it. There is no end, nor beginning, to this scroll. As it is with all great artistic achievements, its rich undeclared meaning will outlive us.

The handscroll finally becomes a hanging scroll when it is fully extended and ready to go on the wall. We now see three seals, all right side up. And the verticality of the mountains at the bottom finally allows us a much needed rest after our dizzy journey. But returning to life on earth, we only find our immediate world more puzzling.

AN ALBUM MAY be a collection of unrelated individual leaves, or a programmed sequence of images to be read with regular cadences. In the latter case, an alert viewer reading an album from cover to cover, aided by the memory of what he has seen and in anticipation of what is to come, transforms the comfortably proportioned rectangular leaves to a scroll, horizontal or vertical, making it much more than the sum of all the leaves it contains. The format of the album, therefore, has indeed drastic proportions! Conversely, a folding screen or a set of *p'ing-t'iao* 屏條 (an arrangement of vertical scrolls),[21] are like giant albums fully opened up. In these arrangements the drastic proportions of the individual panels or scrolls are neutralized. But, as members of a set, they together present a composition in a comfortably proportioned format. However, not all albums have borders around the leaves. A *che-tzu* 摺子 has the outward appearance of an album, but cannot be classified as a *ts'e-yeh* 冊葉 , which means literally "album leaves". Instead, as a format, a *che-tzu* is a scroll folded in zigzag fashion. To the painter, a *che-tzu* is versatile and convenient to carry on trips. He can also get to any section of a long composition instantly without having to unroll each time from the beginning as in the case with a scroll. After the work is completed, a *che-tzu* may be mounted as a handscroll, and indeed many have been so preserved. Taking into consideration the characteristics of all the formats discussed here, it seems then the unique challenge of the true album is in the cadences and the controlled rhythm they suggest. The cadences that struggle not to yield the secrets of the composition all at once are the limitations as well as the inspiration of the album.

I discussed this matter with my old friend, Ch'en Ch'i-k'uan, when he visited me in 1968. It was after a small dinner party following an exhibition of his works at my home. All the guests had left. We talked about how difficult it had become to

---

[21]For an illustration of such an arrangement, see *the Connoisseur*, Roma, 1958, p. 19.
R. H. van Gulik, *Chinese Pictorial Art As Viewed by*

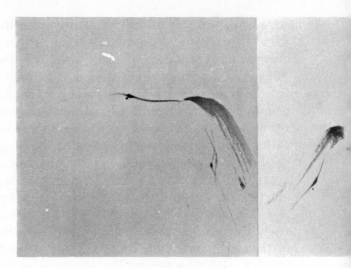

Plate 109
THE CRANE,
by Ch'en Ch'i-k'uan.
Sections a, b, c.

c

have long handscrolls mounted. But albums, and especially *che-tzu*, are still available from Japan, I said. The conversation suddenly became spirited. I urged Ch'en to try his hand on one. He thought about it for few short moments, and then took the small album I placed in front of him and opened it up on the dining room table to its full length. In less than twenty minutes he returned the album to me, and I knew I had in my hands a masterpiece—a breakthrough! By a stroke of genius, he had managed to cooperate fully with the format, thus benefited from it, and yet brilliantly broken all its limitations. Because of his respect for the cadences, he was rewarded with a beautiful and lively rhythm in his work. But, showing even greater respect, he had gone further and challenged his format. As a result, his crane soars high into the sky, its body and wings disappearing above the leaves with only the dangling legs still in the album. And, as the great bird glides, it fills three double-leaves! There is limit-

f

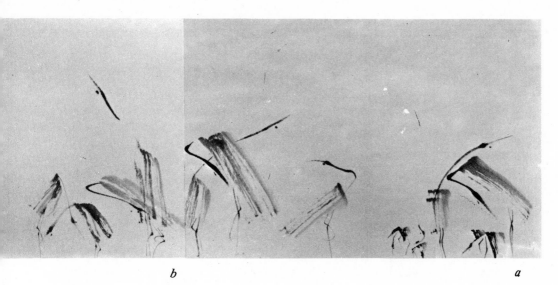

b   a

less imagination and joy in these powerful forms. Here is one *che-tzu* that shall never be mounted as a scroll and stripped of its cadences.

I am a writer, and I know how writers react to the interpretations of their work by their readers and critics. I have interpreted Wu Yung-hsiang's own favorite long handscroll, and Ch'en Ch'i-k'uan's magnificent, dynamic landscape. It is time to let the readers of this article have their own adventures in this untitled album which we shall call "The Crane" (Pl. 109). However, it must be difficult for anyone not to identify himself with the birds, big and small, old and young. Especially when the Great Crane, points his beak at the end of his long and graceful neck at the sky, we contemplate flight with him. And when his velocity approaches the speed of sound, and as his great mass expands, we transcend our physical limitations. But in the end, we return.

The album, as a format, its cadences and all, will never be the same again.

THE CRANE: Sections d, e, f.

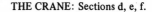
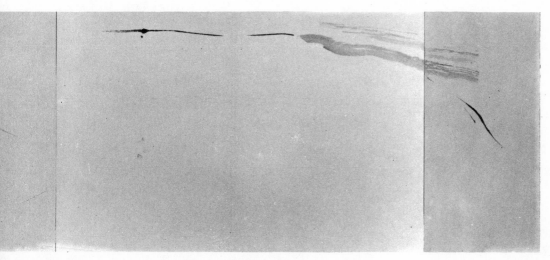

d

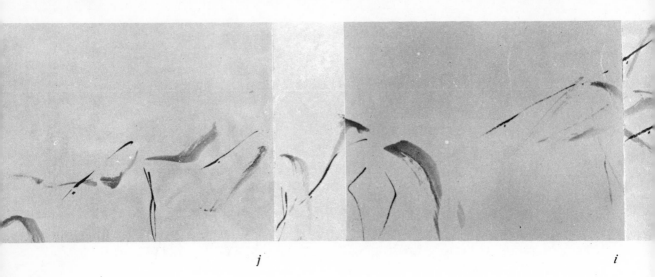

j   *i*

A SEVENTH PAINTING should be discussed here in this article. But such a plate there shall never be. Wu Yung-hsiang, my late sister, plagued by poor health all her life, died in 1970 at age 58 in Taipei. On her deathbed she told a painter friend and student: "I still have a painting to do. It's a new painting, a very, very new painting." What she said has become well known, and most interpret it to mean that this hard-working painter, inventive and resourceful all her life, had only her work on her mind when she died.[22] I think differently. My sister and I talked about the future of Chinese painting at great length whenever we could be together. She was an ingenious

[22]Ch'i, *Biography*, XXV/5 (150), p. 90.

THE CRANE: Sections k, l.

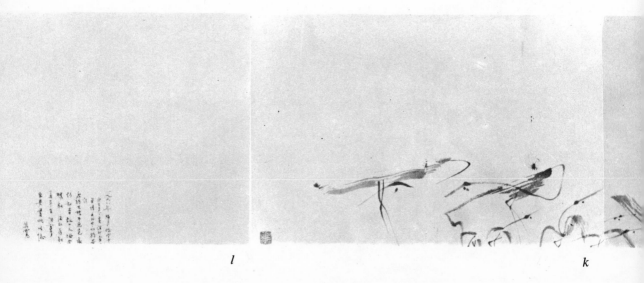

l   *k*

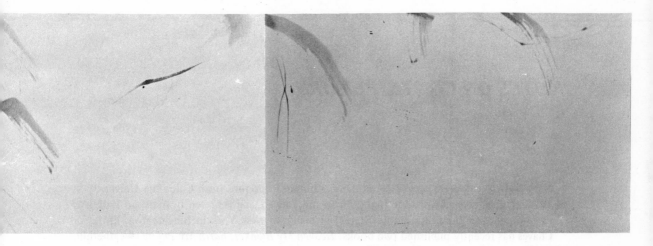

h

g

THE CRANE: Sections g, h, i, j.

and ambitious artist accustomed to excel, and never needed me to urge her to try out any new ideas. She had enough ideas of her own. She had taken a keen interest in the development of Western art when she was a student, but it was near the end of her life that she ventured out of her traditional Chinese environment for the first time and came to the United States with my family. On this trip she had her first exposure to the myriad expressions of modern Western art. Most of the time she was uncomfortable with them, but was attracted nevertheless. Yet she had to decide how she could best utilize her energy and time. We argued about this. I encouraged her to take a vacation from what she had been doing so successfully, and begin something new. If she had been her early self of her student days, she would have agreed to try. But the pressure of daily life and the demand for her paintings finally persuaded her to stay with her established ways. Just for a little longer, she would say; just for this one next exhibition. But her mind, I knew, was already on the new.[23]

So, this article will have no seventh painting. Yet I sincerely believe that so long as our artists continue to experiment and do their part as individuals, and so long as there is always "a new painting, a very, very new painting" on their minds, there will be a future for a painting tradition that is particularly Chinese.

[23]There is a lengthy quotation from her diary in the third installment of *Biography* (*ibid.*, p. 87). In it my sister told of her depression and the thoughts that converged on and burdened her mind. "I often feel lonely and sad, especially when lying awake after midnight. I think of my ambition as a youth, my energies and time invested in copying the ancient paintings, what a waste it now seems! The winds in the field of painting are swiftly changing directions! And, my health is deteriorating! . . . My second younger brother [she is referring to me], with his air of superiority, mercilessly criticizes me. . . ." Of the six of us, three brothers and three sisters, we two were always the closest. I still find it difficult to speak of her in the past tense. I am sure some day when we will be together again, we will enjoy arguing the future of Chinese painting anew.

NOTES ON CONTRIBUTORS

JONATHAN CHAVES earned his Ph.D. in Chinese Literature from Columbia University in 1971. He has traveled widely in India, Japan and Taiwan, and is presently Assistant Professor of Comparative Literature at the State University of New York in Binghamton. Professor Chaves has recently published two books: *Heaven My Blanket, Earth My Pillow* (Weatherhill, 1975), a collection of translations of poems by Yang Wan-li (1127-1206), and *Mei Yao-ch'en and the Development of Early Sung Poetry* (Columbia University Press, 1976).

RICHARD EDWARDS has taught oriental art and archaeology at Boston University, Brandeis University, Washington University at St. Louis, Missouri, University of California at Berkeley, and is at present Professor of Far Eastern Art at the History of Art Department of the University of Michigan. Over a period of thirty years he has traveled widely in China, Taiwan, Hong Kong, Japan, India, Pakistan and Afghanistan. He is author of many articles published in *Archives, Artibus Asiae, Ars Orientalis* etc. and the following books: *The Field of Stones*, a study of the art of Shen Chou (Washington, 1962); *Li Ti*, Freer Gallery of Art Occasional Papers (Washington, 1967); *The Painting of Tao-chi* (University of Michigan, 1967); and *The Art of Wen Cheng-ming* (1470-1559) (University of Michigan, 1976).

ALBERT LOUIS FAUROT (福路), musician, teacher, author and missionary, studied Piano at the Royal Academy of Music in London and received an M.A. in Music History at the Conservatory of Music at Oberlin College in 1940. He studied Mandarin and Chinese music in Peking in 1940, and taught at Foochow College, Hwa Nan College and Fukien Christian University up to 1950. After that, he regularly gave lecture-recital tours in America and the Far East. Besides a number of books on music and piano repertoire, he has written original poetry and has made English translations from Chinese, Japanese, German and French poetry. He is currently Professor of Piano, Music and Art History at Silliman University, Philippines.

MAYCHING KAO (高美慶) graduated from New Asia College, the Chinese University of Hong Kong, and received her doctorate degree in Oriental Art History from Stanford University in 1972. She is at present Lecturer in Art History at the Department of Fine Arts, New Asia College, CUHK.

ELLEN JOHNSTON LAING received her Ph.D. from the University of Michigan, and is presently Associate Professor at Wayne State University, Detroit, Michigan, where she teaches Far Eastern Art History. Her articles on Chinese painting have appeared in *Artibus Asiae, Oriental Art* and elsewhere. She is also author of *Chinese Paintings in Chinese Publications 1956-1968: An Annotated Bibliography and an Index to the Paintings* (Ann Arbor, 1969).

THOMAS LAWTON (羅覃) received his Ph.D. degree from Harvard University in 1970. While living in Taiwan, from 1963-1967, he served as advisor to the National Palace Museum. In 1967 he was appointed Curator of Chinese Art at the Freer Gallery of Art in Washington, D.C., where he is currently Assistant Director. Dr. Lawton is co-author of *The New Chinese Landscape; Six Contemporary Chinese Artists* (New York, American Federation of Arts,

1966); *The Freer Gallery of Art, Part I, China, & Part II, Japan* (Kodansha Ltd., Tokyo, 1971); and author of *Eugene and Agnes E. Meyer Memorial Exhibition*, (Washington, D.C., Smithsonian Institution, 1973) and many articles printed in *Oriental Art, Ars Orientalis, Journal of the American Oriental Society* etc.

Born in Canton, CHU-TSING LI (李鑄晉) received his B.A. in English Literature from the University of Nanking (1943) and his M.A. in Literature and Ph.D. in Art History from the University of Iowa (1955). He also did some post-doctoral work in Chinese art at Harvard and Princeton. After teaching at Oberlin College and the University of Iowa, he served as professor of art history at the University of Kansas since 1966 and chairman of the Department since 1972. He is author of several books, including *The Autumn Colors on the Ch'iao and Hua Mountains: A Painting by Chao Meng-fu* 鵲華秋色 (1965) and *A Thousand Peaks and Myriad Ravines: The Charles A. Drenowatz Collection in Zurich* 千巖萬壑 (1974), both published by the *Artibus Asiae* in Switzerland, and many articles on Chinese art. He taught at the Chinese University of Hong Kong during the academic year of 1972-73, as Visiting Professor of Fine Arts.

HIN-CHEUNG LOVELL (梁獻章) was born in Hong Kong where she attended St. Stephen's Girls' College and read English and History at the University of Hong Kong. After straying into the world of antiquities in the Royal Ontario Museum, Toronto, she studied Chinese Archaeology at the University of London. Since 1968, she has been on the staff of the Freer Gallery of Art, Washington, D.C.

HSIO-YEN SHIH (時學顏) was born in Wuch'ang, China, and educated in the United States. She has taught Chinese archaeology, art history and Chinese cultural history at Bryn Mawr College, Trinity College at Hartford, Connecticutt, York University, University of California at Berkeley, University of Toronto, and the Chinese University of Hong Kong, where she was Visiting Professor from 1973 to 1974. She is now concurrently Curator of the Far Eastern Department of the Royal Ontario Museum and Adjunct Professor of the Department of East Asian Studies at the University of Toronto. Many of her articles on Chinese art and archaeology have appeared in *Artibus Asiae, Arts Canada, World Archaeology, Journal of Oriental Studies* etc.

LAURENCE C. S. TAM (譚志成), a graduate of the University of London in Classical Chinese, obtained his M.A. in History of Chinese Art at the University of Hong Kong and Master in Museology at the University of Toronto. An artist specialized in Chinese ink painting and a teacher of Chinese art history, he is at present Acting Curator of the Hong Kong Museum of Art, responsible for such Urban Council publications as *Kwangtung Painting* and *Ch'i Pai-shih*. His own paintings have been exhibitied in Hong Kong, Japan, England, Scotland, the United States, Canada and Australia.

WANG FANG-YU (王方宇), born 1913 in Peking, was graduated from the Catholic Fu Jen University in that city. He holds advanced degrees from South China University and Columbia University. He taught Chinese Language for many years at the Institute of Far Eastern

Languages, Yale University, and is at present Professor of Chinese at Seton Hall University. He is the author of Chinese language text-books and the compiler of a *Mandarin Chinese Dictionary* (Seton Hall University Press, South Orange, N. J., 1967, 1971). He is also a calligrapher and connoisseur who owns an extensive collection of Chinese rare books and seals.

JAMES C. Y. WATT (屈志仁) was educated in England at King's College, Taunton, and then Queen's College, Oxford, where he graduated in 1959. He is at present Curator of the Art Gallery and Senior Lecturer in Fine Arts at the Chinese University of Hong Kong. He is interested in both Chinese and European literature and occasionally tries his hand at translation of poetry.

WANG TEH-CHAO (王德昭) has been Professor of History since 1943 at National Kweichow University, Taiwan Normal University and Nanyang University successively. Besides his publications on modern Chinese history and political thought, he has translated into Chinese Arnold Silcock's *Introduction to Chinese Art and History* (中國美術史導論, Cheng Chung Press, Taiwan, 1961) and Crane Brinton's Ideas and Men—*The Shaping of Modern Thought* (西洋思想史, Committee for Translation and Compilation of College Textbooks, Ministry of Education, Taipei, 1959). He is currently Reader in History and Associate Director of the Institute of Chinese Studies at the Chinese University of Hong Kong.

AILEEN HUANG WEI (魏黃艾玲) obtained her B.A. from Yenching University in Peking and has taught at the Institute of Far Eastern Languages, Yale University. She is now Professor of Chinese at Seton Hall University.

NELSON I. WU (吳訥孫) is Edward Mallinckrodt Distinguished University Professor of the History of Art and Chinese Culture at Washington University, St. Louis, Missouri. He was born in Peking in 1919, graduated from National Southwest Associated University in Kunming in 1942, and received his Ph.D. from Yale University in 1954. He has taught at San Francisco State College and Yale, and served as Chairman, Department of Art and Archaeology, Washington University, 1968-70, and Visiting Professor, Tokyo University, 1972-73. In 1972, he was made a Senior Fellow of the U. S. National Endowment for the Humanities. A versatile scholar in art, literature and philosophy, Prof. Wu is also a calligrapher and cinematographer. Among his many writings in Chinese and English is the long novel, a spiritual autobiography, 未央歌 (*A Song Never to End*), first published in Hong Kong in 1959 and now in its 12th Taiwan edition; and the allegorical work 人子 (*The Human Child*), Taipei, 1974; both written under the pseudonym Lu Ch'iao (鹿橋).

DIANA YU (余丹) has worked with a number of translation projects before she joined the staff of *Renditions* in 1973. Since then she has served the magazine in its multiple duties of translation, editing and designing. Her own amateur interest in print-making accounts for the appearance of her article in this issue.

略談北魏的屏風漆畫　　　　　　　　志　工

（一）

　　1965年山西大同石家寨發現了北魏司馬金龍夫婦的合葬墓，墓中出土的文物很多，《文物》1972年第三期已有專文報導。墓中的文物羣裏有一件漆屏風，上畫古代歷史人物故事，引起了廣大讀者的注意。因爲它不但給予我們關於古代歷史上人們生活習慣的許多直觀材料，並且還給了我們關於古代工藝和繪畫方面的不少重要史料。

　　由於近代考古工作的普遍深入，發現了若干古代繪畫——從戰國楚帛畫和許多漆器上的繪畫，直到唐代的大量壁畫和紙上、絹上的作品，這些已經足以給繪畫歷史平添了非常豐富的實物證據（宋代以來傳世的繪畫就更多了）；只有南北朝時期的實物比較還不是很多的。敦煌北魏的壁畫是比較豐富、集中的，可是，內容既限於佛教，而大部份畫面的最上一層的顏色又已脫落。現在這件從東漢以來就廣爲流行的歷史風俗題材的漆畫屏風的出現，正好彌補了繪畫史上這一時期的空白。

　　從髹漆工藝上看，在出土的古文物中也有不少精美的成品，自戰國至唐宋，也是極其豐富多彩的，如果研究髹漆工藝的發展歷史，這件屏風也同樣起着重要的史料作用。

　　由於紙絹上的繪畫不易保存，所以探討古代繪畫，常要借助於磚、石、木刻、髹漆、織綉等等，它們盡管或用刀子鐫刻，或以刷子塗飾，或爲針綫刺綉，但還是可以看出所憑借的畫稿的風格和特點。何況用漆描繪，同用筆在紙絹竹木上描繪的效果相差無幾，所以這件漆屏風，既是一件古代工藝成品，又是一幅古代繪畫眞迹。

（二）

　　北魏的皇族，是鮮卑拓跋部中的上層人物，他們到了中原地區，和漢族地主階級相勾結，構成了北魏的統治集團。司馬金龍本爲晉代貴族後裔而成了北魏政治上的重要人物，就是北魏統治集團的特點之一。

　　在歷史上，北魏鮮卑統治階級的軍事組織和語言習慣上還遺留着鮮卑族的痕迹，至於文化藝術，無論傳世的或出土的，幾乎全是漢魏以來的傳統。就拿繪畫和書法來看，把北魏作品同所見的南朝作品相比較，如果說有什麼不同，那只是地區風格的細微出入，而未見有民族的差異。這就反映了，在偉大的中華民族的形成過程中，各少數民族和中原民族融合的歷史情況和共同創造燦爛的古代中國的文化藝術情況。

　　偉大領袖毛主席教導我們，在封建社會中，"只有農民和手工業工人是創造財富和創造文化的基本的階級。"拿繪畫藝術來說，它產生於生產實踐，產生於實用。它的創造者，從原始社會陶器上簡單的動物形象、幾何圖案到漢代"深沉雄大"的雕刻（魯迅語）以及漢魏的屏風上的歷史風俗畫，莫不是勞動人民。文人士大夫畫的出現，是在工匠畫基礎上的一個發展，他們的技法，其最初顯然是從工匠畫學來的。當然，在繪畫藝術的發展過程中，統治階級的文人士大夫畫家在技法上也不斷有所提高和創新，也曾對工匠畫產生過一定的影響。可是，在技術上，不能割斷繪畫發展的歷史，繪畫產生於直接從事生產的勞動者之手，離開了最初的比較古拙的繪畫藝術，便沒有後來繁富的、精湛的繪畫藝術。這裏當然有低級階段同高級階段的區別，但是，凡是技術上有所創新的文人士大夫畫家，總是不斷從工匠的繪畫中受到啓發或以工匠畫作爲借鑒。

民間工匠的繪畫，無論從藝術技巧和作品數量上都占居主流地位，而且自成體系。可是，過去士大夫文人所寫的繪畫史，都往往抹煞工匠畫，置於藝苑之外而不願。這是對繪畫史的歪曲。這件屏風漆畫，以鮮明的色彩、生動的形象顯示了民間藝術的成就，暴露了統治階級編寫的繪畫史的偏見和虛妄。

（三）

讓我們看看這件屏風漆畫的藝術淵源及其風格吧。

從屏風上的畫風來觀察，它的人物形象相當生動，綫條不多，沒有什麼復雜的裝飾性的筆墨，在簡明、扼要的"骨法用筆"中表現了人物的主要動態。大家都盛贊雲崗、龍門的北魏石雕的刀法"簡古"，也就是樸素健康而富有力量，以爲多半是出於刀刻的效果；現在看了這件屏風上人物的畫法，其樸素健康而富有力量，一如北魏的石刻，可以了然當時繪畫的風格基本上就是這樣。

拿這件屏風漆畫同前期的繪畫比較，例如同洛陽、遼陽、望都、安平[①]等地發現的漢代壁畫比較，無論筆法綫條、表現方法，都有它們的血肉相連的關係，就是用色的基本調子，也都有相通之處。

拿這件屏風漆畫與其同時代的作品，例如同南京出土的墓磚上的竹林七賢圖比較[②]，雖然磚刻不能見筆踪和彩色，但兩者人物形象的生動，綫條的簡潔有力，都沒有什麼異樣。盡管磚刻的畫面較大，故事人物的具體內容不同，細節不能不有所差異，但從總的繪畫風格來看，則是一致的。

拿這件屏風漆畫同後來的作品比較，例如同流傳的畫卷《女史箴》、宋摹《列女仁智圖》比較。《女史箴》本是無名畫家的傑作，不知什麼時候被人添上了"顧愷之畫"幾個小字，於是便成了顧愷之的標準眞迹。那卷上分段題字，極明顯晚於北魏；那四個名款小字與每段題字，既非出於一手，而書風更晚，所以我們只能當它是唐代或稍早的筆迹《列女仁智圖》，傳說爲顧愷之作，現存的一卷，由於絹素，筆墨、題字種種特點，很明顯非東晉時的作品，於是有些人只好承認它是宋人摹本，但還要帶上一句顧愷之，說是宋人摹顧愷之的眞迹。我們把屏風漆畫同《女史箴》、《列女仁智圖》對看，很明顯，它們的故事內容既相類，而題材的處理、所畫人物的衣冠服飾、生活器物更多相同。當然，作爲卷軸畫，《女史箴》和《列女仁智圖》在描繪技巧上自然要比漆器上的裝飾繪畫工整細密；而兩個畫卷制作時間又較晚，繪畫的技藝自然更爲精進。從這個比較中我們不難得出這樣的認識:《女史箴》和《列女仁智圖》的畫風，來源於民間工藝，而這兩個圖卷，原來是在工匠繪畫的基礎上加工而成的。

還有兩卷號稱唐代閻立本的畫卷，一是《步輦圖》，一是《帝王圖》，技巧比較工致，許多人物形象、服裝、器物同屏風漆畫也極相近。可見唐代人物故事畫的藝術技巧，同前代民間工匠的漆畫，也是有它的歷史傳統的。

① 《河北望都縣漢墓的墓室結構和壁畫》，《文物參考資料》1954年第12期
《望都漢墓壁畫》,中國古典藝術出版社
《遼陽發現的三座壁畫古墓》，《文物參考資料》1955年第5期
《洛陽西漢壁畫墓發掘報告》，《考古學報》1964年第2期

② 《南京西善橋南朝墓及其磚刻壁畫》，《文物》1960年第8、9期

當然，唐宋以來把這些卷軸說是顧、閻的作品，可能由於畫卷的"底稿"出於顧、閻，或畫風畫法沿襲了顧、閻。但從屏風畫的發現，我們得到了有力的物証，即若干文人士大夫名畫家的師承是其來有自的，他們的師傅就是若干前代無名的工匠及其遺留下來的作品。

（四）

此外，這件漆畫上的題字，也是值得注意的。

我們知道，中國的書法藝術是聞名世界的，不但歷史悠久，而且豐富多彩。從甲骨、籀書、小篆、隸書、草書、行書一直到楷書，幾千年來不斷發展變化，形成一個完整的體系。

書法發展到魏晉南北朝時期，進入了一個新的階段，出現了書法藝術上的千岩竟秀、百花爭妍的局面。晉代著名的大書家王羲之，就生長在這個書法藝術燦若雲錦的時代。魏晉南北朝的書法表現在磚刻、石刻、寫經、簡牘等，有的茂密渾厚，有的駿逸豪放，有的蒼古妙麗，有的雄健逸宕，盡管各有其特色，但都體現出一個共同點，就是由隸書逐漸演變爲楷書的過程。這點，我們只要比較一下北齊天保七年江妙養記磚、北涼寫經殘卷（中國革命歷史博物館藏）、湖北襄陽出土的北齊天統五年造像碑、河南鄭縣出土的南朝甲馬畫像磚側墨書文字以及西涼建初六年侯馥等催箭催鎧文書的文字，便可看出其相通之處了。

司馬金龍墓漆畫題字也是這樣。它十分挺拔俊逸，其形體結構既不是漢代隸書一派，又不是唐代以來楷書一派。它是一種似隸似楷、非隸非楷而兼有魏碑風格的有骨有肉、筆劃稍瘦而圓潤的字體。它氣勢疏朗，給人以優美之感。

還有，書法的筆法和結體，固然每個書者都有自己的習慣特點，但同時代的作品，也必然有着共同的風格。試拿南北朝一些著名的碑刻來同漆畫和題字相比，如北魏的高貞碑和曹望憘題象記，同漆畫上的題字就很接近。只是因爲字上石後筆鋒多受刀刻影響，不如墨迹那末清晰罷了。北魏的寫經多是寫書籍寫經卷的規格，同碑版字體不免有所出入；而這件漆畫題字字迹的體勢却與碑版書法體勢接近，在北魏朱書墨書的碑版原迹尚未發現之前，這份漆畫題字應是印証北魏碑志書風的重要參考材料。

還有南朝的梁始興王肖憺碑，爲南朝書家貝義淵所寫，寫法刻法都相當精緻。從筆流結體的一般風格來看，與北魏高貞碑、曹望憘造像記等，也很相近，這就是說，與漆畫題字也有足以相印証的地方。這些都是值得研究書法藝術時注意的。

明季文人與繪畫　　　　　　　　　　　　　　饒宗頤

引　言

明季文人大都兼擅書畫。詩人吳梅村之爲畫家，（作"畫中九友歌"）人咸知之。至如竟陵鍾惺，亦是能手。嘗見其一幀密林叠嶂，自題：「天啟辛酉夏，戲倣黃子久筆意。」載《神州大觀》第八册。鄧實云：「鍾伯敬以詩名，不謂其能畫；仿大癡得蒼莽之象。晚明士大夫擅文藝者，多兼繪事，亦一時風習使然，董華亭（其昌）提倡之力也。」實則，元季明初，亦有此種現象。劉基爲開國文豪，亦擅繪事，有《蜀川圖》留傳於丹陽孫氏；兼能寫梅，世有藏本。偶一爲之，亦有可觀者；流風餘韻，下逮明之末葉。文人墨戲，初不求工，而自有奇趣，未必由華亭所影響也。

畫人眼中 '畫士'、'士畫' 流品之分野

顧凝遠《畫引》論列明代畫人姓氏，以董其昌崛起雲間，特別目之爲 '中興間氣'。其餘畫

家，分爲以下若干名目：

(一)士大夫名家宗匠（如沈、文、唐）；

(二)文士名家（如陳道復、陸治、徐渭）；

(三)畫名家（周臣四人）；

(四)今文士名家（李流芳、鍾惺五人）。

畫名家大概是指以畫爲專業，非‘文士’者流。所謂‘文士名家’，即文人而兼擅繪畫者，而鍾惺
亦在被稱述之列。

清初周亮工最喜歡蒐集同時人畫品，所作《讀畫錄》，月旦人物，獨具隻眼。（亮工卒於康熙
十一年，此書殆於康熙十二年，由其子在浚編集而成。）故宮博物院藏周亮工《集名家山水册》，
見《石渠》三編著錄。所收畫蹟其中有石溪，而無石濤、八大，可見在周亮工集畫時期，此二位
畫僧尚未成名，不爲人注意。又該册中有龔賢題記，論清初畫壇云：

> 「今日畫家以江南爲盛；江南十四郡，以首都爲盛。郡中著名者且數十輩，但能吮
> 筆者，奚啻千人？然名流復有二派，有三品：曰能品、曰神品、曰逸品。能品爲上，
> 餘無論焉。神品者，能品中之莫可測識者也。神品在能品之上，而逸品又在神品之
> 上，逸品殆不可言語形容矣。是以能品、神品爲一派，曰正派；逸品爲別派。能品
> 稱畫師，神品爲畫祖。逸品散聖，無位可居，反不得不謂之畫士。今賞鑑家，見高
> 超筆墨，則曰有士氣。而凡夫俗子，於稱揚之詞，寓譏諷之意，亦曰此士大夫畫耳。
> 明乎畫非士大夫事，而士大夫非畫家者流，不知閻立本乃李唐宰相，王維亦尙書右
> 丞，何嘗非士大夫耶？若定以高超筆墨爲士大夫畫，而倪、黃、董、巨，亦何嘗在
> 搢紳列耶？自吾論之，能品不得非逸品，猶之乎別派不可少正派也。（使世皆別派，
> 是國中惟高僧羽流，而無衣冠文物也。使畫止能品，是王斗、顏斶，皆可役爲皂隸；
> 巢父、許由，皆可驅而爲牧圉耳。）金陵畫家，能品最夥，而神品、逸品，亦各有
> 數人。然逸品則首推二谿；曰石谿、曰青谿。石谿，殘道人也；青谿，程侍郎也。
> 皆寓公。殘道人畫，龖服亂頭；如王孟津書法。程侍郎畫，冰肌玉骨，如董華亭書
> 法。百年來論書法，則王、董二公應不讓；若論畫筆，則今日兩谿，又奚肯多讓乎
> 哉！」（《故宮書畫錄》卷6，277-278頁）

龔氏又論：

> 「畫有六法，此南齊謝恭（赫）之言。自余論之，有四要而無六法耳。一曰筆，二
> 曰墨，三曰丘壑，四曰氣韻。筆法宜老，墨氣宜潤，丘壑宜穩，三者得而氣韻在其
> 中矣。筆法欲秀而老，若徒老而不秀，枯矣。墨言潤，明其非濕也。丘壑者，位置
> 之總名；位置宜安，然必奇而安，不奇無貴於安；安而不奇，庸乎也；奇而不安，
> 生手也。今有作家、士大夫家二派：作家畫安而不奇，士大夫畫，奇而不安；與其
> 號爲庸手，何若生手之爲高乎？倘能愈老愈秀，愈秀愈潤，愈潤愈奇，愈奇愈安，
> 此畫之上品，由於天姿高而功力深也。宜其中有詩意，有文理，有道氣。噫！豈小
> 技哉！（余不能畫而能談，安得與酷好者談，三年而未竟也？當今豈無其人耶？因
> 紀此而請與相見。）」（《虛齋名畫續錄》卷三龔半千《山水册》）

此二篇爲極重要文字。其論逸品極嚴，清初入選者只二溪而已，不若後來《桐陰論畫》，動輒譽
人爲逸品也。又減六法爲四法，以位置居四者之一；可見今人論畫，喜言構圖，在龔氏眼中，極
不重要，因尚有筆、墨與氣韻三條件，絕不能忽視也。且構圖位置，不在求安，而在求奇。安而
不奇是庸手，作家畫是也；奇而不安是生手，士大夫畫是也。與其取庸手，不如生手之爲高，奇
與安二者之間，安不如奇，惟士大夫畫如能出奇翻新，作家不易辦到，是無異謂‘畫士’不如‘士
畫’。

又其論四法之關聯性：筆欲老而墨欲潤，丘壑欲穩而奇，三者得則氣韻自生，故氣韻乃一綜

合體，離開筆與墨無所謂氣韻，故非筆與墨無以表現氣韻。筆與墨初爲二途，然筆、墨交融之後，即在畫面呈顯氣韻矣。故筆欲老，愈老而愈秀，秀即筆之有神有力處，不秀則疲苶乏神采，不老則稚弱無氣概，何能出奇？秀而且潤，則筆與墨交會，由秀而生潤，益見筆之高妙及墨之光彩；加之構圖之奇而且穩，‘氣韻’自然迴絕。畫之上品，捨此何求？八個‘愈’字，充份說明四法之相生相養，故龔氏四法之說，竊以爲視謝赫尤中肯綮也。

　　龔氏區別清初畫人有三品兩派之說：能品、神品爲正派，逸品爲別派。能品稱畫師，神品爲畫祖，逸品則爲散聖。於逸品推許二谿（石溪、青溪）；能品、神品爲畫士，逸品則爲士畫。是說方亨咸（邵村）有進一步之討論，其與周亮工論畫云：

　　　　「半千‘畫士’‘士畫’之論詳矣，確不可易。覺謝赫《畫品》，猶有漏焉。但伸逸
　　　品於神品之上，似尚未當。蓋神也者，心手兩忘，筆墨俱化，氣韻規矩，皆不可端
　　　倪，仁者見仁，知者見知，所謂一而不可知之謂神也。逸者軼也，軼於尋常範圍之
　　　外，如天馬行空，不事覊絡爲也。亦自有堂構窈窕，禪家所謂教外別傳，又曰別峰
　　　相見者也。神品是如來地位，能則辟支二乘果。如兵法，神品是孫、吳，能則刁斗
　　　聲嚴之程不識，逸則解鞍縱卧之李將軍；能之至始神，神非一端可執也。是神品在
　　　能與逸之上，不可概論，況可抑之哉！半千之所謂神者，抑能事之純熟者乎？總之，
　　　繪事清事也，韻事也。胸中無幾卷書，筆下有一點塵，便窮年累歲，刻劃鏤研，終
　　　一匠作，了何用乎？此眞賞者所以有雅俗之辨也。豈士人之畫，盡逸品哉？」（《讀
　　　畫錄》卷二）

邵村訓神爲筆墨俱化，訓逸爲軼于尋常範圍之外，而以士人之畫，不盡爲逸品。又主神品宜在能品、逸品之上，與半千以逸品居能神之上，大異其趣。此由于對“神”字解釋之不同，故品次亦復不同。

　　方以智則分畫筆有匠筆、文筆二途，而皆未合中道。其言曰：

　　　　「世之目匠筆者以其爲法所礙；其目文筆者，則又爲無礙所礙，此中關棙子，原須
　　　一一透過，然後靑山白雲，得大自在。」（《讀畫錄》卷三“張爾唯傳”）

匠筆爲法所囿，文筆又以法不太具足爲其所累。明季畫人對此二者間之軒輊，持論各有不同，而其輕‘匠’重‘文’，則所見一致，因畫人多爲文士故也。

　　石濤於康熙（三十三年，1694）甲戌秋爲鳴六寫枯樹册題記云：

　　　　「此道從門入者，不是家珍，而以名振一時，得不難哉！高古之如白禿、青溪、道
　　　山諸君輩，清逸之如梅壑、漸江二老；乾瘦之如垢道人；淋漓奇古之如南昌八大山
　　　人；豪放之如梅瞿山、雪坪子，皆一代之解人也。吾獨不解此意，故其空空洞洞木
　　　木默默之如此，問訊鳴六先生，予之評訂，其旨若斯，具眼者得不絕倒乎？」

此册現藏美國洛杉磯（Los Angeles）。（圖見 The Painting of Tao-chi 108頁，安那堡印）。石濤品題之同時畫家，白禿指石谿，青溪爲程正揆，道山即陳舒，（見《讀畫錄》；舒自松江移居金陵）風格屬於高古；查士標（梅壑）、漸江，妙在清逸；程邃（垢道人）長于乾筆，八大特色在淋漓奇古；梅清（瞿山）、梅庚（雪坪子），則以豪放見長。石濤所標揭者，僅此數子，可以代表其一種看法。石濤此文，作于康熙卅三年，與龔賢之爲周櫟園（亮工）題記作於康熙十年，蓋遲廿載，應屬後期之論，此時已不復較量畫士與士畫之分別矣。

文人與畫家相兼之類型

（甲）　散文家兼畫家

侯方域

　　四公子之一，以散文著名，爲陳貞慧之壻，寓居宜興。集中撰“倪雲林十萬圖記”，即貞慧

藏品。論「雲林畫多得之氣象蕭疎，煙林淸曠；此獨峯巒渾厚，勢狀雄強，其皴擦勾斫分披、糾合之法、無一不備，神至之筆。」可謂知言！畫頗罕見。畫家人名辭典不見其名。楊鍾羲曾覩其畫，於所著《雪橋詩話》稱藏有朝宗畫山水，朝宗題句云：「江柳依依江草齊，亂山無語送斜暉，幽人夜把孤篷去，滿載一船春色歸。」(《晚晴簃詩匯》195 "弘智" 條)

王思任

季重好爲古文詞。粵人何吾騶之《元氣堂詩集》卷前即有王思任序。或稱其寫山水林屋，皴染瀿鬱，超然筆墨之外。其評天台山云：「恍惚幽玄，不記何代；片時坐對，人化爲碧。」觀此數語，季重之畫不遠矣(《無聲詩史》語)。可見其對山水體會之深。季重畫，至樂樓藏一軸，胎息子久，爛漫可喜。

(乙)　詩人兼畫家

鍾　惺

伯敬與譚友夏並以詩鳴，其畫論者謂「得之於詩，從荒寒一境入，故神趣冷逸，無一毫喧熱氣。」(《桐陰論畫》)

金陵八家之葉榮木(欣)，評者謂其畫近竟陵之詩：「竟陵之詩淡遠又淡遠，淡遠以至於無。榮木畫似之。每見其所作，斷草荒烟，孤城古渡，令人動秦月漢關之思。」此以詩喩畫，尤覺新穎可喜。

程嘉燧

孟陽詩有《松圓浪淘》等集，錢牧齋譽其照見古人心髓，于汗靑漫漶，丹粉凋殘之後；合轍古人，後生一開心眼，謚之曰松圓詩老。(《列朝詩集》丁集下576頁)朱彝尊則譏其格調卑，才氣弱。漁洋謂孟陽七律，于明末爲一派；舉其警句如「夢裏楚江昏似墨，畫中湖雨白于絲」、「迴峯凍雨皆成雪，出霧危巒半是雲」均可入畫。孟陽畫入逸品，深靜枯淡，意趣開逸，如其詩之娟秀絕塵，不以氣概取勝。惟梔之令人掃除町畦，不得以卑弱爲病。(漁洋《精華錄》五云：「偶得松圓老人畫，愛其風格不減雲林，因用雲林自題『蕭蕭風雨麥秋寒』一首韻題之。」孟陽畫構圖學倪者甚多，宜魚洋之傾倒也。孟陽於崇禎十六年十二月卒於新安，年七十九，雖不得目爲遺民，然以詩人而爲畫家，如孟陽者，不數數觀。)

(丙)　曲家兼畫家

祁豸佳

止祥最工戲曲，周亮工稱其「常自爲新劇，按紅牙，敎諸童子；或自度曲，或令客度曲，自倚洞簫和之，借以抒其憤鬱。嘗于維揚舟中爲其作山水花卉四十葉。」張岱謂其「有書畫癖，有蹴踘癖，有鼓鈸癖，有鬼戲癖，有梨園癖。」又稱其「精音律，咬釘嚼鐵，一字百磨，口口親授。」(《陶庵夢憶》卷四 "祁止祥癖" 條)祁氏一家富藏書，復盡購徐迎慶家藏詞曲書，故於曲藝特精(參《遠山堂曲品劇品校錄》)。止祥山水倣石田，氣勢淋漓，筆力挺拔，有一種不可羈勒之槪。或譏其欠靜趣，豈爲曲家叫囂之習所累耶？

(丁)　畫家兼爲詩人

程　邃

垢道人、穆倩尙氣節，錢牧齋贈序，稱其「蕭森老蒼，眉宇深古，處亂不易方」，以異人目之(《有學集》二十二)。詩不多見，或謂其學杜，如五律警句「黃河冰腹厚，白草馬蹄新。」(《淸詩匯》十六 "過萬年少隰西草堂")一唱三歎。黃賓虹云：「今觀其畫，沉鬱荒涼、澀老生辣之味，俱從身世感慨中出，在在非可磨滅。」洵爲知言。余謂穆倩精篆刻(安徽圖書館藏有其《古蝸篆居印述》，道光四年鈐印四册)，畫復蒼勁古樸富金石味。多收藏。朱彝尊記漸江僧藏題吳道子繪之《光武帝燎衣圖》，後即歸之穆倩云。(《曝書亭集》五四)

胡宗仁

錢牧齋稱其「有詩二千餘首，鍾伯敬爲論定，見其手稿，每自誇其『寒星徹夜疎，明月爲我至」，以爲神來之句，亦可見其淸意。」（《列朝詩集》丁上，467頁）。鍾惺（《隱秀軒集》）謂其有王孟之致，幽澹蕭遠，多人外之趣。《讀畫錄》摘其佳句云「淺雲乍去猶拖水，山月初生不過林。皆詩中畫也。惜其集無力板行。」

惲　格

南田一代畸人，詩畫俱臻妙境，錄其題楊柳一絕「數點昏煙月一潭，綠陰桑火過春蠶；從今移入圖中看，不必攀條憶漢南。」情韵不匱，詩如其畫。故錢飲光（澄之）言：「南田題畫云：筆端點點，俱通元氣，可謂戻工心苦。」「故知南田畫者，當與讀南田之詩。」明季畫人，幾無不能詩者，求知南田之工者鮮矣。

吳　歷

《漁山詩集》曰《墨井集》。嘗學詩于錢謙益，錢序其《桃溪詩稾》稱：「漁山不獨善畫，其于詩尤工，思淸格老，命筆造微，蓋亦以其畫爲之。」（《有學集》48）其句云：「江邊春去詩情在，塞外鴻飛雪意寒。」以寄其冥漠之思，亦頗有畫意。

姜實節

鶴澗畫橅雲林，筆意超雋。張雲章（《樸庵集》）稱「其所居曰藝圃，淸流演漾，古木叢茂。……求其畫者，必得其題句以爲重。雖不識者，見其畫與詩，意其遺世獨立，不讓古之遺民焉。」石濤爲其弟子洪正治寫蘭册，實節甲申夏（康熙四十三年，1704）亦爲之題句。

（戊）　書家兼爲畫家

邢　侗

邢氏（子愿）築來禽館于古犁丘，刻"來禽館帖"，晚歲書名益重，喜作荊草拳石，古秀煙潤（《圖書寶鑑續纂》），獨具一格，以書入畫，自有蒼莽逸趣。《神州大觀》五收其辛亥（萬曆三十九年）作蒲石一幅。

倪元璐

倪氏（鴻寶）行書，從章草取態，或稱其「如番錦離奇，另一機軸，間寫文石，以水墨生暈，蒼潤古雅，頗具別致，文心之餘緒也。」（《無聲詩史》）。陶元藻謂「鴻寶畫幅，山皆峻嶒兀臬，林木則蒼莽鬱葱，皴法喜用大小劈斧，不屑描頭畫角，取媚於人。」（《越畫見聞》）。所作松石氣宇軒昂，以雄深高渾，見其魄力，但多露圭角，習用方筆，畫法與字法，正出一轍。

黃道周

「石齋善畫，人初不知也。臨難前作水墨大畫二幅，長松怪石，極磊落。」（《五石瓠》）。書法運筆多轉折，每從大處落墨。其詩句自云「閱物不至細」是也。山水如《雁宕》等幅，構圖奇特。大潑墨山水，尤覺淋漓盡致。今觀其畫亦如公書，洩天地之奇觀，雖工力非深，亦足令人驚嘆。

明季文人，多兼擅詩文書畫詞曲，惟致力有淺深，故造詣亦異。本文稱之爲詩人兼畫家者，以其主要成就在詩，而畫僅爲副業而已，稱之爲畫家兼詩人者，以其成就在畫且復工詩，餘可類推。

詩格與畫風之對應關係

明季畫人，幾乎無不能詩，而眞詩人之工畫者，更難指數。詩寫情性，由於性分有殊，因習乖異，故詩之爲狀，亦復各具面目。性由天定，習因人力；人之才氣，本乎情性，至於學習則出乎陶染。風力有剛柔之分，體式由研習而得。括而論之，不外先天之性，與後天之習二者而已。詩格之形成如此，畫風亦何獨不然？故畫格之表現，與其詩格之風範，每每有相應之處；無他，由于性分，嗜好，傾向之相同故耳。

此時之畫家，不能一一論述，茲就至樂樓藏品中之畫家，大約區爲三大類論之：

（1）爲才人之畫　作畫不專，而才氣橫溢，偶有著筆，爽氣逼人；或構圖奇特，毫無輕媚習氣，如楊龍友、張大風、黃向堅、傅山、查繼佐之儔是也。

（2）爲能手之畫　術有專攻，工力深至。雖體貌各殊，而爲眞正畫家之畫。陳洪綬、藍瑛、蕭雲從、顧符稹、文點之儔是也。

（3）爲緇流之畫　禪機所觸，不求甚似，發乎性靈，以成自家鼻孔。無可、擔當、髠殘、漸江、石濤、八大之倫是也。

由于學有淺深，習復相異，丘壑殊觀，筆墨異采，綜其畫格，可有八體：

一曰繁縟：峯嶺縱橫，解衣磅礴，吳彬、龔賢是也。

二曰疏簡：蕭寥數筆，斷絕塵襟，程嘉燧、八大是也。

三曰乾渴：乾皴渴擦，神理自足，程邃、戴本孝是也。

四曰濕潤：風雨不來，靑障猶溼，查士標、笪重光是也。

五曰穠麗：工緻精絕，六法全備，藍瑛、王鑑是也。

六曰閒澹：掃除蹊徑，獨出幽異，邵僧彌、沈顥是也。

七曰圓勁：行草中鋒，別有眞趣，鄒之麟、程正揆是也。

八曰險側：不立隊伍，無堅不催，黃道周、倪元璐是也。

劉勰《文心雕龍》論文分八體（"體性篇"），玆略仿其意，非謂畫風止盡于此八種，亦非謂每一畫人僅各獨具一體，玆但從大略言之。明季畫人之成就，石濤花樣，最爲繁出，其他多各握其一端（Extreme），而發揮盡致，大都不喜中庸之道，而危側趣詭，故能標新格。

試觀各家之詩，正可因畫風而闚其體性，沿根討葉，求其會通。李流芳之畫，「略加點染，靈曠欲絕。」（《庚子消夏記》），而詩亦「信筆輸寫，天眞爛然。」（《列朝詩集》）。鍾惺詩幽深孤峭，畫亦如之。李日華小詩跌宕風流，畫亦仗詩以發其妙，錢牧齋謂其「詩以畫壽，非以畫掩。」二者相得而益彰。徐枋畫用筆整飭，詩亦劈嶄，絕無恣肆。漸江畫極枯瘦，寒石生鏽，詩偶亦如香雪，沁人肺肝。傅山詩字，脫盡羈縛，不可響邇，其畫亦如狂士。八大詩如謎語，畫亦時寓寄託，有同諧讔。故知畫人之詩，與其畫正沆瀣一氣，各由天資，摹體成性。詩與畫互爲表裏，舉一可以反三，不遑縷舉。

詩意圖舉例

此時期之畫人，均喜寫'詩意圖'，蓋上承宋明人傳統。（元王惲《秋澗集》卷七三有趙大年畫摩詰詩意，式古堂著錄有《摩詰句圖》、《明人詩意圖册》。）間以古人詩句入畫，試舉數例如次：

（1）戴本孝：《杜詩山水册》

凡十二幅，引首吳雲題"秦山吳水"。用杜詩"白鹽崖"、"再過吳氏"、"夜宴左莊"、"東柯谷"、"瞿唐崖"、"麥積山寺"、"仇池"、"東屯"等爲題材，每詩後附有跋語，自云「近于六法，惟緪汲于陶、杜句中，每爲眞鑒者首肯。」時在庚午（康熙廿九年，1690），鷹阿年七十，蓋晚年之作。吳雲題記云：「其詩中之畫，畫中之詩，合而爲一。」「此不是詩，不是畫，即其人耳。」陸氏《續穰梨》十一著錄。

（2）傅山：李商隱《詩意軸》

題李商隱"晚晴詩"。字有小異，首句「夾城」作「邨城」，第五句「併添」作「併臨」，取「天意憐幽草，人間重晚晴」兩句意，綾本水墨，《續穰梨》十一著錄。

（3）邵彌：《唐人詩意册》

共十頁，設色，題王維「空山不見人，但聾（聞）人語響。」柳宗元「黃葉復溪橋，荒村惟古木。」孟浩然「松月生夜涼，風泉滿淸聽」等句。自跋云：「爲暑所苦，松月生涼之境，令人夢想，故復寫此，不厭其重出。」《穰梨》二十九著錄。

（4）高簡：《陶酒詩意册》

至樂樓藏絹本八開，寫陶公詩小册，如讀《山海經》句，簡淡可愛。

（5）葉欣：《百陶詩》

葉爲金陵八家之一，嘗爲周亮工摘陶句作小景百幅，周爲作百陶舫藏之，事見《讀畫錄》。

（6）查士標：《書畫合璧册》

八對幅，題曰「士標畫邵邨先生詩意。」似寫方亨咸詩句。《故宮書畫錄》卷六著錄。

所謂‘詩意’，不特寫前人佳句，亦寫時人詩句。明末清初，此風甚盛，如至樂樓藏石濤寫《黃研旅詩册》，其尤著者也。

投贈、題詠詩什與畫史資料

各家文集及總集中，作者與畫家交往投贈題詠之什，不少爲畫史重要資料，涉覽所及，略述其概：

丁雲鵬：

吳江兪安期有"丁南羽畫維摩説法圖長句"云：「更兼秘本久不傳，丁生創出遙齊肩；神手疑懸造化力，慧眼應破天人權。」（《明詩紀事》庚籤卷25，2554頁）。詹景鳳有"丁南羽畫山水歌"云：「丁生傲兀思離奇，登樓十日衆不知。科頭獨坐靑松古，坦腹空山白日遲。興來大噉忽高踞，援筆熻赫生風雨。千里移來屋壁看，江山香靄知何處？」（《明詩紀事》庚籤卷7下2243頁）。詹氏工書畫，具眼睥睨一世，獨推丁生，自非同于尋常之阿好。

魏學濂

子一論畫，屢爲方以智所稱引。黃宗羲撰"子一魏先生墓志銘"云：「加之旁通藝事，章草之書，倪黃之畫，陽冰之篆，孤姿絶狀，觸毫而出，無非詩書之所融結，學侶挹其精微，詞宗稱其妙絶，一時盛名無出其右。」惜其早世，未獲大成，亦明季畫人之具風骨者。

黃道周

漳浦于獄中寫《孝經》百卷，夫人蔡氏寫《心經》百卷配之。蔡夫人亦工畫，全祖望記仁和小山堂趙氏有葉子一册，末題曰：「石道人命蔡氏石潤寫雜花凡十種，時崇禎丙子（九年，1636），鈐以「玉卿私印」，夫人之字也，「石耕」則石齋先生之章也。」全氏記此畫卷幷錄其詞，載《鮚埼亭詩集》卷二，爲明季畫史，增一故實。

楊龍友

錢牧齋《有學集》卷五有"爲（趙）友沂題楊龍友畫册"、邢昉《石臼集》有"觀楊龍友畫山水册子董宗伯書跋作歌"及"題楊日補所藏楊龍友畫雲山圖"二長古，可爲研究楊畫之助。龍友自題畫云：「胸中自寫塊壘氣，筆底何妨斧鑿斑。生卷老雲皴白石，不將媚骨點靑山。」（《明詩紀事》辛籤卷6上2776頁），眞能自道其甘苦者。

陳洪綬

老蓮畫《水滸葉子》，流行于代。彭孫貽《茗齋集》有七古題其《水滸葉子》云：「吳後千年有陳子，更開生面尤絶倫。觀其下手萬象變，神鬼觸案窺纖新。離奇衣紋古面貌，愈拙愈秀無前人。」（《明詩紀事》辛籤卷12，2905頁），可供參證。

惲格

太倉沈受弘有"贈毗陵惲正叔一百韵"（《清詩紀事》卷3，405頁）。記惲格早歲經歷，有關隆武‘史事’，極爲重要。

顧符稹

王士禎有昭陽顧符稹"畫棧道圖歌"云：「顧生畫學李思訓，尤工棧道兼騾綱。丹靑金碧妙銖黍，近形遠勢窮毫芒。」（《精華錄》卷2，20頁），可見顧氏畫以金碧工細見長。《畫家辭典》誤其名，稹字誤作禎，宜據正。

蕭尺木

桐城方授（子留）贈蕭尺木一律云：「眼枯未忍望鍾陵，早見鍾山梅下僧。四海情空入畫，千秋何事欲傳燈。敢當倒屣憐貧病，聊與科頭數廢興。我夢不離靈谷樹，欲隨君往白雲層。」（《明詩紀事》辛籤卷16，3012頁）。子留明亡後逃之四明山，悒鬱而死，年才二十七，與尺木同抱滄桑之痛。王漁洋有 "蕭尺木楚詞圖畫歌長古" 句云：「蕭梁王孫筆倔儷，攀掣顧陸提僧繇。丹黓粉黙寫此本，墨花怒捲湘江潮。」（《精華錄》卷一），可作蕭氏《離騷圖》解題讀也。

程 邃

惲南田有 "醉歌吟贈黃海程穆倩"，自注稱程君爲（楊）機部，黃石齋門下士。曹溶與程遇於維揚，作長歌以贈。富平李因篤有 "高歌行寄程穆倩" 句云：「君有長歌二千字，兩京板蕩須臾事。」（《清詩匯》41，10頁），詩中頗有關晚明史事。

漸 江

湯燕生（岩夫）詩皆唐音，篆書古淡入妙，"訪漸江大師朔園" 一律，有「藥欄秋興閒今古，留客聽泉蔓草坡」之句（《明詩紀事》辛籤卷31，3338頁），知漸江所居，有朔園一處。燕生又題漸江丁酉寫岑嘉州逸句，贊云：「偶然落筆，標格奇至。梧樹挺森，峰巖峭邃。中有高齋，亢爽孤寄。」謂此畫彷彿有清閟閣困學齋遺意。圖見《神州大觀》第三册。

沈 顥

朗倩畫以小幅爲佳。錢牧齋有題石天《石厓秋柳小景》云：「刻露巉巖山骨愁，兩株風柳曳殘秋；分明一段荒寒景，今日鍾山古石頭。」（《有學集》卷1，19頁），王漁洋有和作，其爲文士所重如此。

戴本孝

務旃遊華山，漁洋贈詩云：「捫蝨雄談事等閒，餘情盤薄寫孱顏；洛陽貨畚無人識，五月騎驢入華山。」（《精華錄》79頁）。粵程周量《海日堂集》有 "送戴務旃遊西岳" 五古四首，又 "送本孝之蘭州" 云：「去年送君華山去，一杖冥冥入烟霧。自寫眞圖篋底歸，今來又指蘭州路。歎君馬首何太頻，天都白石情相親。即今大雪滿天地，猶作騎驢行路人。」秦隴之行，亦畫苑之佳話。

大 汕

其《離六堂集》，世頗罕覯。集中有 "乞高望公畫詩" 七絕，自題畫之作甚多，又題王石谷、高澹遊畫，題白水（鏡）、石谿、高謜園畫册、龔半千畫册，均有裨畫史。

瀏覽所及，偶舉一二以示例，其他資料有待同好之鈞索研討耳。

結 語

明季文人，不作匠筆，貴爲士畫，而耻爲畫士，大都以山水爲園林，以翰墨爲娛戲，以文章爲心腑，而以畫幅爲酬酢。信手拈來，朋友之間，以藝互相感召，題句者蓋以詩答畫，贈畫者實以畫代詩。得其人之畫與詩，可慰相思之飢渴。王士禛記畫家宋珏一絕句云：「來時梅瘦未成花，別後垂楊金作芽。他日相思如見畫，板橋西望是吾家。」見畫如見人，畫之爲用，駕乎友情之上。故畫之至佳者，往往爲贈與至交之作。如至交而兼爲畫人者，則其畫必更佳，而其意義爲更深，以其爲眞正知音故也。（程邃爲查士標作畫題云：「我梅壑乃畫中之得禪者也，想必有以教我。」非相知之深，孰肯爲此言乎？「音實難知，知更難逢，逢其知音，千載其一。」（《文心雕龍》語）。明人作畫題詩，非以沽利釣名，但求知音之賞，此張怡所云「乃能於中得解」、「於此道大有神會」者（周亮工《讀畫錄》序），正謂此耳。

RENDITIONS Books

A GOLDEN TREASURY OF CHINESE POETRY: 121
Classical Poems. *Translated by* John A. Turner

THE TRANSLATION OF ART: Essays on Chinese Painting and Poetry

AN ANTHOLOGY OF YUAN PLAYS (*in preparation*)